Rationing Medicine

Rationing Medicine

Robert H. Blank

Columbia University Press
New York

Library of Congress Cataloging-in-Publication Data

Blank, Robert H.
  Rationing medicine.

  Bibliography: p.
    1. Medical care—United States—Utilization.
  2. Medical innovations—United States. 3. Resource
  allocation. I. Title [DNLM: 1. Delivery of Health
  Care—United States. 2. Ethics, Medical. 3. Health
  Policy—United States. WA 540 AA1 B57r]
  RA410.7.B56 1988   362.1'0973   87-15803
  ISBN 0-231-06536-1
  ISBN 0-231-06537-X (pbk.)

Columbia University Press
New York   Oxford

Copyright © 1988 Columbia University Press
All rights reserved
Printed in the United States of America

Clothbound editions of Columbia University Press are Smyth-
sewn and printed on permanent and durable acid-free paper

To Maigin

Contents

Preface

This book is about the excruciating and complex decisions that must be made as we allocate increasingly scarce health care resources. I have purposely introduced controversy here because I believe that only through debate and deliberation over these sensitive issues will we be able to minimize the emerging crisis in medicine. Although as a society we may never reach a consensus on how best to distribute health care, we can at least agree to engage in an open dialogue among all affected parties and come to agreement on some of the steps necessary to ameliorate the situation. Unless we act to limit the current expectations of the public and make hard decisions now, the scope of the problems we will pass on to our children is staggering.

"Rationing" is a term that incites strong reactions from many persons and groups. When applied to health care, the idea of rationing generates even more severe opposition on ethical and political grounds. The suggestion that we shift our emphasis away from curative medical technologies toward primary care and prevention contradicts the powerful cultural and economic forces that favor a "technological fix" for health problems. To argue further that this preventive approach be designed to include consideration of individual responsibility for ill health caused by personal behavior is to risk condemnation. On all of these points, this book will elicit controversy. I hope that it will also contribute to the rational discussion of these volatile issues and provide a useful addition to the dialogue on the allocation and rationing of health care in America.

In order to illustrate the dilemmas facing us, four areas of health care are followed throughout the book: organ transplantation; treatment of seriously ill newborns; reproductive technology; and fetal health. I have intentionally avoided the inclusion of AIDS. Although it represents perhaps the most cogent example of an emerging crisis, I felt that its inclusion would detract from the broader themes of the book rather than clarify them. The enormity of the AIDS problem, however, dramatically demonstrates the scope of the policy issues raised in this book. The reader is challenged to go beyond the examples enumerated in the book and to analyze critical allocation/rationing concepts as applied to AIDS.

Acknowledgments

Although many individuals had an impact on this book, three scholars deserve special acknowledgment. Lynton K. Caldwell of Indiana University and Conrad Rosenberg of the Long Island Jewish Medical Center reviewed the manuscript and made invaluable suggestions that strengthened this final product. Marvin Henberg of the University of Idaho provided valuable insights, particularly for the discussion of individual responsibility in chapter 5.

Ann M. Miller, of Columbia University Press, did a superb job of editing and helped transform academic writing into a readable book. Karen Meyer deserves special thanks for the countless hours she put into research and preparation of the manuscript. I would also like to thank Carolyn Cradduck and the whole staff at the Program for Biosocial Research at Northern Illinois University. Finally, I thank Kate Wittenberg of Columbia University Press, without whose help and encouragement this book would not have been written. Although the final product is substantially stronger because of their contributions, any remaining shortcomings are my sole responsibility and should not reflect on any of these persons.

I also want to thank my wife, Mallory, for her patience and understanding, and Jeremy, Mai-Ling, and Maigin for being adaptive and largely cooperative.

Rationing Medicine

1

The Context of Health Care in the United States

In preparation for the inevitable, plans must be made and the techniques developed for the effective allocation and rationing of health care resources (Evans 1983).

Economic incentives such as those embedded in current cost-containment measures are not a substitute for social decisions about health care priorities and the just design of health care institutions.... These hard choices must be faced publicly and explicitly (Daniels 1986:1383).

Unless we decide to ban heart or liver transplantation, or make them available to everyone, some rationing scheme must be raised to choose among potential transplant candidates (Annas 1985:187).

It is in high technology areas where we face the stark reality of patient need against scarce resources in life and death situations that we see rationing with all its sharp edges exposed (Mechanic 1986:217).

It is becoming increasingly clear that major alterations in the health care system of the United States will be necessary in the coming decades if we are to avert a crisis of immense proportions. Many seemingly unrelated demographic, social, and technological trends in actuality constitute a concatenation that promises to accentuate traditional dilemmas in medical policymaking. The aging population, the proliferation of high-cost biomedical technologies designed primarily to extend life, conventional schemes of retroactive reimbursement by third-party payers, and the realization that health care costs are out-stripping society's perceived ability to pay, all lead to pressures for expanded public action. At the same time, public institutions appear both unable and unwilling to make the difficult decisions in an area traditionally viewed as outside the political arena.

The constraints on economic resources already apparent in the United States are bound to be compounded by the confluence of the trends noted above. Even with all that is being done to contain costs, health care expenditures will increase from $387 billion in 1984 to an estimated $660 billion in 1990 and $1.9 trillion by 2000, repre-senting almost 15 percent of the GNP. According to Blendon (1986:67), this means a doubling of the nation's health spending every seven years and an increase in per person expenditures from $1,500 in 1984 to almost $7,000 by the year 2000. Moreover, health care costs in the United States are now over $1,500 per year per person; the comparative figure for Britain is $400. The increased competition for scarce resources within the health care sector will necessitate re-source allocation as well as rationing decisions. In turn, these actions are certain to exacerbate the social, ethical, and legal issues and in-tensify activity by affected individuals and groups. Although public officials might continue to avoid making the difficult decisions and attempt to resolve long-term problems with piecemeal solutions, they soon will be forced to become major participants in the health care controversy.

This book examines the multitude of problems for policymakers raised by these issues and analyzes why biomedical issues are partic-ularly problematic and sensitive within the American cultural and institutional context. Central to our value system is a tendency to look for the easiest solutions. We have become dependent upon increasingly higher levels of technology in order to avoid more difficult changes in lifestyle. Should society continue to encourage this tendency and de-velop technologies to provide a "fix" for all health problems, or should we make efforts to discourage such hazards as obesity, smoking, and sedentary life found in an affluent society? Few technologies arouse greater controversies concerning individual rights, social needs, and responsibilities than biomedical technologies, since they deal with hu-man life and death directly. As the scope of fundamental rights has expanded in society, conflict is accentuated by the introduction of technologies that contrast rights and responsibilities across a variety of divisions in society. Basic questions arise concerning the scope of individual rights, the extent to which society ought to intervene in these freedoms, and how constraints might be justified. If a person abuses him- or herself, what responsibility does society have toward that individual? Ought the concept of community be expanded to take into account the responsibilities of an individual toward the unborn, toward future generations, toward other species? This chapter outlines the framework within which these formidable yet compelling dilemmas must be resolved.

Traditional Notions of Health Care

Health care in the United States, as in any country, is the product of many cultural, social, and political factors. It is impossible to explain the reaction of a citizenry or its leaders to health issues without an understanding of these factors. Although it is not feasible here to examine all of the complex historical and cultural determinants, there are several factors which are critical and which largely define the unique context of medical decision making in the United States.

Central to this framework are the political structures, institutions, and processes that define the boundaries of policymaking. Full understanding of this political context is essential if we are to comprehend the particular priorities and the apparent inconsistencies found in the health care system. In the United States, this context includes the basic institutions of federalism, separation of powers, and popular consent, as well as the actual procedures of policymaking. It is difficult to envision a national health policy in a country where each of fifty states is responsible for public health and there is no single locus of power at any level. Moreover, what rules of the game must be followed to achieve a particular goal, and what constraints are there on the government in bringing about these ends? This political context of health care policy is discussed at considerable depth in chapter 4. Attention here is focused on the value system which both reflects and shapes the political framework.

Political culture is the complex of beliefs, values, and attitudes concerning government held by the population. To focus on those elements of political culture which influence health policy, we must look at beliefs concerning definitions of health, the role of the government in the health arena, and the extent to which health care represents an individual right or a privilege granted by society. Although it is always dangerous to generalize to entire populations, cultural orientations that largely define the framework for health care policy in the United States are deep and consistent across much of the citizenry.

Observers of American society since Alexis de Tocqueville have commented on the uniqueness and the diversity of values among American citizens. This pattern of values has been viewed as a reflection of the historical development of the United States, especially the break from the feudal system and the continuous westward expansion (Hartz 1955). American values have been seen as products of, alternately, heavy dependence on the liberal tradition, or a fundamental consensus on the value of individual human life. As a society, we place much emphasis on individual autonomy, self-determination, personal privacy, and a shared belief in justice for all humans. Individuals in a liberal society are free to determine for themselves their preferred lifestyle and then, as long as they do not harm others, to live it. With this general consensus of support for certain general values, however, the belief has developed that each person's views should be heard and that all interests should be represented. The result has been a proliferation of competing views on issues of public concern. Given the diverse population and our tradition of individualism, social and political institutions have proved remarkably resilient and adaptable. Still, cultural pluralism has produced a large number of potential lines of stress in society that are reflected in health care issues.

In addition to the significant emphasis in the liberal tradition on individual autonomy and a broad range of rights, American culture is also predisposed toward progress through technological means. Alexander Capron (1975:123) suggests that this value extends to medical technology through a deep commitment to the belief that medicine will progress and give us ever greater powers over disease. A reinforcing value, according to Marc Lappe, is a "deep-seated aversion to chance in the Western psyche" (1972:413). This desire for control is crucial to understanding our characteristic health care decisions. Presumably, equating the reduction of uncertainty with progress facilitates acceptance of a wide range of technologies. The result, unfortunately, has been an unrealistic dependence on technology to fix our health problems at the exclusion of nontechnological solutions. For instance, in their comparison of British and American doctors' views toward technology, Miller and Miller conclude:

British doctors are trained to be much more skeptical than their U.S. counterparts about the technological imperative—the notion that more sophisticated medical procedures are synonymous with better health care. In part this is because the British health establishment gives far greater credence to what good primary care can accomplish than do most U.S. doctors. In addition, however, British health professions and the population itself simply tend to cast a more critical eye on the promises of technology. (1986:1385)

Reiser (1984:171) cautions that technology can be addictive and compelling because it takes on a life of its own. We build into machines our aspirations and needs. Like humans, technologies once created seem to acquire a right to survive and to make their mark. Because they have powerful symbolic meaning, medical devices, such as the artificial heart especially, are difficult to limit once they are introduced. Reiser (1984:173) argues that the technological fix approach is generally wrong because it does not adequately account for these complex effects of technology. As we will see later, this technological orientation, along with the belief that good health is the right of every individual, contributes to the emerging health care crisis in the United States.

As a society, we place considerable emphasis on the individual's right to medical care. The patient-physician relationship has been seen largely as a private one, beyond the public realm. Although in the aggregate we are willing to cut costs, when it comes to the individual patient we have been ready to expend all resources without consideration of costs. There is a not-so-implicit assumption that every person has a right to unlimited expenditure on his/her behalf, despite the understanding that in the aggregate this is unfeasible. The problem of unlimited individual claims in the context of limited societal resources produces the dilemma of health care today. As stated by Schramm, "If society's task is to improve the health of the many, disproportionate spending on acute care for a small number of persons must come into question" (1984:730).

However, the suggestion that we somehow limit medical expenditures on an individual in order to benefit the greatest number contradicts the traditional patient-oriented mores of medicine. There are strong pressures for intensive intervention on an individual basis even in the last days of life; this, despite the enormous cost for very little return in terms of prolonging the patient's life. Colorado Governor Richard Lamm's suggestion that terminal patients have a duty to refuse intensive and expensive medical intervention and to die was met with widespread criticism by the press, health professionals, and the public. Despite its cost-benefit logic and its attractiveness for the aggregrate, Lamm's proposal directly challenged the tradition of not withholding care from a patient in need, with no concern as to cost.

In addition, supporting this maximalist approach to medical care, we have created an intricate mechanism for minimizing the amount any single individual will pay for these benefits. Private health insurance allows individuals to protect themselves by spreading the risk of requiring expensive medical treatment across many persons. The real cost of the services is therefore obscured, since individuals seldom must bear the costs directly or fully. This insulation of the individual patient from cost encourages the maximalist approach and supports the presumption that cost should not be a concern in the treatment of the patient. No matter how much is spent on the patient, the payment will usually be made by the amorphous third-party payer.

The belief that individuals have the right to unlimited medical care should they so choose it; the traditional acceptance of the maximalist approach by the medical community; and the insulation of the individual from feeling the cost of treatment have together placed severe limits on the extent to which proscription of expensive and often ineffective intervention is possible. Arguments in favor of containing the costs to society of health care, while acceptable at the aggregate level, tend to fail when applied at the individual level. Although a large proportion of the population supports some type of cost containment in theory, traditional beliefs in the maximalist approach remain strong when their own health or that of their family is at stake.

It has been suggested that no matter to what extent health care facilities are expanded, there will remain a steady pool of unmet demands. According to the Office of Health Economics (1979), additional manpower and money are not the answer to the health care crisis. Instead of resolving the problems, this approach increases the demand for solutions to an ever-expanding range of technical medical problems. Although wealthier countries devote substantially higher proportions of their wealth to health services than do poorer countries, demand for such services does not abate. Instead, the public comes to expect a level of medical care not expected by persons in less wealthy countries. Moreover, as more of these expectations are met, demand for expanded health services actually escalates.

In a system where third-party reimbursement insulates much of the public from the real cost of meeting these higher expectations, it is not surprising that the public strongly supports increased development of medical technologies. Schwartz comments, "However jaundiced the medical care experts have become about the excesses, inefficiencies, ineffectiveness, and irrelevance of much medical care, the fact is that the public does not share this perspective. Increased investment of medical care continues to be highly valued by the public" (1984:24). Instead, the public demands more front-end insurance coverage to pay for high-cost medical care. As a society, we have come to expect the best that science can offer when it comes to medical care for ourselves or our loved ones. Although we complain about the high cost, when our health or life is at stake, we expect no expense to be spared. The preferred solution for many consumers is simply to shift the basis of payment to the government and private third-party payers. These demands clearly prevent any simple solution to the problems of health care.

Another concern of the American public which shapes demands for expansion of health expenditures is its obsession with prolonging life. Franz Ingelfinger concludes that too much money is spent to "convert Western octogenarians to nonagenarians" (1980:143). The determinants of death are many, and to pour untold millions into defeating one merely shifts the opportunity to others. Saving an elderly person from one illness might very well expose that person to an even more debilitating disease. Although the quality of life of many persons at advanced ages is questionable and extensive technological intervention might prolong life only briefly, American society has an excessive concern with staying alive at all costs. Although there is considerable evidence that this mentality is changing, by far the most expensive year of life for most persons is their terminal year. Still, our system hesitates to withhold treatment no matter how costly, if only it extends life. Moreover, as Norman Daniels (1986) argues, in the health care system of the United States there are no assurances that beneficial treatments or procedures withheld from one patient will be put to better use elsewhere, or that the resources will be used to meet the greater needs of other patients. It is especially difficult to justify saying no to a patient under these circumstances—with the frequent result that treatment is offered even in marginal cases. Often physicians who personally realize that the aggressive treatment of a terminally ill patient is pointless still continue because of pressure from the patient's family, fear of a malpractice suit, or simply because it is easier within our value system. Yet prolongation of life is bound to become even more expensive, because we are approaching an asymptote: we are reaching that point where no matter how much we spend on extending the life span of the aged, the return—in the number of years of life gained—still diminishes unrelentingly.

According to Brandon (1982:949), the result is a vicious circle which continues to escalate costs. Rising health costs combined with the heightened expectations of the public make it necessary for people to obtain adequate medical insurance. However, the availability of more comprehensive insurance encourages overuse of medical care, which consequently drives prices up and makes it necessary to have even more insurance. The demand for expensive medical diagnostic and therapeutic technologies exaggerates this pattern.

The situation is even more complex, however, because it is not the public that creates the initial demand for more advanced technology. Instead, the initiative for medical research and development comes from the scientists themselves. The artificial heart, for instance, was never demanded by the public, not even by an interested segment of it. Instead, it was developed to meet a need perceived by the medical researchers (Office of Health Economics 1979). The scientists thus hold out promises that can be fulfilled only if new resources are made available. Once developed, media attention dramatizes medical innovation, and demand increases among both physicians and patients. Once an innovation passes the experimental stage, consumers come to expect that it will become available for their benefit.

Public expectations may also be raised unrealistically because of a tendency to oversell medical innovation and overestimate the capacities of new medical technologies for resolving health problems. Often the initial response of the media is to report innovations as medical "breakthroughs." Because most health care is routine and therefore not newsworthy, the media naturally focus attention on techniques that can be easily dramatized. This is especially true in the United States, where our underlying "technological fix" mentality places tremendous emphasis on finding the cure for cancer, creating the bionic person and, to many, discovering a technological fountain of youth. According to Ingelfinger (1980), organized medicine is also to blame for the overselling of medicine because as a whole it has encouraged the belief in the omniscience, rather than the ignorance, of the medical profession. He also targets politicians who promise too much, and voluntary health groups who suggest in their fund-raising campaigns that if only more money were thrown into the research mill, the major diseases would be contained. Despite the failure of medicine to deliver on many counts, as a whole the public continues to support the continuing search for perfect solutions to health problems through technology.

Without doubt, these expectations and perceptions of medicine have resulted in an overutilization of and reliance on technology in American medical practice. Patients demand access to the newest technologies because they have been oversold on their value. Popular health-oriented magazines and television shows extol the virtues of medical innovations. Physicians have been trained in the technological imperative which holds that a technology should be used if it offers any possibility of benefit, despite its cost. Whether to protect themselves from malpractice suits, to provide the most thorough workup for their patients, or to increase profits, many physicians would rather err heavily on the side of overusing diagnostic and therapeutic technologies. The heavy investment of medical providers in expensive diagnostic equipment such as CAT scanners—often merely to stay ahead of the competition—encourages their use even when their benefit is marginal or nonexistent. Third-party retrospective reimbursement provides no disincentive to this overutilization of medical technology. According to Wildavsky (1977), the patient seeks care up to the level of his insurance, and our system encourages this pattern.

Social Trends Contributing to the Health Care Crisis

The strong emphasis placed on the autonomy of the individual and the sanctity of human life in American political culture, as well as rising public expectations regarding health care, helps to explain why the infusion of expensive life-extending technologies creates a severe policy dilemma. In order to understand the full scope of the emergent health policy problems facing the United States, however, several further contemporary trends affecting American health care must be explicated, including the rapidly escalating costs of medicine, the aging of the population, the expanded role of the government in health care, and the growing share of the health care system controlled by for-profit corporations. Another crucial factor, the rapid advances in medical technology, is discussed in more detail in chapter 2.

Rapidly Escalating Cost of Health Care

One of the issues heightening the political sensitivity of medical innovation is that of funding. From basic research to applied medical care, the government and other third-party payers increasingly pay a major portion of the costs of health care, at a time when the escalation of medical costs continues largely unabated. In 1950 the total health care cost in the United States was $12.7 billion, approximately 4.5 percent of the gross national product (GNP). In 1980, that figure rose to $245 billion or 9.3 percent of GNP, and by 1984 the cost was $387 billion or 10.7 percent. As noted earlier, it has been estimated that health care expenditures in the United States will rise to $690 billion in 1990 and $1.9 trillion by the year 2000 (over 14 percent of the GNP), even if all the piecemeal cost containment efforts now being introduced continue. The proportion of these costs paid for by the government is certain to increase in the future, as private mechanisms prove unable to deal with the continuing escalation of the cost of medical care.

Kressley (1981) contends that two trends in the American medical care system are headed on a collision course. One is the rapid growth and diffusion of sophisticated biomedical technologies which are driving up costs, and the other is the call for cost containment to reduce the economic burden of medical care on society. Medical technology is unique among technologies in its economic role. Most nonmedical technologies are introduced to increase output and reduce production costs, but biomedical technology's effect on output cannot be measured with any precision. More often than not, medical innovations increase the costs of medical care, at times drastically. The only clear exceptions are vaccines and pharmaceuticals, which tend to reduce the cost of treatment. Furthermore, consumer decisions are not a major factor in the market for biomedical innovations. There is no true market mechanism in biomedicine because consumers of medical care have their needs defined by the suppliers. Moreover, the retrospective reimbursement mechanism of third-party payers is designed to accept prices set by the producers.

Further complications arise from the fact that distribution of medical resources in the United States is skewed toward a very small proportion of the population. More and more medical resources have been concentrated on a relatively small number of patients in acute care settings. Substantial questions about the just distribution of scarce resources in a society are therefore accentuated in the establishment of biomedical priorities. For instance, in 1975, 55 percent of all hospital expenses were incurred by only 4 percent of the patient population, less than 1 percent of the entire population. Furthermore, intensive care and coronary care costs alone account for approximately 15 percent of all hospital costs (IOM 1979:20). Similarly, in 1982, patients with end stage renal disease, who represent less than .25 percent of all Medicare Part B beneficiaries, accounted for over 9 percent of the total Medicare Part B expenditures (Evans 1983:2209).

The Aging Population

Elderly persons are the leading users of hospital care on a per capita basis and have the highest expenditures for health care. Ironically, because of medical improvements and technologies that prolong life, chronic disease requiring frequent medical care has become a greater problem. Obviously, the demand for such care will continue to increase in an aging population. At present, 11.4 percent of the U.S. population, or approximately 25.6 million people, are 65 years of age or older. By the year 2035 the elderly population will double in size. Moreover, those persons over 80 now constitute about one-sixth of the total elderly, a proportion which is increasing in large part because of the high expenditure for medical care during that stage of life. Life expectancy at age 75, for instance, increased by 2.2 years, to 81.0, between 1965 and 1979. Because of the concurrence of multiple and often chronic conditions, the cost of prolonging life at older ages is usually higher than at younger ages, increasingly so since the introduction of antibiotics in the 1940s reduced the incidence of death from specific illnesses such as pneumonia (Ricardo-Campbell 1982:7). It is estimated that by the year 2000 the number of elderly aged 80 and over will increase by about 50 percent, and that by 2035 approximately one out of every ten Americans will be over 85 years of age. This aging population already has put a tremendous strain on the health care system to provide acute and especially chronic care facilities for a population which is heavily dependent on these services. These pressures are certain to intensify as the elderly come to constitute over 15 percent of the population by the year 2000.

Recent studies have confirmed that the elderly are high-cost users of medical care, much of which is funded by the federal government through Medicare and Medicaid. In 1980, for example, 63.9 percent of the health care expenditures for those over 65 years of age was paid for by the public sector. This contrasts with 28.6 percent for those under 65 (Lawrence and Gaus 1983:365). Anderson and Steinberg (1984:1349) cite findings that users of high-cost medical care are more likely to be persons with chronic medical problems who are repeatedly admitted to the hospital than persons with single cost-intensive stays. According to Zook and Moore (1980), persons over 65 years of age are disproportionately represented in this high-cost group. Of the 30 million people who in 1976 had a debilitating illness that lasted three months or more, the rates per 1,000 population varied considerably by age: for those under 45 it was 67; for those 45–65 it was 242; and for those 65 and over it was 453 (Lawrence and Gaus 1983:366). Furthermore, Medicare expenditures are highly concentrated on a small percentage of elderly beneficiaries who are repeatedly admitted to the hospital. Almost 60 percent of Medicare's inpatient hospital expenditures between 1974 and 1977 were attributable to the 12.5 percent of the patients who were discharged three or more times during that period, and 20.3 percent of inpatient expenditures were attributable to 2.6 percent of beneficiaries discharged more than five times (Anderson and Steinberg 1984:1351).

As a result of these patterns of use, the increasing proportion of the elderly in the population will have a substantial impact on future health care costs. The elderly now represent a significant political force certain to gain in strength as they come to represent a larger minority making vocal demands on the system. Both Medicare and Social Security projections indicate severe disruptions of these programs in the coming decades. The only point of debate is when the impending crisis will arrive. Congressional Budget Office predictions in 1983 noted that without major changes, the Hospital Insurance Trust Fund of Medicare could collapse by the end of the decade. With the move of Medicare away from fee-for-service reimbursement to the predetermined diagnosis-related groups (DRGs) in the 1983 amendments to the Social Security Act, more optimistic projections now estimate that the trust fund will be solvent until 1994 (Demkovich 1984a). Although this would delay trust fund bankruptcy by several years, it is becoming clear that piecemeal solutions are unlikely to divert disaster indefinitely. The aging population, along with the heavy dependence of the elderly on expensive long-term care, is creating ever-more-critical health care problems that exacerbate the other factors contributing to the escalating cost of medical care. Harron, Burnside, and Beauchamp agree that this difficult problem could become a crisis, and they raise the critical allocation question: "Could we arrive at a point in the future when there is either an overt or covert policy to withhold certain lifesaving health care resources from citizens older than a certain age?" (1983:122).

Government Involvement in Medicine

All governments are concerned about the health of their citizens, if only through the need to have a healthy labor or military force. Government involvement in public health in the United States can be traced to early attempts to use the police power of the state to improve sanitation and reduce the spread of contagious diseases. To this day, the fifty states have primary responsibility for taking those measures necessary to protect the public health of their residents and for setting policy priorities in the provision of public health programs. Throughout this century, the national government has become more and more active in establishing minimum health care standards and in funding biomedical research into particular diseases. It was not until 1965, however, that Congress became directly involved in health care policy. Through Medicare, Medicaid, and active funding of biomedical research, the federal government has quickly become a major participant in the health care process. Despite this flurry of government activity, the United States has yet to develop anything resembling a comprehensive national health policy. To date, the response of the government to medical care has been piecemeal, haphazard, and at times contradictory.

Although the United States lacks a national health policy, the trend toward increased government involvement is accelerating. At present over 42 percent of the costs of health care are paid by government at the national, state, or local level. Estimated government funding of health care for 1988 approaches $225 billion (HCFA 1986). The single largest federal program is Medicare, passed in the House of Representatives on April 8, 1965 by a 313 to 115 margin as a compromise between Democratic and Republican congressmen and the American Medical Association (AMA). Actually, Medicare encompasses two distinct programs. The hospital insurance coverage (Part A) is financed through payroll taxes placed in a trust fund. The optional supplemental medical coverage (Part B) is funded by a combination of general revenues and premiums paid by the beneficiaries. Medicare costs have risen from $1.35 billion in 1966 to $64.6 billion in 1984 and a projected $95.8 billion by 1988 (HCFA 1986). Medicare now represents approximately 5 percent of the total federal budget. Because of its size and the continuing controversy that surrounds it, Medicare is a tempting target for budget cutting.

The sister program of Medicare, part of the 1965 Social Security Act, is Medicaid. Unlike Medicare, which is a federal insurance program for the elderly middle class, Medicaid is a state-federal partnership for low-income people, primarily women and children. Although minimum standards are set by Congress, Medicaid is a state-run program financed through a federal matching formula which varies according to each state's ability to pay. The total estimated cost of Medicaid in fiscal 1986 was $45 billion, of which approximately $21 billion came from participating states (all but Arizona, which has its own program). In 1966, the first year of Medicaid implementation, the total national expenditure for the Medicaid program was only $734 million, although even that figure was twice the original estimate.

The exponential increase in the cost of Medicaid and Medicare has not only placed a severe financial burden on the government, but has also contributed to the steep rise in hospital and medical costs since 1966 and raised questions of effectiveness. According to Goggin:

Medicare and Medicaid, then, proved not the panacea for the health problems associated with cost, access, and quality of the 1960s, but were partly to blame for creating new problems of the 1970s, especially run-away costs of health and medical services. In spite of improved access to health and medical care for the elderly and poor...their actual performance did not come up to political and legislative promises. (1984:74)

Contributing to the inability of the government to control the rapid escalation of health care spending is the necessity of supporting the interests of those very elements of society—the health care providers— who must be regulated. An explicit political promise was made in the 1965 amendments to the Social Security Act not to interfere with the free enterprise system of medicine and not to dictate to physicians how to practice medicine. Although this promise has been infringed upon in recent years, it illustrates the extent to which health providers exert substantial influence over any attempts by the government to regulate the health industry. Any move by the government is met by threats of noncompliance by powerful elements in the health community who view the proposed action as against their best interests. Pressures by these interests to relax the freeze on physician reimbursement and to reverse the administration's proposal to reduce DRG payment rates (Demkovich 1984b) have succeeded, demonstrating the need for the acquiescence at least of physicians, hospitals, and other health providers to governmental action.

Conversely, the health providers are heavily dependent on the continuation of Medicare, Medicaid, and other government funding of health care. Substantial reductions in government expenditures for health care would have catastrophic effects on the health care industry. Despite current cost containment strategies designed to restrain government reimbursement of health services, many physicians and hospitals could not exist without Medicare and Medicaid funding. The $120 billion-plus per year that these programs offer goes directly to the health providers. Not surprisingly, an early study of the policy impact of these programs (Stuart and Bair 1971) found that the individuals who gained the most from them were the providers of medical services, not the recipients. Obviously, the health industry has a high stake in being responsive to reasonable cost containment policies considered by the government. Just as clearly, the medical care community will fight hard to minimize losses that might confront them through such policies. The danger, of course, is that patients specifically and the consumer public in general may find themselves shortchanged by bargains struck between the well-organized medical community and the government.

Corporate Medicine

Another major trend in American medicine is the growing share of health care controlled by profit-making businesses. Profit-making conglomerates now own chains of hospitals, clinics, nursing homes, kidney dialysis units, pharmacies, diagnostic laboratories, medical office buildings, shopping mall emergency centers, and other health-related enterprises. By 1982, 10 percent of the 6,300 community hospitals in the United States were owned by these profit-making chains, with another 5 percent managed under contract to them. As of 1985, Hospital Corporation of America (HCA), the largest such chain, owned or managed 431 hospitals accounting for over 60,000 beds (Mechanic 1986:12). Nearly 80 percent of the nursing homes in the United States are operated by profit-making corporations, and these corporations are becoming increasingly visible in the home health care industry as well. Early in the 1980s, Humana, Inc. initiated the idea that health care, like any product, could be marketed, managed, and distributed nationally. Humana was the first hospital chain to advertise its name and logo on all of its hospitals and ambulatory care centers. In May 1986, the company unveiled a nationwide advertising campaign, including television commercials, promising to make Humana "the McDonald's of the health care industry" (*American Medical News*, June 20, 1986, p. 3). Not to be outdone, HCA is investing $8 million annually in its advertising effort to market its hospital and subsidiary operations, which extend to all facets of health care.

Nonprofit community hospitals and publicly supported clinics, which traditionally have accepted those unable to pay, increasingly are finding themselves unable to compete financially with their profit-motivated competition. According to Starr (1982), new medical corporations show little propensity to serve those persons from whom a profit cannot be made. This situation contributes to the evolving two-tier system of health care, where those without sufficient insurance coverage or personal wealth are unable to gain access to significant medical care.

The growth of the medical-industrial complex represents a profound change in American medicine that threatens traditional notions of the physician-patient relationship and the role of the medical community. Starr (1982) sees a resulting decline in the capacity of physicians to define the standards of judgment by which medicine is evaluated. Instead, corporate managers concerned primarily with turning a profit for their investors will shape the institutions that provide medical care. The corporation evaluates the doctor's performance according to its own criteria of profit. Together with the powerful insurance conglomerates, these businesses are taking medical decision making away from the primary health providers and placing it in the hands of the managers and their computers. To the extent that these changes provide efficiency and cost containment, they are encouraged by the current government regulatory process.

The growth of the profit-making sector in medicine is to some extent the product of a centralization of health care. Even among nonprofit hospitals, multihospital chains or multi-institutional systems are commonplace. Over 30 percent of all hospitals in the United States are part of these enterprises. Control continues to shift from local institutions to regional or national ones. Standardized decisions are made at corporate headquarters and applied at the local level without an appreciation of the possible uniqueness of local values and needs. Government moves toward DRGs and various prepaid health plans encourage this standardization and centralization of medical decision making. Although nonprofit hospitals have always set policy, usually they were controlled by physicians. Today, the corporations control the physicians, and increasingly, the medical marketplace.

Competitive Disadvantage

One cause for concern over the escalation of health care costs in the United States that is less obvious is the effects of these costs on the capacity of the United States to compete economically with other developed nations. The United States does not exist in isolation, nor does it any longer enjoy an insurmountable productive advantage. We spend more on health care than do our major competitors in the world economy, whether measured in dollars or in proportion of GNP. Although the inflationary costs of health care is a problem in all countries, the retrospective reimbursement system of employer-paid insurance raises American labor costs substantially.

According to Joseph Califano, former Secretary of the Department of Health, Education, and Welfare and now a Chrysler board member, Chrysler Corporation paid $6,000 per active worker in health insurance costs in 1983 (1986:82). When tax contributions to Medicare and the health insurance costs of supplier firms were included, Chrysler's total health care costs represented $600 per car, more than 10 percent of the price of its smaller cars. Moreover, the $375 million in health insurance premiums that Chrysler paid Michigan Blue Cross/Blue Shield in 1983 made the insurer the company's largest supplier, a situation that is likely to continue because of strong resistance from the United Auto Workers to changes in coverage that would produce savings. While other companies have instituted co-payments and deductibles and provided incentives for employees to join health maintenance organizations (HMOs), the auto workers are unwilling to give up their comprehensive, and expensive, insurance coverage.

Importantly, health care costs are not as significant a problem for auto producers in other countries, such as Japan, that have nationalized health care. Obviously, the cost of such coverage is paid for indirectly by industry in these countries, but it is nothing on the order of $600 per car. Although the U.S. auto industry, and particularly Chrysler Corporation, spends more than other American businesses on workers' health insurance, health care costs for labor help place American industry in general at a competitive disadvantage that is difficult to overcome by other cost-cutting efforts. Clearly, health care costs to employers represent a drain on American industry. Continued increases in insurance premiums above and beyond the inflation rate promise to accentuate this problem.

The Etiology of the Health Care Crisis: A Model

Unfortunately, there is no simple model that explains the etiology of the emerging health care crisis. The concept of health care itself is intricately interwoven with the most fundamental values of any society. It has evolved over generations and, thus, is difficult to alter without threatening the basic values from which it came. As a result, many of the most difficult problems in medicine today are ethical, not technical ones. What is the value of a human life? What is the most fair or just way to distribute medical goods and services? Who ought to make life/death medical decisions? Although there is considerable literature on medical ethics and a recent presidential commission addressed such concerns in detail, many persons in the health care profession would prefer to deal with the medical aspects apart from the broader moral dilemmas.

At substantial risk of oversimplification, figure 1.1 illustrates some of the major factors that must be incorporated into any effort to explain the emerging health care crisis in the United States. Although this model includes what I believe to be the most critical elements, it fails to explicate the complicated interactions among them that are essential for a full understanding. Also, the simple arrows in the model represent very complex reciprocal relationships among the elements of the model.

Despite its limitations, the model does demonstrate the extent to which any health policy decision is the result of multiple pressures from the providers and the consumers as well as the constraints imposed by demographic factors and the structure of the government itself. Many of the unique problems encountered in the United States can be traced to the absence of any single locus of health policymaking and the fragmented policy process. Also, the strength of the health care provider in the United States is immense: any successful policy must have at least the tacit support of those being regulated. Moreover, because the population of the United States is large and diverse, any attempts to achieve a homogenous pattern of allocation of health care resources will encounter severe difficulties.

The hard decisions that we as a society face in the coming decades must be made within this complex and often contradictory context. Although many observers today offer rational suggestions for resolving the health care crisis, particularly by controlling runaway costs, I argue that decisions made in the health care arena are unlikely to be founded on fully rational grounds. Health care is a very personal issue for most persons: what might be logical from an economic standpoint on the aggregate level often is unattractive from the emotional perspective of

Figure 1.1
A Model of Health Care Policy in the United States

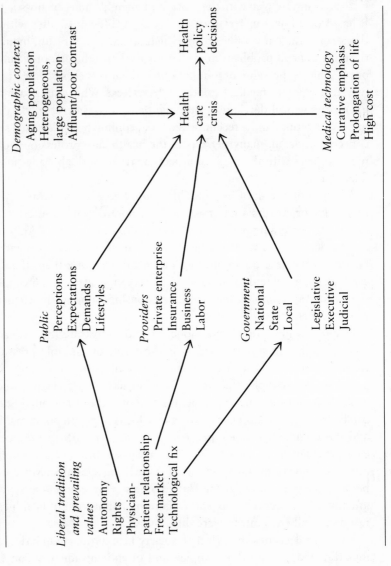

the individual. As Klien notes, a great many users of health care are "hardly the rational shoppers required to make the competitive private market model work" (1981:299). One of the dangers of even positing the need for some type of rationing system for medical care is that in applying any criteria to specific cases, the outcome will appear harsh and even inhumane. Many of the issues discussed in chapter 2 elucidate this discrepancy: decisions that are deemed rational in the aggregate seem unfair when applied to specific individuals, given our prevailing values. This inherent conflict helps to make health care policy issues among the most demanding we have yet to confront.

In addition to the irrational element of individuals' demands, powerful health groups naturally defend their own best interests, even if the overall results run counter to the long-term interests of society. Given these conditions, it is no surprise that public officials do not see comprehensive alterations in the health care system as politically feasible. No-win issues are not amenable to dramatic or drastic political action.

As a result, in the United States we have largely avoided making the difficult decisions regarding the distribution of scarce medical resources. Most often the "solutions" merely shift costs from the individual to the government, or from one agency to another. For instance, Aaron and Schwartz (1984) see a tendency of policymakers to rely simply on a shift toward prospective reimbursement schemes to solve health cost problems. Although giving the appearance of resolving the problem, these shifts only delay the need to make the hard choice. As Brandon (1982) notes, however, we are running out of easy options and supposed panaceas. These interim shifts in the burden of payment fail to approach the critical issues of establishing policy priorities and setting limits on the use of certain high-cost medical technologies. Neither our policymakers nor the public are willing to pierce this cost-shifting facade and make the difficult choices.

In many ways, the fundamental difficulty preventing development of effective public policy to reduce costs arises from the unreasonable expectations of both health care consumers and providers that an unlimited availability of medical technology is possible. These expectations fuel demands by the public, but the public, in turn, is encouraged by the providers of health services. There is little doubt that the suppliers of high-technology goods and services have a large stake in the continued growth of the health care industry. The infusion of corporate medicine and for-profit hospitals into the health care community illustrates the extent of these stakes. Moreover, insurance providers are the beneficiaries of this expansion in the short run, even though eventually, uncontrolled costs might well undermine their interests.

Although most consumers have yet to experience directly the ramifications of the cost crisis in medicine, as expensive medical innovations continue to proliferate and public expectations rise, these problems will escalate to crisis proportions for all consumers. It is characteristic of our political system that we refrain from making hard choices in politically volatile areas until a crisis is obvious. Although this approach is shortsighted, it is understandable, because most policy decisions are made on a very short time frame. Public officials are not reelected on the basis of their efforts, no matter how legion, to resolve future problems. Therefore it is not surprising that their attention is directed toward either effecting policies which are painless for their constituencies, or toward dealing with unavoidable crisis issues. This nonresponsiveness of legislatures to the primary causes of the emerging crisis in health care is analyzed in detail in chapter 4.

Trade-Offs in Health Policy

All political decisions involve trade-offs when goods and services are distributed across a population. No matter what allocation scheme is used, some elements of society will benefit and others will be deprived. Philosophical debate has long been devoted to what criteria ought to be used to determine whether or not a particular policy is just or fair. Do we select those policies that maximize the good of the greatest number, help those who are least well off, or concentrate goods in a small elite on the assumption that somehow benefits might "trickle down" to those on the bottom? Since Plato first argued in the *Republic* that health resources should not be wasted on the sickly and unproductive, the distribution of these limited resources has been part of a public policy debate. Although historically the dominant policy in the United States has been to minimize direct government intervention in the allocation of health care resources, for reasons discussed above this policy perspective is now undergoing drastic revision.

Table 1.1

Trade-Offs in Health Care Allocation

Preventive medicine	v.	Curative medicine
Improved quality of life	v.	Extension of life
Young	v.	Elderly
High-incidence diseases	v.	Rare diseases
Marginally ill	v.	Severely ill
Cost containment	v.	Individual choice

Table 1.1 presents some of the clearest trade-offs currently debated in the health policy literature. Whether contrasting a preventive with a curative approach, care for the young with care for the old, or an emphasis on quality of life with extension of life, it is unfortunate that the debate often is framed in "either-or" terms. Obviously, it would be more comfortable to place high priority on all categories or, alternately, to balance them out in an equitable way. Unhappily, the options are narrowing, and health care resources dedicated to one category do, in reality, reduce the resources that can be committed to others. Writes Knaus,

As more and more of our national wealth is being allocated to sophisticated medical services like intensive care, it becomes more likely that the extraordinary demands of a few desperately ill individuals or the indiscriminate application of a new expensive treatment will threaten the availability of basic medical services. (1986:1177)

The stakes in how these resources are allocated among the possible categories have therefore become quite high, particularly for those in society who lack the personal resources essential to protect their own interests. This situation makes the need to establish meaningful social priorities for health care allocation even more critical.

Programmed Medical Decisions: Computer Rationing

The ultimate solution to rationing decisions in a technologically oriented society might be the use of computers to make a binding decision based on a multifaceted medical profile of the patient. Computers are used today to help in the diagnosis of certain diseases and in measuring the risk of various treatment strategies. Many observers, including Roger Jelliffe (1985) and Victor Pollak (1985), believe that computers and intelligent machines should do more to improve the quality and cost effectiveness of patient care. By using computers to plan and manage therapy and by linking them with intelligent machines to deliver such therapy, patient health would be improved and the cost of medical care reduced (Freiherr 1985).

Computers have the advantage of providing useful information drawn from extensive data banks—information any single physician or even team of medical specialists does not so readily have. One of the many new programs is Aesculapius, which engages the computer's diagnostic capabilities through a two-step process. Gapen describes its functioning:

First, a physician interviews and examines a patient to obtain a thorough history and physical.... When lab values are obtained, they are added to the computerized record, a neatly typed history and physical is printed for inclusion in the patient's permanent medical file.

Aesculapius also has a useful feature that vastly simplifies the laborious process of recording the data generated in a patient interview. When a physician lists the patient's major complaints and their possible causes, the program can pull up a list of signs and symptoms associated with the differential diagnoses.... The physician then simply checks off the findings the patient is manifesting.

In the second phase ... Aesculapius searches a data bank called the Knowledge Base for illnesses that exhibit the same symptoms as the patient being interviewed. When diagnostic assistance is desired, Aesculapius permits the computer to weigh clinical data found in the history and physical. Like the mind of a physician, the computer's reasoning processes are molded so flexibly that a variety of uncertainty factors can be juggled to identify a disease, based on the strengths and weaknesses of the evidence at hand. (1984:18)

Sophisticated analytical programs using this wealth of data could be written to incorporate not only medical-risk data but also any lifestyle or social information that the policymakers wanted to include. As a subject of this decision-making process, the prospective patient would undergo a complete diagnosis similar to that of Aesculapius. His medical history, current health status, and relevant medical diagnostic data would be fed into the computer, as would demographic data, emotional status, and a range of lifestyle data relevant to the medical decision. The latter would vary depending on current medical knowledge. As understanding of the genetic bases of particular diseases broadens and the capacity to identify with precision genetic traits that predispose carriers to these diseases improves, these data would also be included. On the basis of this complex of information, the computer would return the verdict: a supposedly dispassionate, logical, and unbiased decision. The computer would specify whether or not the patient was an acceptable risk and, if so, what treatment was warranted.

This system would have the benefit of removing from the physicians or authorities the difficulty of personally making a decision not to treat. If such use of a computer were strongly supported by society, physicians would be able to point out to their patients their inability to counter or even appeal before a higher authority the official decision. The computer rationing system (COMRATS) would relieve the physician of making painful decisions and justifying them to patients for whom the verdict is "no treatment," but obviously it is the antithesis of the current system, which centers on the patient-physician relationship. COMRATS would replace a human decision—far preferable to most of us, no matter how fallible—with a statistical conclusion based on the assumptions and logic written into the software. Although the ultimate decision would be unemotional, and might in fact maximize the cost effectiveness of medical decisions, it would deprive medicine of any trace of an ethos of treating patients as individuals. The discretion of the doctor would be excluded from such a process and replaced by a set of statistical equations that would define and weigh the multitude of factors that must be part of any life/death decision. The physician would thus become nothing more than a glorified data processor whose job it would be to ensure that all relevant data make it into the computer.

Although COMRATS more clearly fits the world of the ever-logical Mr. Spock of "Star Trek" than the pluralist world of Dr. Spock, it represents one possible solution to the emerging health care crisis in the United States. In spite of its threat to the traditional practice of medicine and to the individual autonomy of patients and physicians, unless less drastic allocation and rationing schemes are initiated, COMRATS or some similar system might not remain simply a futuristic fiction. The computer capacity is already present, and the medical data banks necessary for such a system are well underway. All that is needed is the motivation to institute the process. A perceived uncontrollable crisis in medicine, if sufficiently onerous and widespread, might be enough. Conversely, the threat of a COMRATS might be enough to initiate serious efforts to develop a comprehensive rationing system that would be more congruent with our prevailing belief in the human factor.

Confronting the Difficult Choices: Toward Long-Term Solutions or Impending Crisis?

In order to avoid scenarios involving the use of COMRATS or, alternately, a collapse of the health care system, vigorous action must be forthcoming on several fronts. Although it might be helpful to continue or to expand current efforts to establish pro-competitive health delivery systems, regulate medical costs, and selectively reduce government support, long-term solutions necessitate major alterations in our basic orientations toward medicine outlined earlier in this chapter. We must rethink our social priorities and attempt to come to at least some broad agreement concerning what we as a society expect from the health care system.

Lasting solutions require difficult policy decisions at several levels. First, there must be a realistic appraisal of how much of society's resources we are willing to allocate to health care: 10 percent of the GNP? 12 percent? 15 percent? What priority does society place on medical care as opposed to education, housing, defense, leisure, and so forth? Once that appraisal is made, choices must follow as to how these resources are to be allocated among the various categories examined above. Do we wish to continue to place our emphasis on sophisticated but expensive technologies designed to extend life, or should we shift our emphasis to preventive medicine and primary care? Are we willing to fund research on some diseases far in excess of the mortality or morbidity they are responsible for, while virtually ignoring research on other, perhaps less "glamorous," diseases? Finally, hard rationing decisions at the individual level are unavoidable. This will require educating the public about the limits of medicine, moderating public expectations concerning health care, and shifting our priorities toward preventive approaches in which the individual has an obligation to order his or her life in a way that maximizes health and minimizes the need for expensive treatment.

Those individuals who oppose any rationing of medicine deceive themselves by denying its present existence. The fact is that medicine has always been rationed in some way. Although the United States to date has largely rejected any explicit rationing system, less direct forms are common. Decisions constantly are being made in medicine as to who shall receive medical goods and services. In the words of David Mechanic:

Although rationing is sometimes evoked by critics of change as a new impending threat and aberration, rationing of health care has always existed but it has remained sufficiently embedded in common modes of thinking to attract little attention. . . . Given the complexity and generosity of the American system of care, we have successfully maintained the illusion that rationing is foreign to it. (1986:63)

Elsewhere, Mechanic (1977) contends that the marketplace traditionally has been a natural device for rationing services. This rationing-by-fee system distributes health care services based on ability to pay. However, because of the trends discussed earlier, particularly the escalation of costs brought on by medical high technology and growing public demand unfettered by cost considerations, rationing by fee has broken down. This breakdown has been accelerated by physicians trained in the technological imperative which disdains considering the costs and benefits of a particular procedure for a particular patient before prescribing it.

Instead of focusing on whether or not some form of rationing is necessary, the debate more properly should be directed at the extent to which the government and its agents should take a direct role in establishing rationing procedures and structure. Should the haphazard, inequitable, and often contradictory private rationing continue, or should the government accept responsibility for the allocation and use of medical resources and take active steps to design and implement a comprehensive rationing system? I argue here that the government has this responsibility and must soon act upon it if a health care crisis is to be averted. Chapter 3 discusses in detail the various options that are presently available for distributing health care resources in the United States.

Revising Public Expectations: The Urgent Task of Public Education

Although the United States is far from the ideal model of democracy, public opinion traditionally has been a major factor for shaping the political boundaries within which public policy is made. Decision makers enjoy considerable discretion as long as they remain inside the broad parameters of public opinion. However, should they dare violate the public trust and transgress the opinion boundaries, they will find that change in the status quo comes only with considerable difficulty and at heavy political cost. Any alterations of the health care system, particularly alterations that might involve possible intervention into individual choice and lifestyle, will necessarily be constrained by the perceptions and expectations of the health care consumers themselves.

According to Klein (1981:292), the present American health care crisis may be primarily a matter of excessive expectations on the part of the public. He suggests that the dynamics of the U.S. political process generate expectations which cannot be realized, thus producing a gap between promise and performance. In order to change a policy, leaders must magnify its shortcomings to such an extent that the public will accept a change. For Klein, "the dramatic presentation of problems— the rhetorical language of crisis—may therefore be the price paid in the American political system for mobilizing sufficient support for action" (1981:292). This tendency is aggravated in the case of health policy, because the health care system itself generates excessive expectations among consumers eager to see each new medical "breakthrough" as corroboration of the technological progress whose benefits they expect to share, despite the costs.

Reinforcing the problem of unreasonable expectations is public ambivalence about what, if anything, should be done to control the escalating costs of medicine. According to Blendon and Altman, "The public is neither sufficiently concerned . . . nor sufficiently single-minded about what should be done to make adoption of a solution to the health-cost problem a realistic possibility" (1984:615). Although the public wants the problem of health care costs addressed by the policymakers, it appears unwilling to favor a solution that would dramatically alter the present health care arrangements. Jeffe and Jeffe comment, "There is little evidence that the public is prepared to lower its standards for health care quality and convenience. Thus, cost-saving measures that are perceived to reduce quality and accessibility are not likely to be palatable to the consumer" (1984:55). This national schizophrenia is evident in a growing data base of public opinion on the U.S. health care system. A brief review of these survey data exemplifies the difficult task facing policymakers in devising health decisions that will enjoy the necessary support of the public consumers.

Perception of a Health Care Problem

Despite all the attention placed on the problems of the health care system in the United States, neither the public nor its elected officials rank the health care issue very high among the most important problems facing the nation. National surveys taken by the Gallup Organization (1986) demonstrate that health-care-related problems do not appear among the top ten most important problems. Foreign policy, unemployment, inflation, excessive government spending, moral decay, and crime all rank higher in the view of the public. This view was also reflected in responses of governors to the same question as it relates to the state (National Governors' Association 1983). They, too, failed to rank the health issue in the top ten. It was ranked eleventh overall, well behind jobs, education, and public safety. This is particularly revealing, because outlays for health care are already the second or third largest expenditure for most states and, moreover, are usually the fastest growing.

When asked whether we as a nation were spending too little or too much to improve and protect the nation's health, two out of three Americans believe federal spending for health care should be increased (Blendon and Altman 1984:613). Only 14 percent feel that our society is spending too much for health care. Again, most Americans, unlike many economic analysts, do not seem to be overly troubled by the growing proportion of the economy devoted to health care. Indeed, they feel that we are spending too little for these services. Concern over health care in general is reflected also in a 1983 Louis Harris survey that found that only 21 percent of the public agreed that "on the whole, the health care system works pretty well and only minor changes are necessary to make it work better." In contrast, over 75 percent of the public felt that the health care system is in need of fundamental changes: a quarter of the respondents saw so many things wrong with it that in their opinion "we need to completely rebuild it" (Harris 1983).

Individual Experience with the Health Care System

In spite of a solid consensus that the medical system as a whole is in bad shape, most individuals surveyed are satisfied with the care they themselves receive. In a recent Yankelovich study (1982), 88 percent of the respondents were satisfied with the quality of care they received from doctors, 81 percent with the quality of hospital care, and 81 percent with their access to health care. These figures are consistent with the 1983 Harris findings of satisfaction, ranging from 70 percent for insurance benefits to 77 percent for the quality of health care in general, and they are in agreement with a recent Gallup survey (1986a), where 70 percent of the respondents rated hospital service on the high to very high side.

Although 78 percent of the public feel that the cost of medical care is unreasonable (Tarrance 1983), and 70 percent are somewhat or very dissatisfied with the cost (Yankelovich 1982), third-party payment shields a large proportion of the public from the real costs of health care, thus decreasing the public's immediate stake in lowering the costs. Yankelovich (1982) found that 63 percent of Americans have private health insurance coverage, 24 percent have Medicare or Medicaid coverage, and 13 percent are on prepaid health plans. Overall, 81 percent are very or somewhat satisfied with their present coverage. So, despite their concern over rising costs, most Americans accept the concept of third-party payers and are comfortable with the current system of payment. A study conducted for the American Hospital Association concluded that only 8 percent of the public lack some form of private or government health insurance coverage (Jeffe and Jeffe 1984:46).

Cost Containment and Regulation

Seventy-six percent of the public agree that one of the problems with health care is that there is no real competition holding prices down

(Harris 1983). This is not translated into public support for government attempts to regulate health care, however. Only 8 percent of Americans give a high priority to enactment of a national health service (Harris 1983), and only 40 percent would like to save money by giving up their personal doctors and being treated at a clinic (Tarrance 1983). By a margin of 38 percent to 30 percent, respondents felt that the cost of health care was more likely to increase with total government regulation than to lessen (Jeffe and Jeffe 1984:55). Similarly, 40 percent felt that the quality of health care would suffer by government regulation, while only 14 percent thought quality would improve. Again, these data appear to be in conflict with data presented earlier which demonstrate support for more government spending on health care. Also, 61 percent of the respondents to the 1983 Harris survey would support government controls of doctor and hospital fees. Not surprisingly, 90 percent of a sample of leaders of physicians' groups and 74 percent of the hospital administrators surveyed found the idea of such intervention unacceptable.

A final instance of ambiguous public soundings is the discrepancy between the public's view of the medical profession in general and of their own physicians. A similar discrepancy has been discovered between perceptions of Congress in general and of an individual's own congressman. In a study conducted for the AMA, while 66 percent of the sample said that "doctors are too interested in making money," only 28 percent said their own doctors were. Likewise, while 62 percent said doctors spent too little time with their patients, 77 percent felt their own physicians spent enough time with them (Tarrance 1983). In other words, when directed at the amorphous medical profession, public perception is negative; when members of that public consider their own physicians, however, their levels of trust and confidence remain high. This reflects the continuing importance to the public of the unique physician-patient relationship which obscures dissatisfaction with the impersonal medical bureaucracy.

The Knowledgeability of Health Care Consumers

Americans traditionally have viewed health care primarily from the perspective that "when you get ill you go to a physician to get better." Preventive medicine and holistic health care, although more salient today than in the recent past, remain minority approaches for both the medical community and the public. Moreover, the average health care consumer does not know how to use the health care system well. There is too much dependence on the professional medical community for health tasks that an educated person should be able to do for him- or herself. According to Brown (1978:149), uninformed people demand services they do not need, particularly if these services are offered as providing cures. In a majority of cases that physicians see, there is nothing they can do to cure the illness, and the person would get better without professional treatment. Third-party reimbursement has encouraged this misuse of health care.

Also, our population as a whole is ill-prepared to deal with emergency situations. Even simple first aid, which is largely common sense, is beyond the capacity of many citizens. The result is overuse of emergency room facilities and, again, third-party reinbursement. Despite active campaigns to teach CPR and other emergency life-saving techniques, most of the population remains ignorant. It is clear that health education in prevention, emergency aid, and in the use of the health system continues to be of low priority in our society. To a large extent, this reflects our heavy dependence on the technological, curative approach to health care outlined earlier. The proportion of the health dollar designated for education is minute. Only recently have patients been encouraged to obtain second opinions. Still, it is difficult for much of the public to even consider comparison shopping when it comes to health care. It may be that many persons put more thought into buying a pair of shoes or a new winter coat than into undergoing medical treatment.

Setting Limits on Health Care: Personal Responsibility for Health

As noted earlier, the prevailing value system in this country places heavy emphasis on the notion of rights. Although the Constitution makes no mention of a right to health care, the courts have often interpreted the right to life to include an inherent claim of all citizens to health care and to autonomy in making decisions concerning health. Although there has always been friction between individual rights and the common good or societal welfare, when these values conflict the individuals' claims to health care generally have taken precedence. Within the context of greatly expanded technological possibilities and the accompanying high costs, however, attention now has shifted to determining what, if any, limits should be placed on such claims upon society by individuals for health care. Harron, Burnside, and Beauchamp remark,

As the cost of health care has escalated, our expectations of medicine have expanded. It seems that the more successful medicine becomes, the more we expect from it. In some quarters, the definition of health has expanded to include an all-inclusive concern for human well-being—physical, mental, and social. At the same time, the demands of "rights" to health and health care have extended to all segments of the population....

In addition to deciding how much of our resources will be committed to health care, we also must face the fact that full and complete care cannot be given to everyone in the society. By what system, then, shall individuals qualify? If exclusion is necessary, then by what system shall persons be excluded? (1983:114).

There remains a strong belief that all persons in an affluent nation such as the United States should have a decent standard of health care, and that society, in the name of justice and fairness, has a responsibility to guarantee this standard to those who cannot attain it in the private sphere. Disagreement centers on the definition of a "decent standard" of health care: what does it include and what might reasonably be excluded from its purvey? According to the President's Commission for the Study of Ethical Problems in Medicine and Biomedical and Behavioral Research (1983a), no one has the right to have life extended at all costs. Although everyone is "entitled to an adequate level of care," no one is entitled to a "maximum level that would bankrupt the nation," according to Morris Abram, chairman of the commission. No one, it would seem, has the right to extraordinary health care, if such care necessitates public expenditures that would preclude or dilute a more minimal level of health care for others in society. The distinction between ordinary care necessary to meet the "standards of sound medical practice" assured to all persons, and extraordinary care which is not assured to all, is of course a policy decision of great magnitude. As noted by Engelhardt (1984), there are moral as well as financial limits to society's protection of its members from the risks of poor health. The major policy problems center on what the boundaries of health are and who defines them.

As with all rights, even the most fundamental ones, the right to health is far from absolute. There are many instances where the state might be morally justified in denying extraordinary medical care even if its decision condemns the individual to death. No matter how difficult to accept in an individual case, as Abram points out, an absolute entitlement to a maximum level of care could bankrupt the system and, more importantly, substantially reduce the level of health care available to the population as a whole.

Although a prevailing emphasis in contemporary American society is the right of the individual, it must be remembered that any right also implies a corresponding obligation. The right of one individual vis-à-vis other individuals in society carries with it the notion of an obligation to respect the corresponding rights of those others. In the area of health care, then, it could be argued that a person has an obligation to care for himself in a way that promotes good health. A shift of emphasis from the individual's rights to his responsibilities is in evidence in much of the current health care literature and promises to be at the vortex of the public policy debate over the allocation and rationing of medical resources. The Office of Health Economics, for instance, suggests that there might "need to be a fundamental shift in public and professional attitudes toward health in which the individual would have to accept a very much greater degree of responsibility for his own well-being" (1979:387). If one has a claim on society for some minimal level of health care, then one also has a responsibility to minimize the overall costs to others in society by living as healthful a life as possible. Without this explicit balance between rights and responsibilities, those who take their obligations seriously will suffer unfairly. This issue will be addressed most directly in chapters 3 and 5.

Preventive Medicine and Lifestyle Change

The preference for curative medicine over preventive medicine in the United States is well documented (Murray 1984). According to the Idaho Health Systems Agency,

Medicare demonstrates preference for high technology over prevention. Illustrations:

—Magnetic resonance imagery diagnoses, which costs between $360 and $1,400 per scan, is covered. Outpatient prescription drugs are not.
—Renal dialysis for persons with end stage kidney disease is covered. Flu shots and dental services are not.
—Heart transplants for disabled persons under age 55 are covered (costing $10 million to treat 63 people). Routine gynecological exams, including PAP smears and breast exams, are not. (1986)

Moreover, the medical profession has developed primarily around the search for cures for disease, rather than for ways of preventing disease. Often, however, advanced technologies are supportive rather than curative; that is, instead of curing a disease, they preserve a particular level of personal health by creating a continual dependence on further medical treatment (Ricardo-Campbell 1982:6). Considerable evidence suggests, however, that the most significant improvements in health have come from preventive, not curative or supportive efforts, even though these latter efforts are the more dramatic and are therefore more readily funded. Furthermore, most advances in the preventive area have come from outside medicine, primarily in the areas of improved sanitation, nutrition, housing, and education.

Although many preventive efforts such as detection and treatment of hypertension are not cost effective according to Russell (1986:4), if well planned and executed, preventive medicine often can provide a high return on investment. Conversely, curative medicine, at present the prevailing approach, is often of questionable utility, particularly near the end of life. But here again, society's obsession with keeping the individual alive forces us to invest huge amounts of scarce health dollars in the quest to prolong life even for a short time. Moreover, often the life we are "saving" is of questionable quality, spent attached to tubes and machines in a sanitized hospital setting. The recent moves toward hospice care and the refusal of heroic lifesaving measures represent a repudiation of the high-technology extension of life which has become a major aspect of our health care system.

Despite the disenchantment felt by many with the prevailing focus on life extension at all costs, and the view of some that death has been dehumanized in the process, billions of dollars continue to be expended on the development of life-extending technologies. In the words of

Lester Thurow, "modern technology makes it likely that everyone will die of an illness that requires immense amounts of money except those lucky to die quietly in their sleep" (1985:611). The medical community as a whole, with strong support from the public, still favors curative medicine. If, as argued earlier, health dollars expended in one area come at the expense of funding in other areas of medicine, this preoccupation with high-cost curative technologies raises serious questions as to whether or not we are making the best possible use of our limited health dollars. From a cost-effectiveness standard alone, it is clear we are not. According to Saward and Sorensen, "When viewed from an economic perspective, it would appear that in curative medicine we are spending more and more for less and less improvement" (1980:49).

If, upon close scrutiny, prevention proves more effective than curative efforts, then preventive medicine must be given high priority in a social policy that attempts to distribute scarce resources most fairly. A multifaceted preventive approach would require that substantial attention be given to improving the environment by reducing environmental pollutants, to eliminating unsafe working conditions, and to continuing to improve housing, health education, and early detection programs. Inadequate nutrition continues to contribute to a variety of health problems and would also have to be addressed in a comprehensive health care program.

The most difficult preventive measures are likely to be those in which the individual has prime responsibility: cutting down on smoking and on alcohol and drug use, improving diet, getting adequate exercise, using seat belts, and so forth. Together, for lack of a better term, these behaviors and habits are here labeled "lifestyle" decisions. For reasons to be examined in detail in chapter 5, attempts by the government to intervene in lifestyle decisions are inherently controversial in American culture and bound to fail if there is any evidence of government coercion. For instance, laws requiring motorcyclists to wear safety helmets have been attacked as paternalistic and unwarranted government interference in behavior that is not threatening to the health of others. Many such mandates have either been rejected by the courts as violations of individual autonomy or rescinded by legislatures under constituency pressure. A premise of this book, however, is that pressures emerging from the health care crisis necessitate a much closer look at the role individuals play in contributing to their own health problems; a shift of responsibility for health toward the individual; and a renewed emphasis on the individual's obligation to society to do those things that maximize health.

2

Critical Health Care Issues

This chapter introduces four specific areas of health care that promise to exacerbate the emerging crisis in medicine: organ transplantation; the treatment of disabled infants; the use of reproductive innovations; and the provision of adequate fetal environments. Although they involve different life stages, from preconception to near death, these health care areas share many characteristics. All clearly illustrate the extent to which new medical technologies and medical knowledge produce excruciating ethical and public policy impasses. They also raise questions of individual rights and obligations and of the extent to which societal good might negate personal autonomy. Together, these issues demonstrate the political difficulties we face in defining the proper role of government in making health care decisions in a pluralist society.

The discussion here is designed to describe the technical advances in each of the four areas and to explicate their policy implications. It does not analyze directly the accompanying ethical problems, nor does it specifically discuss questions concerning the possible rationing of medical resources as applied to each area. Also, examination of the role of government in these substantive areas is here kept brief: it is covered in considerably greater detail and in a more integrated fashion in succeeding chapters.

Human Organ Transplantation

One of the most dramatic of the medical technologies, and the most expensive on a per case basis, is the transplantation of major human organs, primarily heart, liver, and kidney. The recent extension of transplant possibilities through the use of artificial organs and organs from other species has created serious policy dilemmas that are bound to become more intense. The subject of organ transplant surgery also offers an opportunity to analyze the implications of public policy, because there has been direct government subsidy of kidney transplantation. This section examines the technological advances which define the medical boundaries of organ transplant surgery. It also describes the current debate over developing a national policy concerning organ transplantation and the implications such a policy would have for health care in the United States. Because heart and kidney transplantation have been dealt with more extensively in the literature, focus is placed primarily on liver transplants here, although some comparative data on other procedures are included.

Medical Parameters of Organ Transplants

Advances in surgical procedure, organ preservation techniques, tissue matching, and drug treatment have combined to accelerate the frequency and magnitude of organ transplantation. As survival rates continue to improve, the demand for transplant surgery has multiplied. Patients are now queuing up for new livers, hearts, kidneys, pancreases, and heart-lung combinations as their original organs fail. (In 1986, Thomas Starzl of the University of Pittsburgh Health Center announced that he was ready to attempt the first total gastrointestinal transplant into a man who had only six inches of intestine left. If approved by the hospital's institutional review board, the procedure would involve simultaneous transplant of the small intestine, liver, pancreas, spleen, stomach duodenum, colon, and rectum.) Although the number of transplant candidates remains small, the demand for transplant surgery is potentially unlimited in a population that would prolong life at great expense. Also, the number of transplant facilities has expanded rapidly to keep up with this demand. The number of medical centers doing liver transplants has climbed from 3 to 34 in four years. Similarly, the number of heart transplant centers has multiplied from 5 in 1982 to nearly 60 in 1987. At present, more than 180 medical centers are performing some type of transplant surgery.

Table 2.1 presents data on transplant procedures in the United

Table 2.1
Organ Transplantation in the United States

	Kidney	Pancreas	Liver	Heart	Heart-Lung
First transplant	1954	218	1963	1967	1981
Number performed (1984)	6,968	218	308	346	37
Cost	$20,000 to $35,000	$35,000 to $60,000	$100,000 to $300,000	$ 70,000 to $250,000	$100,000 to $300,000
One-year survival rate with cyclosporine	80–90%	35–40%	60–70%	75–80%	
Approximate number of centers (1985)	110	19	34	58	8
Estimated number who could benefit per year	7,000	5,000	10,000	50,000	—

Source: Unpublished 1984, 1985 reports of the American Council on Transplantation.

States. By far the organ most commonly transplanted is the kidney. The moderately low cost of the operation, its reimbursement through Medicare, and the relative availability of donor organs ensures continued expansion of this program. Kidney transplants are clearly the most routine of the procedures, although even here, up to 20 percent of the transplant patients die within one year and about 40 percent die within three years. It is obvious from table 2.1 that the potential costs of heart and liver transplants far exceed those of the kidney program, primarily because of the large initial cost of the former. Also, the survival rates continue to be lower for heart and especially for liver transplants. Although survival rates undoubtedly will rise for liver transplants, this surgery also will continue to be problematic because of the nature of the organ and the difficulty of obtaining suitable donor organs. (Because there is only one liver and one heart, obviously the use of living donors is not an option as it is with kidneys.)

The Cyclosporine Controversy

The most recent development to substantially improve the survival rate of transplant patients is the introduction of the drug cyclosporine (originally cyclosporin-A). Cyclosporine is one of the most potent and specific immunosuppressants so far discovered. Approved by the Food and Drug Administration in 1983 for routine use, it suppresses the body's natural immune system and keeps it from rejecting the transplanted organ. Cyclosporine is unique in that while it suppresses production of the white blood cells responsible for organ rejection, it does not grossly interfere with the activation of antigen-specific suppressor T-cells or B-lymphocytes which destroy bacteria.

Not only has cyclosporine dramatically reduced the incidence of organ rejection, but when rejection does occur, the process is slowed. As a result, episodes of rejection are less dangerous and easier to treat. According to Austen and Cosimi, both "survival and rehabilitation have improved markedly in cyclosporin-treated patients" (1984:1437). Cyclosporine has roughly doubled the overall one-year survival rate for kidney transplant patients (from 50 percent to about 85 percent), and for liver recipients (from 35 percent to 70 percent). A Stanford University trial of cyclosporine in cardiac transplant patients has proven its superiority over conventional immunosuppression. Stanford now projects survival to be 75 percent at two years, up from 58 percent without the drug. Also, because of accelerated rehabilitation, the cardiac transplant patient's average hospital stay has been cut from 72 days to 42 days, and hospital costs have fallen from over $100,000 to $67,000 (Austen and Cosimi 1984:1437). Certainly, the introduction of cyclosporine has revolutionized the transplant field.

Despite its effectiveness in suppressing the immune system and in markedly improving survival rates, cyclosporine, like all medical innovations, also has its drawbacks. For one thing, it is expensive. Maintenance doses for transplant patients cost anywhere from $4,000 to $10,000 per year. Although this cost undoubtedly will be reduced in the future, it will remain high. More important, however, are the severe side effects of this drug. The major toxic effect of cyclosporine is impaired kidney function in virtually all patients who have used it (Strom and Loertscher 1984:728). It has also been linked to liver damage, to hypertension, and to an increased risk of the cancer lymphoma (Austen and Cosimi 1984:1437). Considerable research activity is underway to determine what combination of cyclosporine therapy and conventional immunosupression will reduce the risk of such damage. Also, continued development of new analogues of cyclosporine with comparable potency but less toxicity is expected in the future. In the meantime, the difficult question is whether or not the long-term benefit of cyclosoporine use outweighs the long-term risks, particularly the risk of hastening kidney failure. Not to be lost is the irony in using an agent which eventually destroys the very organ it saved.

Unanswered Questions

In addition to the questions raised by the use of cyclosporine, organ transplantation raises many other serious policy questions. A major one arises from the problem of guaranteeing a sufficient supply of organs. This is especially critical for those organs, such as the heart, pancreas, and liver, that require a brain-dead donor. Austen and Cosimi (1984:1437) estimate that the number of suitable heart donors is currently about 2,000. Although this pool is satisfactory now, if the indications for heart transplants are substantially improved, a major donor shortage is anticipated.

The donor problem is complicated by the fact that the families of many suitable donors refuse permission. The figure of 2,000 cited above represents only about 10 to 15 percent of the people who suffer brain death each year and could serve as organ donors if permission was forthcoming. Although the rate of donations may be increased through education campaigns, the overall size of the pool might actually shrink as medicine learns to save more of these people (Wehr 1984b:458). Also, with good reason, the government is hesitant to intervene and encourage procurement of organs from unwilling or even undecided donors. The Uniform Act for the Donation of Organs requires the documentation of consent before organs can be transplanted. The question today is whether or not the Act could be amended to presume consent in the absence of any documents to the contrary. According to Mark Cwiek:

The solution seems clear: action must be taken now to promote the availability of needed human organs and to avoid creating greater social and moral problems. The passage of presumed consent laws in all of these fifty states must become a priority of the highest order. (1984:99)

Although this approach, presently used in Belgium (*American Medical News*, March 13, 1987, p. 24), might resolve the supply problem, it contradicts our basic values concerning personal autonomy. According to Engelhardt, "the more one presumes that organs are not societal property, the more difficult it is to justify shifting the burden to individuals to show they do not want their organs used" (1984:70). Although Engelhardt considers it unfortunate that potential recipients may die if insufficient organs are available for transplantation, he does not consider this unfair, because other values (i.e., keeping the body intact for burial) must be protected in a free society. "Free societies," Engelhardt writes, "are characterized by the commitment to live with tragedies that result from the decisions of free individuals not to participate in the beneficent endeavors of others" (1984:70–71).

A related problem that is reaching crisis proportions is the diminishing blood supply. On the one hand, the eligible donor pool has contracted, in part due to the public's fear of AIDS. On the other hand, the demand for blood continues to escalate as more surgeries and organ transplants—some of which require over 100 units of blood—are performed. Alfred Grindon, director of American Red Cross Blood Services in Atlanta, predicts that fewer units of blood will be available in the future (Bosy 1987:2). The result, he contends, will be ethical arguments over who should have access: those with money, or family, or friends who can arrange donations, versus those who cannot make special arrangements. This scarcity of blood also raises broader allocation questions as to whether surgeries that represent extraordinary strains on the blood supply should continue to take precedence.

There is also the broader policy question of the social value of high-cost procedures such as liver transplants. In fact, organ transplants provide a cogent example of the conflict between the prevailing ideal in our culture that no expense be spared to save an individual, and the reality that in the aggregate the costs of such allocations might detract from more productive uses of limited health care resources. According to Albert Jonsen, for instance, the development of the artificial heart threatens to deprive many persons of access to needed medical care:

The threat appears first in the likelihood that public expenditures will be drawn to this technology, rather than toward preventive measures that would have, overall, a more beneficial effect on health.... The added burden on publicly financed health care will force certain budgetary reallocations. These are likely to affect less visible, less "urgent" expenses such as those for health education, screening, prevention, community clinics, hospital stay, and so forth. (1986:10–11)

The trade-offs here are very clear. Rita Spence, president of Emerson Hospital in Concord, Massachusetts, estimates that the hospital bill for William Schroeder's artificial heart operation represents 790 days of care at her hospital, or full treatment for 113 patients at an average stay of one week. More dramatically, the cost of one liver transplant would finance one year's operation of an inner-city clinic in San Francisco that provides 30,000 office visits in that time (Friedrich 1984:76). Arnold Relman, editor of the *New England Journal of Medicine*, sees the emphasis on organ transplants as threatening to bankrupt us or at least divert money from pressing social needs such as housing, education, and the environment (Rodgers 1984:63).

All investments in expensive lifesaving treatments raise questions of social priorities. Do such treatments represent the efficient use of health care resources, and what trade-offs are required to provide the requisite amount of resources? Do we have the moral authority to use state powers to redistribute financial resources, or scarce organs themselves, so as to provide transplant surgery for all those who would benefit? Finally, does the individual in a liberal society have a right to a new organ if the alternative is death? If so, how far does this right extend when it conflicts with the rights of others to receive more basic health care needs? These difficult questions of fairness, equity, efficiency, and cost are inescapable.

One final point about the use of organ transplantation must be made. In spite of all the technical advances, it is still unclear how many people really have their lives meaningfully extended by new organs. Even under optimal circumstances, 30 to 40 percent of liver transplants will fail within a month, during which the patient endures considerable physical and emotional pain. But even if the patient survives for a year or two or more, post-transplant existence is usually quite difficult for the patient and his family. Hale illustrates the post-surgical emotional and psychological ordeals of patients who have undergone transplant surgery and must now live "tethered to medical treatment for life" (1984). She cites the high incidence of suicide among kidney transplant patients as well as more tacit forms of revolt, such as noncompliance, that stem from the loss of control over their lives following surgery.

There is a danger that in our quest to prolong life at all costs, we lose sight of quality-of-life concerns. According to Kenneth Vaux, "we are going to have to temper our ambitions and learn to accept the inevitability of the disease, the inevitability of death itself" (Friedrich 1984:75). We must learn that everything that can be done, that is technically possible, need not be done to prolong a life if the quality of that life will be so poor as to negate those things which make a human a human. We must first develop the capacity to distinguish between those cases in which the benefit to the person will be marginal at best, and those in which his or her life will be as meaningfully extended. Even in the latter cases, we must be aware of the trade-offs implicit in any large single investment such as an organ transplant. Again, this returns us to the realm of government policy, where such decisions ultimately rest.

Government Involvement in Transplantation

By 1972, kidney dialysis had improved dramatically, and demand for this treatment far outstripped its availability, thus necessitating a private rationing system. In passing the end stage renal disease (ESRD) program that year, Congress took the easy way out. After witnessing the public relations campaign of the proponents, which included the dialysis of a patient during a Ways and Means Committee hearing, Congress extended Medicare coverage to all kidney patients. It took this action at the same time that it increased taxes to bail out Medicare, which faced imminent bankruptcy. Eighty percent of kidney dialysis and transplant costs are now borne by the federal government.

The ESRD program is often cited as a case in disastrous medical policymaking. Because original projections severely underestimated the number of eligible patients, the first-year costs of $241 million far exceeded the estimate of $135 million. By 1983, the cost of the ESRD program exceeded $2 billion per year for approximately 70,000 patients. As a result, these patients, who represented about .25 percent of all Medicare beneficiaries, accounted for 13 percent of total Medicare expenditures for outpatient care and almost 10 percent of all Medicare B costs. The advent of federal funding not only allowed the dialysis population to become considerably larger, but also sicker and older. In 1967, only 7 percent of dialysis patients were over 55; by 1983, the percentage had climbed to 45. Many dialysis patients suffer from other diseases that would disqualify them from treatment in Britain and other countries with a national health service. According to Robert Rubin, a kidney specialist who is Assistant Secretary for Planning and Evaluation in the Department of Health and Human Services, any sort of transplant entitlement program could force the government to pour money into the treatment of patients with little chance of survival: "You might not want to transplant someone with cancer beyond the margins of the liver but if it's a federal program, heck, you do it" (Wehr 1984b:458). The hesitancy of Congress to rush into support for federal funding of liver and heart transplants is therefore understandable. According to Annas, however, the decision of Congress in 1972 to fund kidney treatment "simply served to postpone the time when identical decisions will have to be made about candidates for heart and liver transplantation" (1985:187). That time has now arrived.

On the other hand, there are significant political pressures on policymakers to guarantee new organs to those who need them. Just as the ESRD program was the result of strong and emotion-laden lobbying efforts, so today public officeholders increasingly are becoming the targets of constituents who appeal for public aid in obtaining and paying for expensive transplant surgeries. Most difficult to resist are the pleas for lifesaving transplants from the parents of young children. House Speaker Tip O'Neill, CBS's Dan Rather, and President Reagan, among many other notables, have succumbed to these emotional pleas and interceded on behalf of particular patients who have made it into the public spotlight. At the local level as well, it is not unusual to see the news media carrying these appeals to the public and from there to local, state, and national officials.

In a well-publicized case, the parents of 11-month-old Jamie Fiske led a campaign in 1982 to obtain funding for her liver transplant. With the leverage of the local press and politicians, the Fiskes forced Blue Cross/Blue Shield to agree to pay for the surgery. Once successful at that stage, the Fiskes appeared at the national convention of the American Academy of Pediatrics to ask for a live donor. Although initially their request was refused, the story made it into the national news, and Jamie had a new liver in eight days. There was a similar case in 1983 involving a military family; when Adriane Broderick needed a new liver, her parents were able to manipulate the system to get Congress to order the military medical program, CHAMPUS, to finance such procedures. It was reported that White House aide Michael Batten estimated that his activities in pressuring private health insurers and state Medicaid directors to finance liver transplants have "forced 20 states to pay for liver transplantations when they otherwise might have declined" (Wehr 1984b:455).

As a result of this access to surgery through public relations, the distribution of organ transplants makes very little sense from a medical or fairness standpoint. In one case, for instance, a child who was judged to be a poor medical risk was given two transplants partly because congressional and media attention made the patient a cause célèbre (Rodgers 1984:63). Recently, parents who followed the formal procedures for obtaining a donor heart for their infant were outraged when publicity over the denial of a heart transplant for Baby Jesse gained her immediate access to treatment, over those patiently waiting in the queue for a suitable organ. For every person who obtains a transplant through these methods, scores of others die for lack of same, even though they might be better medical risks.

Until recently, one rationale of third-party payers for not reimbursing patients for the costs of liver transplants was that the transplants represented experimental, not therapeutic, procedures. Because reimbursement is generally made only for those procedures which are shown to be reasonable and necessary therapeutic measures, many insurers have refused to pay. In 1983, however, a National Institutes of Health panel proclaimed liver transplants therapeutic, thus opening the way for a flood of potential transplant patients. Writes Rodgers, "Armed with NIH's blessing, transplant boosters began demanding more operations, tried prying funds from reluctant insurers and pressed Congress and the Reagan Administration for medicare coverage. Governors and legislators hurried aboard the transplant bandwagon" (1984:62). Continued attempts of third-party payers, including the government, to avoid payment on grounds that liver transplants are still experimental are bound to be viewed as nothing more than an effort to avoid facing the enormous costs.

In response to the growing dispute over liver transplants, on October 4, 1984 Congress passed a bill (S. 2048) designed to ease the difficulties of patients and their families seeking organ transplant surgery and to take these decisions out of the realm of public relations. Interestingly, a provision that would have financed cyclosporine treatment for patients who could not afford the drug was omitted from the final bill. As passed by Congress, however, the bill created a task force to study and report on the ethical, legal, financial, and other questions associated with organ transplants. The final report of the Task Force on Organ Transplantation was issued by the Department of Health and Human Services (HHS) in July 1986. Specifically, it deals with the allocation of transplant surgery and the limited supply of human organs, the extent of insurance coverage, the medical value of immunosuppressive therapy, and payments for such therapy.

The bill also authorizes the expenditure of $2 million annually to support a national computerized system for matching patients with donors of scarce organs. This is especially critical with the proliferation of transplant centers across the country and the more than 120 existing organ retrieval agencies. As an effort to save more of the many organs reportedly wasted for lack of skilled teams to save and transplant them, S. 2048 moreover authorized $5 million in fiscal 1985, increasing to $12 million in 1987, for grants to create or upgrade local and regional agencies that procure human organs for transplantation and that participate in the computerized matching network. This bill also provides for a national registry of transplant patients to facilitate scientific evaluations of transplant procedures and directs the Secretary of HHS to assign responsibility for administering organ transplant programs to the Public Health Service or another appropriate body. Finally, this bill prohibits the purchase or sale of human organs for transplantation and authorizes sentences of up to five years for knowingly violating this provision. This latter provision is likely to be critical as the proliferation of transplant centers produces a demand for suitable organs that outstrips the limited supply. It also demonstrates government's compelling interest in protecting individuals from economic incentives for selling their organs by imposing actual penalties on such a choice. Although Senate Bill 2048 certainly does not appear to threaten a repeat of the ESRD experience, it will be very difficult for Congress to escape the growing pressures from constituents, interest groups, and the media to fund an expanding array of organ transplants.

Treatment of Seriously Ill Newborns

In a press conference held to announce guidelines for infant bioethics committees (IBCs), Robert J. Haggerty, vice president of the American Academy of Pediatrics, asserted that who decides how to treat newborns with severe disabilities and how those decisions are made "has become the moral issue of our time." Ironically, as with organ transplants, it is the success of medicine in treating these severe disabilities that has itself produced the controversial moral and financial public policy dilemmas. Until very recently, nature largely did the selecting of which infants would survive and which would die. Today, however, increasingly sophisticated neonatal treatment is altering the course of nature. A variety of physical conditions that in the near past were considered fatal and untreatable are now treated. In some cases the results of aggressive neonatal treatment are good and the infants survive to lead fulfilling lives. However, in a growing number of cases the quality of life of the surviving infant is so questionable as to raise doubts about the use of the lifesaving treatment. The result, according to the President's Commission, is that

medicine's increased ability to forestall death in seriously ill newborns has magnified the already difficult task of physicians and parents who must attempt to assess which infants will benefit from various medical interventions and which will not. Not only does this test the limits of medical certainty in diagnosis and prognosis, it also raises profound ethical issues. (1983:198)

Moreover, these ethical issues soon become policy issues because, for reasons discussed below, a large proportion of interventions are paid for by public funds, and neonatal care is extremely expensive and in many cases of marginal long-term benefit.

The Technological Context: Neonatal Care

In the decade between 1970 and 1980, the death rate of neonates (infants 28 or fewer days old) was almost cut in half, the greatest proportional decrease in any decade on record. A significant portion of this improvement occurred among the smallest of infants, those with birth weights below 1,500 grams, or about 3.3 pounds (1,000 grams is approximately 2.2 pounds). Among infants weighing between 1,000 and 1,500 grams, the survival rate has increased from 50 percent in 1961 to over 80 percent at present. Furthermore, over half the infants born weighing less than 1,000 grams now survive, compared with less than 10 percent in 1961. This impressive increase in the survival rate has been made, however, only at great monetary and personal expense. These costs are examined here for each of the two general categories of newborns in which decisions whether or not to use life-sustaining treatment must be made: newborns with low birth weight, and those with congenital abnormalities.

Approximately 230,000 infants, or 7 percent of all live births in the United States annually, are classified as low birth weight. Of that number, approximately 18,000 weigh less than 1,000 grams (Bernbaum and Hoffman-Williamson 1986:22). Although infants weighing less than 1,500 grams constitute less than 1 percent of all live births in the United States, they account for almost 25 percent of all admissions to neonatal intensive care units and half of all infant deaths (OTA 1981:11). While the average length of hospital stay in the neonatal period for normal weight infants is 3.5 days, the corresponding figure for infants weighing less than 1,000 grams is 89 days. Besides the prolonged hospitalization at birth, a substantial proportion of infants with very low birth weights are rehospitalized during the first year (McCormick 1985:87).

Most low birth weight babies are premature, although a minority are small despite a normal gestation period. Premature birth is caused by a variety of factors, including poor maternal nutrition and cigarette smoking as well as many other aspects of the fetal environment. Failure to thrive, or growth retardation of the fetus in the uterus, is found in a higher proportion of infants born to women from the lower socioeconomic groups, particularly young, single, nonwhite mothers who lack proper prenatal care (Eisner et al. 1979).

Low birth weight is strongly associated with illness and mortality in the neonatal period. The lower the birth weight, the more serious the problems. According to Shapiro and associates (1980:363), low birth weight infants are forty times more likely than infants of normal weight (over 2,500 grams) to die in the neonatal period, and five times more likely to die between one month and one year of age. Despite the improvement in survival rates cited earlier, a large proportion of infants born weighing less than 750 grams die even though aggressive treatment improves their chance of survival. One recent study showed survival rates of 45 percent for infants in the 700- to 800-gram range and 8 percent in the 500- to 600-gram range (Bowes and Simmons 1980:1080). Moreover, many of the survivors have severe long-term health problems. In summarizing a series of studies, Strong (1983:16) found that the percentage of survivors among 500- to 1000-gram infants who have a major handicap (such as severe mental retardation, cerebral palsy, major seizure disorders, or blindness) ranges from 7 percent to 30.2 percent. An additional 21.9 percent to 55 percent have some lesser degree of handicap (learning disabilities, hyperactivity, verbal delay, minor hearing loss). The proportion of these infants with a normal neurological outlook varies from 5.6 percent to 29.1 percent. Many of the problems experienced by very low birth weight babies arise from the fact that they have been deprived of a very critical maturation period in the womb. Although the major organ systems are in place after 20 weeks of gestation, they remain immature in development and function. When the fetus is separated from the functional development of the uterus and its natural life-support system, aggressive medical intervention is necessary to sustain life.

The most common complication of premature birth is hyaline membrane disease, a consequence of immature lung development. Machine-assisted ventilation by means of respirators is used to supplement the insufficient oxygen supply caused by this disease, but even so 50 to 70 percent of deaths among premature infants can be linked to lung disease. Low birth weight infants are also at high risk for birth asphyxia, which can cause permanent brain damage of varying degrees. Hypothermia, hypoglycemia, retarded bone growth due to calcium deficiency, and a susceptibility to infections due to an immature immune system are also common. Severe jaundice can result from an immature liver, and underdeveloped kidneys and gastrointestinal tracts make feeding difficult. Maintaining the delicate balance essential to proper development of the fetus outside the womb is the task facing health care providers for low birth weight babies.

The second category of seriously ill infants are those afflicted with congenital abnormalities requiring major medical attention in order for the infants to survive. About 4 percent of the infants born in the United States have one or more detectable congenital abnormalities. Although they account for only a small fraction of the neonatal intensive care cases, the Baby Does and Baby Faes dominate the discussion in the media as well as in the medical literature. Most common among congenital abnormalities are neural tube defects (NTDs) such as spina bifida and anencephaly, and Down's syndrome. Neural tube defects are present in approximately two out of every one hundred live births in the United States. The most common NTD, spina bifida, causes physical and/or mental disabilities that vary widely in severity and may involve many organ systems. Because of the wide variation in effect, difficult decisions must be made as to whether or not aggressive surgical treatment is warranted and, if so, what treatment is most appropriate.

Another congenital abnormality that has raised substantial debate within the medical community as well as among the public is Down's syndrome. Individuals with Down's syndrome are mentally retarded, although the degree of retardation varies widely and cannot be determined in early infancy when the decision whether or not to treat is crucial. A difficult issue, and one which has fueled the debate over treatment of the infant with a severe handicap, concerns the significant minority of Down's syndrome children born with gastrointestinal blockages, congenital heart defects, or both. Although surgical treatment in these cases often is routine, as opposed to treatment for severe spina bifida, where the results of surgery are problematic, many parents and physicians reject intervention to preserve the life of such children. Survey research data (Gallup 1983) in fact reflect an even division of the public over the question of allowing a Down's syndrome baby to die rather than using medical intervention to save its life. While 40 percent favor treatment in such circumstances, 43 percent oppose it.

Neonatology

In 1975, the American Board of Pediatrics gave the first neonatology certification examinations. During the decade since, over 1,000 neonatologists have been certified. Along with the growth of this medical subspeciality, high-technology neonatal intensive care units (NICUs) have opened across the country. Over 600 hospitals now maintain NICUs. Some, such as the Children's Hospital in Denver, a level III facility with the latest in maternal, fetal, and neonatal technologies, have become regional centers specializing in highly aggressive treatment of newborns with low birth weight, congenital abnormalities, or other problems. Upon birth, the baby is resuscitated if necessary and sped (often by helicopter) to an NICU where the latest technical equipment and procedures are available. Fetal monitoring is often used to identify fetuses at risk; when a fetus is identified as such, the mother is transported to a hospital with an NICU so that immediate treatment will be available. Once an infant has been admitted to an NICU, the almost universal approach is to initiate aggressive treatment, because neonatologists are trained to use technologies to save lives. The Office of Technology Assessment (OTA 1981:15) estimates that 6 percent of infants are admitted to NICUs, staying on the average of eight to eighteen days. The total cost for NICU care in 1978 was approximately $1.5 billion.

Issues in Treating Seriously Ill Infants

Our heavy use of highly sophisticated and expensive neonatal intensive care again illustrates the tendency of our society to place emphasis on curative medicine at the expense of prevention. A large proportion of low birth weight infants are victims of environmental factors which can be controlled. Still, as stated by Miller, "efforts to treat the problem have gained support far in excess of efforts to prevent it" (1984:553). Instead of spending relatively small amounts of money to educate pregnant women and to provide adequate prenatal care and nutrition, we continue to place emphasis on treatment, at a very high cost to society and especially to those individuals directly affected. This latter point is especially critical because many of the infants who are saved have life-long diseases or handicaps requiring long-term commitments of effort and resources, should these survivors leave the hospital. Although the medical community and public officials appear willing to support NICUs, there is minimal support for less dramatic but crucial follow-up care.

I agree with Mathieu (1984:610) that it is "short-sighted and potentially disastrous to mandate sophisticated and costly medical care for severely handicapped newborns" without addressing the hard decisions of who cares for and pays for them after the initial lifesaving medical treatment is given. Many of these children will require extensive medical care throughout their lives. Are the parents expected to bear full responsibility for this downstream care? If so, they should have the final choice whether or not to initiate aggressive treatment at birth. What if the parents are not equipped to care for such a child? Until now, state support has been lacking. As the number of severely ill infants we save increases, we must be willing to expend considerably more resources to care for them throughout their lives. Responsibility does not end once they cease to be newborns. Once aggressive medical treatment ends, aggressive social care is essential. Ironically, even as we have encouraged aggressive medical intervention for neonates, we have actually allowed cuts in funding for social programs designed to cover the downstream needs of the infants we save. Mechanic links this tendency to our infatuation with technology: "As a culture, we do far better in the application of a 'technological fix' than in building complex social arrangements that must be sustained over time in coping with expressive, frustrating, and often intractible problems"(1986:207).

Opposition to this dependence on aggressive medical intervention to save the lives of seriously ill infants comes from several quarters, and is based primarily on either quality-of-life or cost-effectiveness considerations. Sylvia Schechner (1980:142), a pediatrician, suggests that such efforts be withheld from infants weighing less than 750 grams because of the poor quality of life among many of those surviving. Care should be provided to keep the infant comfortable but no steps should be taken to prolong its life. Young agrees that aggressive therapy should not be initiated for infants weighing less than 750 grams unless "strong, countervailing medical or social reasons" can be offered. Instead, we must strive for a better balance between investments in initial aggressive treatment and the resources currently allocated for the long-term care of the disabled. To that end, limits must be set on "technological expansionism" and resources channeled into the prevention of conditions that at present we are "inclined to remedy, ex post facto, by highly aggressive technology (Young 1983:18). Just because a technology is available, we do not have to use it under all circumstances. William Kirkley (1980:873) raises the question of cost effectiveness by asking whether public funds might not be put to uses which would better promote the interests of society. Should society reallocate funds now expended on treatment for very low birth weight infants? This question is a matter of public concern in part because a significant portion of the overall cost of caring for very low birth weight infants is paid for through Medicaid (Strong 1983:16).

Although there is agreement that there are cases in which it is wrong to initiate or continue life-support procedures on certain infants (Duff and Campbell 1973), there is disagreement concerning the nature of those cases, the procedures for dealing with them, and the decision-making criteria (Robertson 1975). In addition to quality-of-life arguments, there are the considerations of the economic and emotional pressures on the family, as well as the cost to society of maintaining a growing number of severely handicapped children saved by aggressive treatment.

Carson Strong rejects cost-effectiveness arguments against aggressive treatment of newborns with severe birth defects: "Vigorous lifesaving medical care is required in the best interests of the patients.

In clinical decision making this consideration outweighs the financial burden to society, which ought to continue paying for this kind of medical care, out of considerations of justice" (1983:19). Although Strong contends that the decision to initiate aggressive treatment at birth does not commit us to providing continuous intensive care, it is very difficult to withdraw treatment once it is begun. Paul Ramsey (1970) argues that we have a duty to maintain neonatal life, despite any social costs, because the newborn is a human being. Diamond (1977) agrees that even the child with serious birth defects has the right to live and that the parents and physicians cannot decide to terminate that right, which takes precedence over all others.

Until very recently, the decision as to whether or not to intervene to save the life of the newborn with severe abnormalities supposedly was made exclusively by the parents in consultation with their physician. In actuality, the decision frequently was made unilaterally by the attending physician in the delivery room, based upon his medical judgment as to the potential quality of life for the infant. The President's Commission found that the prevailing opinion in the medical community is still that such decisions should be left to parents, because they are the ones who must bear the burdens of the decision: "Physicians confirmed that decisions to forego therapy are a part of everyday life in the neonatal intensive care unit; with rare exceptions, these choices have been made by parents and physicians without review by courts or any other body" (1983:207). The official stand of the AMA is that "the decision whether to exert maximal efforts to sustain life should be the choice of the parents" (American Medical Association 1982:9).

Seldom is treatment continued over parental objections. Moreover, there is little evidence of parents' demands for continued treatment being dismissed. There are, however, data to indicate that some parents feel they have been pressured to accept the advice of physicians. According to one report, manipulation of the situation by the health care providers for their own benefit does occur in the process: "Consultation with the family is used in part as a method of ensuring that they will accept the decision and not take legal action against the physician later. It is not considered appropriate for the family to make the final decision" (Crane 1975:76). Even taking into account such qualifications, until recently decisions as to how to medically treat infants with severe disabilities has largely been within the private domain. Events of the last several years, however, have placed these life/death decisions squarely at the center of public policy.

Government Involvement in Treating Disabled Infants

As noted earlier in this section, in April 1984 the American Academy of Pediatrics urged all hospitals to establish infant bioethics committees (IBCs) to make decisions on neonatal treatment (Annas 1984). The AAP guidelines were developed as a response to the Reagan administration's Baby Doe regulations. These regulations, in turn, were a reaction to the well-publicized case of a Down's syndrome infant with an incomplete esophagus who was allowed to die with parental consent. Under a federal law banning discrimination against the disabled (section 504 of the Rehabilitation Act of 1933), HHS issued regulations in 1983 to ensure that treatment was not deliberately withheld from handicapped infants. Hospital staff and others were urged to report apparent violations through a specially set up "hot line." In May 1984, however, the courts struck down the original regulations as well as attempted modifications.

In September 1984, after months of emotional hearings and difficult negotiation, Congress passed a child abuse bill (H.R. 1904-PL 98-457) which included controversial Baby Doe provisions. As a condition of receiving federal child abuse aid, the bill requires states to have procedures for responding to reports of medical neglect of handicapped infants in life-threatening situations through existing state child protection agencies. Also, hospitals are encouraged, but not required, to establish committees to review problematic cases. The bill also delineates special circumstances within which withholding treatment does not constitute medical neglect. Doctors do not have to take heroic measures when treatment is "virtually futile" in saving the infant's life, when the infant is "irreversibly comatose," or when the treatment itself is "inhumane."

Obviously, the wording of these exceptions, as well as references to "reasonable medical judgment," are ambiguous and open to a variety of interpretations (Rhoden and Arras 1985). This is understandable, because the Baby Doe provisions were backed by a coalition of medical, handicapped rights, and right-to-life groups, and had strong support from the Reagan administration. The American Hospital Association would have preferred to see the federal government stay out of this area, but they accepted the compromise version over previous ones. Despite backing by the AHA and by the American Academy of Pediatrics, the infant care provisions were not supported by the AMA because it felt they left no room for considering the quality of life severely disabled infants would face if they were kept alive indefinitely (Hook 1984a and 1984b).

In May 1985, the latest Baby Doe regulation went into effect in the form of the HHS's final rule implementing the child abuse amendments to the 1933 Rehabilitation Act. Through the wording of the regulations, it was clear that the Reagan administration intended to interpret the provisions of the act as narrowly as the courts would allow. The HHS regulations used the vague and flexible language of the act to justify a narrow and rigid interpretation of its medical indications policy, again rejecting any consideration of subjective quality-of-life judgments.

On June 9, 1986, the Supreme Court struck down the administration's Baby Doe rules (*Bowen* v. *American Hospital Association*). In a five to three vote, the Court ruled that the federal law prohibiting discrimination against handicapped individuals in activities receiving federal funding does not give the Secretary of HHS the right to intervene in decisions regarding medical treatment of handicapped infants. Justice Stevens, writing the plurality opinion (Justice Burger concurred with the judgment but disagreed with the reasoning), stated: "Section 504 does not authorize the secretary to give unsolicited advice either to parents, to hospitals, or to state officials who are faced with difficult treatment decisions concerning handicapped children." The laws of the fifty states regulating intervention in cases of medical neglect were not affected by the decision. The extent to which this decision will affect the treatment of handicapped newborns remains to be seen. Opponents of the Baby Doe rules hailed it as a return of discretion to parents and physicians, while proponents viewed this decision as undermining the right of the newborn to be treated aggressively.

The entry of the federal government into neonatal care decisions corresponds closely to recent initiatives in organ transplant legislation. I will analyze the implications of this pattern in later chapters. Suffice it to say here that medical decision making never again will be a fully private matter. The government is already heavily involved in setting public guidelines for what until very recently were decisions made by parents and physicians. According to Shapiro and Rosenberg: "Until now, such situations have been managed, with a great deal of caring and anguish, by a process involving primarily physicians and families. It has been suggested that the involvement of the federal government in this process could be disruptive to the usual medical and psycho-social processes" (1984:2033).

Reproductive Technologies

Both organ transplantation surgery and neonatal intensive care raise questions concerning the use of scarce medical resources. They also introduce the difficult issues of determining the proper role of the government in health care decision making, and of the rights and responsibilities of individuals with regard to medical care. Finally, it is clear from these two areas that the trade-offs necessary in order to allocate medical goods in a just and equitable manner are often painful ones, because not everyone can have the maximum treatment that is now technically possible. Hard policy decisions on transplant and neonatal care must be made, however. No longer is medicine a fully private matter. Nowhere is this shift towards the public sphere more pronounced than in the area of reproduction.

Reproduction has always been assumed to be a central right in a liberal society. Although some limits are placed on procreative choice in all societies, in most western societies procreation is viewed as a fundamental right inherent in the very concept of the individual. In recent decades, the U.S. Supreme Court has formalized the right to privacy in reproduction. Justice Douglas, in *Skinner* v. *Oklahoma* (1942), applied the concept of "fundamental interests" to procreation when he interpreted the equal protection clause of the Fourteenth Amendment as applying to protection from compulsory sterilization: "We are here dealing with legislation which involves one of the basic civil rights of man. Marriage and procreation are fundamental to the very existence and survival of the race." Since that time, the constitutional protection of reproductive choice has been expanded. Justice Goldberg, in a concurring opinion in *Griswold* v. *Connecticut* (1965), viewed the marital relationship as a fundamental area of privacy protected by the Ninth Amendment. The state can interfere with marriage and procreation only upon proof of a "compelling state interest." In addition, any proposed state action is subject to strict judicial scrutiny in terms of violation of the equal protection clauses. This philosophy was reiterated in *Roe* v. *Wade* (1973), in which the Court ruled that a state cannot dictate to a pregnant woman whether or not she may have an abortion during the first trimester of pregnancy. In *Eisenstadt* v. *Baird* (1972), the Court recognized "the right of the individual, married or single, to be free of unwarranted government intrusion into matters so fundamentally affecting a person as the decision whether to bear or beget a child." Although the individual's decision concerning reproduction is still valued, new technologies have begun to complicate what once was presumed to be a straightforward and natural process, thereby creating critical policy issues.

The growing arsenal of human genetic and reproductive technologies offers couples and individuals an increasing range of options for increasing fertility, limiting fertility, and exercising "quality control" over their potential progeny. Fertility-enhancing technologies are being developed, along with increasingly precise prenatal diagnosis and genetic screening techniques and an expanding variety of sex preselection methods. These reproductive technologies raise significant questions. At the same time as they expand individual choice, these innovations also heighten the possibility of societal control over reproduction. Several of the major innovations are discussed here, before these questions are addressed.

Technologies Aiding Conception

Infertility is a growing problem for many American men and women. In 1982, an estimated one in six couples was infertile. Although the causes of infertility are complex and poorly understood, environmental, heritable, pathological, and sociobehavioral factors are recognized contributors. Drug therapy and microsurgical intervention are effective in reversing infertility in some instances, but increasing numbers of couples are turning to reproductive technologies such as artificial insemination and in vitro fertilization. According to the OTA, the demand for these technologies is attributable to several factors:

1. Couples are delaying childbearing, thereby exposing themselves to the higher infertility rates associated with advancing age.
2. An increased proportion of infertile couples is seeking treatment due to an increased awareness of the availability and successes of modern infertility services coupled with a decreased supply of infants available for adoption. In 1983, about 50,000 adoptions took place in the United States, but an estimated two million couples wanted to adopt.
3. A greater number of physicians offer infertility services than in previous years. An estimated 45,600 physicians provide infertility services, a statistic that exceeds by 25 percent the number of physicians providing obstetric care. (1987:1)

The technique most widely used to aid conception is artificial insemination (AI). Approximately 10,000 to 15,000 children per year are conceived through this method, in which a syringe is used to deposit semen in or near a woman's cervix. AI is a relatively simple medical procedure; in fact, one researcher suggests that a home insemination kit might not be far off. Biologically, it is irrelevant whether the sperm is the husband's or a donor's, but the ethical, psychological, and social problems surrounding third-party insemination are considerable. Artificial insemination by donor (AID) is usually employed when the husband is wholly infertile or is known to suffer from a serious hereditary disorder such as Huntington's disease. AID may also be used by single women wishing to bear a child.

Although the first reported AID of a human took place a century ago, its use has been widened in the last several decades by the introduction of cryopreservation techniques which freeze and preserve sperm indefinitely by immersion in liquid nitrogen. Cryopreservation has led to the establishment of commercial sperm banks, some of which now advertise their products to the public. Sperm banks make it possible for a man to store his semen prior to undergoing a vasectomy, as a form of "fertility insurance." More importantly, they also facilitate eugenic programs where the sperm of "superior" men are sold to consumer couples or to single women.

In vitro fertilization (IVF), another technique now available to couples unable to conceive, is a procedure by which eggs are removed from a woman's ovaries, fertilized outside her body, and reimplanted in her uterus. This procedure is called for when the oviducts are blocked, preventing the egg from passing through the fallopian tubes to be fertilized. The National Academy of Sciences estimates that up to 1 percent of all American women who are otherwise unable to bear children might be able to do so through IVF.

In order to be successful, IVF entails a series of well-timed and executed procedures. The first stage is to obtain an egg from the woman's ovary. A small incision is made in the woman's abdomen and a fine hollow needle is inserted, so that follicular fluid containing a well-developed egg may be drawn out. The fluid is then deposited in a medium that allows the egg to mature completely prior to fertilization. Similarly, semen is placed in a carrier solution that capacitates it so that it will be able to fertilize the egg. The mediums containing the egg and the sperm are then diluted to simulate conditions found in the fallopian tubes and then mixed in a petri dish (the "test tube"). A few hours after the fertilization occurs, the fertilized egg, or zygote, is transferred to a solution that supports cell division and embryo maturation. When the embryo reaches the 8- to 16-cell stage, it is transferred to the uterus of the egg donor, or to another woman, a surrogate mother.

In vitro fertilization therefore expands considerably the possible egg-and-sperm combinations and further complicates the concept of parenthood. It also illustrates the speed at which a technology can become widely available. In 1978, the first in vitro baby, Louise Brown, was born in England. In January 1980, after considerable political debate, Norfolk General Hospital obtained government approval to make the technique available in the United States. In its first year of operation the Norfolk In Vitro Fertilization Clinic treated 41 patients, 15 percent of whom did become pregnant. On December 28, 1981, Elizabeth Carr became the first in vitro baby born in the United States. By 1987, the number of clinics in the United States offering in vitro fertilization exceeded 140, and the number of children born through this method was well over 1,000. Moreover, most clinics continue to have long waiting lists of infertile women who are willing to pay $4,000 to $5,000 for the chance to become pregnant. In some cases, the final cost of pregnancy has been in excess of $20,000.

A technique which promises to replace IVF as the method of choice for many women is embryo lavage. In this process, the menstrual cycle of a woman donor is first synchronized with that of the infertile woman who wishes to bear a child. Sperm from the husband of the infertile woman is then used to artifically inseminate the donor. Approximately five days after insemination, the uterus of the donor is lavaged, or flushed out, and the solution is microscopically screened to identify and isolate the embryo. The embryo is then transferred to the uterus of the wife to implant itself and be carried to term. In the first application of embryo lavage in 1983, 12 women donors were utilized and the "best" of the resulting embryos was transferred, leading to the birth of a healthy baby. Although this process was originally developed for cases in which a woman is unable to produce viable eggs, because it does not necessitate the costly and risky egg retrieval procedure of IVF, it is attractive to women with blocked fallopian tubes who are not concerned with being linked genetically to their babies. These market considerations were not lost to Fertility and Genetics Research, Inc., which holds patents on both the procedure itself and the computer software needed to synchronize the women's menstrual cycles.

One social innovation made possible by reproductive breakthroughs is the phenomenon of surrogate motherhood. An infertile woman and her husband enter into an agreement with another woman, the surrogate, that she will be artifically inseminated with the sperm of the husband. After conception, she carries the fetus to term; once the baby is born she relinquishes her right to it, giving it to the couple. Surrogate motherhood raises new legal and moral problems because the surrogate must be willing to be inseminated by the sperm of a stranger, carry his baby for nine months, and then give the baby to the couple. Both the physical and emotional commitment of a surrogate mother is substantial. The couple must rely totally on the good faith of the surrogate to keep her promise because they cannot be assured of any legal right to the child. The proliferation of lawsuits involving surrogate motherhood (e.g., *Stern* v. *Whitehead*) is bound to continue.

In addition to the techniques for overcoming infertility currently in use, far more revolutionary methods are under development. Egg fusion, or the combination of one mature egg with another, would eliminate the need for male genetic material and would always produce a female. In an extension of this technique, both eggs could be obtained from the same woman, thus producing a daughter who is totally hers genetically. Another possibility for a childless couple is a fetal transfer from a woman considering abortion. Theoretically, abortion does not preclude supplying the developing fetus with a life-support system other than that of its natural mother's womb. Intensive care innovations for the newborn are constantly improving the probability that artificial wombs might become available in the not-so-remote future. With the availability of such technologies, abortion would not necessarily result in the death of the fetus but merely in its transfer to another womb, mechanical or human. The technique of fetal transfer would allow a pregnant woman who does not wish to have a child to have the fetus transferred to the womb of a woman who wants it. Under these circumstances, fetal adoption might replace abortion.

Policy Issues Concerning Reproductive Technologies

At the very least, these rapid advances in reproductive technology force us to reevaluate our beliefs concerning reproduction and the right of procreation. In a broader sense, they challenge traditional notions of parenthood. Now we must learn to distinguish among the genetic parents, who contribute the germ material, the biological mother, who carries the fetus to term, and the legal parents, one or both of whom might also be the genetic parents. Moreover, the extent to which these artifically induced methods of conception involve considerably more individuals than the natural method means that procreation is no longer purely a private matter between one man and one women.

One shared characteristic of all reproductive technologies, from AID to gene therapy, is that they introduce a third party into what has been until now a private matter between a man and a woman. The more complex the intervention, the more mediators are necessary. Embryologists, geneticists, and an array of other specialists become the new progenitors. Although the desire of these specialists to help desperate patients may be genuine, their very presence takes control of procreation away from the couple. The willingness of many infertile couples to do (and pay) anything to have a child also encourages commercialization of procreation. The heightened demand raises the potential for exploiting the consumers of these services. Third-party involvement raises critical questions about who has access to the technologies. The danger, as in all health care, is the development of a tiered system in which the technologies serve primarily the upper middle class.

Supreme Court decisions on procreative privacy culminating in *Roe v. Wade* (1973) and reiterated recently in *City of Akron* v. *Akron*

Center for Reproductive Health (1983) clearly support the right of a woman not to have a child if she does not so desire. Access to contraception and abortion are legally guaranteed for all women, whatever their age or marital status. Abortion continues to be a volatile issue, but the complementary question of whether all women, whatever their age, marital status, or other conditions, have a corresponding right to have children is even more problematic. If there is a right to have children, are there any limits that can be imposed on the number or health of progeny? Just as the right to abortion is not abolute, it might be that the right to have children could be denied under some circumstances. If so, who should set such limits, and on what basis?

Furthermore, if a right to have children is granted, can all infertile couples or singles legitimately claim access to technologies such as in vitro fertilization, embryo flushing, and so forth? Although the cost of AID and even of in vitro fertilization does not approach that of an organ transplant, in the aggregate—with a potential of 200,000 in vitro procedures per year—the amount could become staggering. Should Medicaid or some similar public program fund these procedures for women who cannot themselves afford the high costs? Or does this right, if recognized, apply only to those who can pay for it? What if a couple requires the services of a surrogate mother in order to have children—who pays? A public furor arose recently in response to a case in which a woman on welfare had a child via artificial insemination by a donor (Hastings Center Report 1983). Not only did the woman have the procedure paid for by public funds, she also received $161 in monthly pregnancy welfare assistance and $401 a month from Aid to Families with Dependent Children after the child's birth. Although this case may be unusual, it is a very real illustration of the dilemmas that arise in interpreting reproduction as a positive entitlement.

Leon Kass (1981:466) sympathizes with the plight of infertile couples and their desire to utilize these new techniques, but he does not believe they are entitled to reproduction through these techniques at public expense. Once in vitro fertilization, embryo flushing, and similar techniques become routine medical procedures, however, denial of aid to infertile parents seems unlikely. I agree with Kass that this problem is symptomatic of our entire approach to health care:

It represents yet another instance of our thoughtless preference for expensive, high-technology, therapy-oriented approaches to disease and dysfunctions. What about the prevention of tubal obstruction? We complain about rising medical costs, but we insist on the most spectacular and the most technological—and thereby the most costly—remedies. (1981:464)

It is also important to note that infertility is often the result of the practices of the affected person, particularly when it has been caused by unchecked venereal disease. This raises particularly sensitive questions regarding lifestyle choices and personal responsibility for health care which are discussed in chapter 5.

Fetal Health: Preventing Disease by Protecting the Fetal Environment

The three critical health care areas discussed so far largely involve curative medicine. Organ transplantation, neonatal intensive care, and fertility technologies raise similar problems regarding availability, allocation, and possible rationing. Although prevention of the conditions which require consideration of these treatments is not always possible, the need for such care could be reduced significantly if proper emphasis was directed toward prevention. One area in which tremendous strides toward identifying and isolating the causes of disease have been achieved in the last decade is prenatal development. The availability of precise and efficient prenatal diagnostic techniques such as amniocentesis, ultrasound, and fetoscopy, and recent innovative treatment in utero including fetal surgery, has rescued the fetus from the secrecy of the womb. In combination with advances in knowledge about fetal development, these diagnostic techniques are revolutionizing treatment of the fetus and challenging traditional assumptions. Together, they evoke serious questions about maternal responsibility for the health of the unborn child.

Effects of Maternal Action on Fetal Development

From the moment of conception, a developing human organism is exposed to a multiplicity of environmental factors, all of which are capable of affecting its health. These factors include the womb con-

ditions, i.e., the temperature, pressure, character, and turnover of am-
niotic fluid; maternal emotions as expressed in hormonal changes that
reach the embryo or fetus; all drugs administered to the mother, prescription and nonprescription; radiation; noise (Verni and Kelly 1981);
nutrition; infections; and maternal-fetal incompatibilities, such as Rh
blood factor. Any one or a combination of these factors significantly
affect the developing fetus and can cause congenital deformities, high-
risk pregnancies, and numerous other problems.

Recent innovations and refinements in biomedical research and data
collection have produced growing evidence of the potentially deleterious effects of the immediate environment of the fetus on its development. The behavior of the mother during gestation, and in some
instances prior to conception, has been linked to a variety of congenital
disorders, ranging from reduced IQ and impaired motor coordination,
to mental retardation, high-risk premature births, and in some cases,
physical deformation or prenatal death (Harrigan 1980:292). Although the data suggesting the causal nature of environmental factors
in many cases remain tentative and inconclusive and the effects of
such factors appear to be interrelated with the mother's individual
physiology, the evidence of fetal damage resulting from the behavior
of the mother is mounting. Most troubling is the data on maternal
malnutrition, alcohol consumption, smoking, and venereal disease,
because the often devastating results are avoidable. Before discussing
the health care context of fetal development, current data on these
problems are summarized.

Maternal Malnutrition. All fetal nutrition comes from the mother's
blood through the semipermeable membrane of the placenta and the
umbilical cord. The fetus is therefore totally dependent on the mother
for all nutrients necessary to proper development and growth. When
the fetus is deprived of an adequate and balanced supply of critical
vitamins, minerals, and other nutrients, a wide range of developmental
problems may result. It is hardly surprising that a mother's malnutrition during pregnancy can have adverse affects on fetal growth and
infant vitality. What is surprising is that until the last several decades,
the adverse effects of maternal malnutrition on the fetus were not
commonly recognized. It was not until the 1940s that substantial
evidence became available linking malnutrition with reduced birth

weight and a range of other harmful effects. Extensive statistical studies of the Dutch famine (Smith 1947) and the Leningrad seige during World War II (Antonov 1947) distinctly demonstrated that severe fetal problems are associated with malnutrition during pregnancy and provided the impetus for nutrition research using animal models and human population statistics.

Most attention currently focuses on the retardation of fetal growth that results in low birth weight infants. Insufficient levels of nutrition during fetal development substantially increase the risk of small-for-date or small-for-gestational-age births. Unlike true premature babies, who are the right size for their fetal age but are born too soon, these infants are born on time, but are small upon delivery because they have not developed properly. According to Winick (1976:29), 20,000 extra calories are required during pregnancy to provide the requisites for a proper birth weight. This means that approximately 2,000 calories, carefully selected to provide protein and other essential components, are needed each day for the mother and fetus.

Although adequate nutrition is important throughout pregnancy, exposure to malnutrition during the third trimester is most clearly related to a low birth weight syndrome due to retarded fetal growth (Susser and Stein 1980:184). The deleterious effects of malnutrition in late term are serious and well recognized, but there is considerable evidence that inadequate maternal nutrition in the first trimester as well is related to shortened gestation periods, a heightened risk of central nervous system disorders, a sharp increase in perinatal, or newborn, death, and a retardation of fetal lung development (Naeye 1980:201). Moreover, nutrition throughout pregnancy has a direct effect on brain growth, because without sufficient nourishment, the rate of brain cell division is slower than normal.

Although crucial questions remain unanswered and findings are as yet inconclusive, according to Annis, "many authorities in the field of prenatal development feel that inadequate nutrition still constitutes the greatest potential threat to optimum development of the unborn child" (1978:63). Prenatal malnutrition is clearly associated with a broad assortment of serious and sometimes severe fetal developmental defects that are especially distressing because in most cases they could have been averted. In light of our emerging understanding of the importance of adequate maternal nutrition, it is vital that prospective

mothers be fully educated as to their role in providing a safe environment for the fetus they plan to carry, and that adequate prenatal care
and nutrition be made available to all pregnant women.

Maternal Alcohol Consumption. There is a high risk that any drug
ingested by a pregnant woman will cross the placenta and enter the
bloodstream of the vulnerable embryo or fetus. Even if the mother
has built up immunities to particular drugs, the fetus does not have
similar protection. The fetus appears especially susceptible to danger
early in gestation when it is a rapidly growing and differentiating
organism, "constantly changing in size, cell type, percentage of cells
in mitosis, length of cell cycle, dependence on the maternal organism,
and ability to replace dead cells" (Brent 1980:147).

Although concern over the adverse effects of maternal alcohol consumption on the developing fetus can be traced back at least to the
early Greeks (Warner and Rosett 1975), it was not until the last decade
that researchers were able to delineate a recognizable pattern of fetal
abnormalities associated with chronic maternal alcohol abuse (Council
on Scientific Affairs 1983). The fetal alcohol syndrome (FAS) has since
received considerable attention, and effort is now being directed at
better understanding the sources of variability in the effect on the fetus
of alcohol consumption and the role played by timing. Chernoff
(1980:321) notes that findings about FAS are especially significant
because of the magnitude of alcohol abuse in the western world.

According to Jones and associates (1973), 43 percent of infants born
to chronic alcohol abusers might have significant structural malformations. Chernoff (1980:324) notes that FAS is the third most commonly recognized cause of mental retardation, exceeded only by
Down's syndrome and neural tube defects. In addition to the striking
facial appearance of FAS children, growth deficiency, both gestational
and postnatal, is common, resulting in a failure to thrive (Hanson et
al. 1976). Growth in head circumference is below normal, and the
incidence of mental retardation, ranging from minor deficiences to
severe retardation, is increased. Poor coordination, hyperactive behavior, and tremors are also frequently reported in FAS babies (Hanson 1981). Although progeny of chronic heavy drinkers are at highest
risk of manifesting extreme FAS symptoms, considerably less maternal
alcoholic intake is also linked to a variety of fetal problems. Con-

sumption of as little as one ounce of pure alcohol per day results in 11 percent of the offspring exhibiting FAS features. At consumption levels above two ounces this increases to 19 percent (Jones et al. 1973). Because these latter two categories represent a substantially larger proportion of the population than the chronic problem drinkers, prevention of FAS requires considerably more awareness of the effect of these lower consumption levels on the fetus.

There is also a complicating factor concerning maternal alcohol consumption. Crucial—though preliminary—evidence suggests a relationship between the timing of fetal exposure to alcohol and the seriousness of the resulting damage. Hanson et al. (1978) found that the consumption level in the first month of pregnancy was a better predictor of the severity of FAS than the amounts of alcohol consumed later in the pregnancy. Such findings, indicative of a critical stage for major nervous system malformations, hold devastating implications for efforts at preventing FAS, since they suggest that FAS can be far along before most women are even aware that they are pregnant. By the time a woman learns that she is pregnant, damage may have already taken place, in which case it would already be too late to avert the most severe malformations.

What is required for the prevention of FAS, suggests Chernoff, is to "have all women of childbearing age who are not practicing contraception modify their drinking habits to be compatible with normal prenatal development" (1980:326). Obviously, this is an unlikely possibility, even if considerably more money is spent on public education efforts. Given the aggregate of evidence demonstrating the deleterious effect of alcohol consumption on fetal development, however, it is certain that significantly greater attention will be directed toward the responsibility of the mother for providing an ethanol-free environment for her developing fetus.

Maternal Smoking. The increased incidence of smoking by women of childbearing age in recent decades has stimulated considerable research on the effects of cigarette smoking on the development of the fetus. Although data remain inconclusive concerning the full impact of maternal smoking, several decades of major research studies and substantial statistical findings confirm a variety of deleterious effects of tobacco on fetal development and pregnancy outcome.

The most clearly corroborated finding to date is that mothers who smoke run a higher risk than nonsmoking mothers of giving birth to underweight babies (Longo 1982). Basing its conclusions on over 45 separate studies, the U.S. Surgeon General's report *Smoking and Health* (HEW 1979b) confirmed that maternal smoking reduces birth weight, even when findings were statistically controlled for a broad range of demographic and situational factors. The average weight of a smoker's baby was 200 grams less than a nonsmoker's across all categories. A significantly greater proportion of smokers' infants weighed less than 2,500 grams at birth, putting them at higher risk for a range of potential complications (Miller et al. 1976). Research also shows that the greater the number of cigarettes a woman smokes during pregnancy, the greater her chances of bearing a low birth weight baby (Van Den Berg 1977).

In addition to slowing fetal development, maternal smoking has also been linked to shortened gestation periods (Meyer 1982), increased incidences of complications in pregnancy and of spontaneous abortion, and a higher risk of late term and newborn deaths (Rush and Kass 1972). Significantly, Meyer et al. (1976) found that the risk of perinatal death increased as the number of cigarettes smoked increased. For those smoking at least one pack a day, the risk was 35 percent higher than for nonsmokers. At least a portion of the increased mortality of smokers' babies is attributable to complications which arise during pregnancy, including premature rupture of membranes, bleeding during pregnancy, and premature detachment of the placenta (Coleman et al. 1979:L14).

One consolation that emerges from research on the teratogenic, or malforming, effects of maternal smoking is that smoking prior to pregnancy appears to have no appreciable effect on birth weight (Butler et al. 1972). Moreover, unlike the effects of alcohol, the effects of tobacco are not concentrated in the early pregnancy period. Therefore, a woman who quits smoking or even reduces the amount she smokes during pregnancy can reduce the risk of fetal developmental retardation and increase the birth weight and length of the infant (Sexton and Hebel 1984). On the other hand, the proportion of female teenagers who smoke has increased significantly over the last decade. Given the increasing incidence of pregnancy among teenage women, already considered a high-risk group, this trend is not encouraging.

Maternal Illnesses. All maternal illnesses during pregnancy and birth are potentially dangerous to the fetus. Although the most striking reminder of the potential affect of maternal illness on the fetus is the rubella epidemic of the 1960s, during which over 50,000 fetuses were affected, numerous organisms are capable of crossing the placenta and damaging the developing fetus. Of infants infected by congenital toxoplasmosis, a parasite transmitted by cats and contaminated meat or soil, for example, 10 to 15 percent die, and 85 percent of the survivors display psychomotor retardation between the ages of two and four (Devore, Jackson, and Piening 1983). Likewise, hepatitis B virus heightens the risk of prematurity, stillbirth, and perinatal mortality. Although few exposed infants develop acute hepatitis or chronic liver disease, for those who do, life is difficult. For the 150 to 400 infants born annually with congenital syphilis, little can be done to ameliorate the damage done during gestation. Transmittal of syphilis to the fetus is associated with brain damage, cardiovascular system abnormalities, blindness, and increased rates of spontaneous abortion and perinatal death. Evidence indicates that the fetus is at high risk for damage throughout the gestation period and that nearly every organ can be affected.

Although the teratogenic effects of herpes are not nearly as striking as the effects of syphilis, the frequency of genital herpes (simplex B) infections has reached what some observers call epidemic proportions, thus threatening a large number of unborn children. Recently, there has been considerable publicity over the problems of integrating children with congenital herpes into the schools. Until a cure is found, they are faced with a life of health problems and social stigmatization. In addition to the possibility of chronic herpes infection in offspring, herpes is clearly associated with heightened risk of microcephaly (abnormal smallness of the head), retinal dysplasia (abnormal development of the retina), mental retardation, and perinatal death. Whether or not the infected mother has visible lesions, 30 to 50 percent of newborns delivered through the birth canal and contaminated with herpes virus become infected, and of these, half will die or be severely damaged. Approximately 70 percent of all neonatal herpes infections are disseminated, or spread throughout the body, affecting the internal organs, especially the liver, adrenals, and central nervous system. Of the infants who contract the disseminated form, 60 to 90 percent die (Devore, Jackson, and Piening 1983:1661). Although disseminated herpes simplex virus infection during pregnancy is uncommon, when it occurs it is accompanied by high maternal and fetal mortality and morbidity (Peacock and Sarubbi 1983).

Sever (1980:174) contends that herpes infections will require considerable emphasis in the 1980s because of the explosive increase in the rate of infection among women of reproductive age, the recurrences of infection after dormant periods, and the current lack of satisfactory treatment. Corey (1982) recommends virologic surveillance of pregnant women. He advocates that women with a history of genital herpes, or whose current or past sexual partners have had herpes, be monitored to identify those with the most virulent stage (clinical or asymptomatic viral shedding) at or very near term. Those who test positive would be candidates for a caesarean section.

Maternal Lifestyle Choice: A Summary. Despite the complex nature of the fetal environment and the variation of effects any single stimulus might have on a specific fetus, the evidence demonstrates that there are many ways in which maternal behavior and health can impair the proper development of the fetus, causing irreparable harm in some cases. Although data remain inconclusive, there is growing evidence of the importance of providing as risk-free a fetal environment as possible. Maternal smoking, drinking, eating, and general lifestyle can and do have an effect on the fetus. As more is learned about the specific deleterious effects of certain behaviors, it is likely that increased attention will be directed toward the responsibility of the mother for providing the fetus with a safe environment throughout gestation. Unlike most other prenatal disorders, such threats to the fetus and newborn as maternal malnutrition, FAS, and congenital illnesses are completely preventable.

Within the context of the growing knowledge about these hazards, a real question arises concerning the right a child may have to a safe fetal environment and as normal as possible a start in life. But in turn, there is a potential conflict between the rights of the developing fetus and of the mother. It is certainly tragic that in as affluent a country as the United States, children continue to be born with birth defects caused primarily by a lack of proper nutrition or by the harmful behavior of the mother during pregnancy. However, in a democratic society, freedom of action, and the primary responsibility for that action, remain with the individual pregnant woman. She alone is the direct link to the fetus, and she alone makes the ultimate decision whether or not to smoke, to use alcohol or other drugs, to maintain as good nutrition as she can, and so forth.

Lest the emphasis here on the responsibility of mothers be interpreted as sexist, the plain fact should be stated that where fetal environment is concerned, it is the actions of the mother, not the father, which directly affect the fetus. In recognizing the rights of women, not men, to reproductive choice when abortion is at issue (*Roe* v. *Wade*, 1973), the Court has not-so-tacitly agreed that the woman also has the prime responsibility for the fetus. While this does not excuse a father from playing a positive role in guaranteeing a risk-free environment for the fetus, the final choice and responsibility will always be the woman's.

Drawing the Lines: Where Do These Issues Take Us?

This review of health care issues emerging from the diffusion of new medical knowledge and technologies illuminates the characteristics of the policy problems that we face in the coming decade. As noted in chapter 1, our potential expenditure on health care is unlimited under a system that has at its base a belief in the prolongation of life. The continuous expansion of medical capabilities serves primarily to fuel the expectations and demands of the public. As Kass (1981:468) notes, it is hard to oppose federal funding of baby making in a society which increasingly demands that the government supply all needs. Moreover, it becomes even more difficult to refuse to guarantee access to expensive transplants, neonatal care, and fertility technologies when health care is considered a fundamental human right. Under such circumstances, it becomes tremendously difficult to deny access on the grounds of inability to pay or any other rationing approach.

Despite the difficulty of this task, the facts dictate that boundaries must be drawn in the near future if we are to have any chance of averting a major health care crisis. Simply put, society cannot afford to fulfill the insatiable medical demands of the population, particularly in light of the trends discussed in chapter 1. I argue in the following chapters that only government action at the national level can provide a framework within which meaningful social priorities in health care can be established. Government cannot regulate the problem away, but only decisive and consistent action on the part of our political institutions can shift the momentum in the direction of solving those problems. As a society we must learn to curb our demands: we cannot afford to pay all of the medical costs for all of the people who demand maximal technological intervention to meet their health goals. Given our cultural framework and the prevailing views of medicine in this society, the task is one of the most challenging the United States has yet to face.

3

The Allocation and Rationing of Medical Care

Long-term solutions to our emerging health care crisis will require major alterations in basic orientations toward medicine in the United States. Reevaluation of our social priorities is crucial at three levels. First, we must come to some consensus as to how much of society's limited resources we are willing to allocate to health care. Most observers contend that when the cost of health care exceeds 10 percent of the GNP, efforts to stabilize it are essential, but we continue to expend vast sums of money on goods and services that we can largely agree are less worthwhile than health care, and on some that actually are costly to our health. What priority do we place on health care as compared to education, national defense, housing, leisure activities, pets? How much are we willing to take from these competing areas and transfer to medical care? These first-level macro-allocation decisions entail basic politics, since the funding pie is apportioned according to societal priorities.

Second, once a consensus is reached as to how high a priority ought to be put on health care as compared with other expenditures, the resources available for health care must be distributed within the many areas of health care. Assuming that society refuses to make major alterations at the first macro-allocation level, hard decisions will be necessary in order to allocate limited medical resources in the most just and equitable way. What proportion of the health budget should go to primary care and preventive medicine, as compared with high-technology curative medicine? It is at this second allocation level that the trade-offs examined in chapter 1 must be appraised and choices made that will drastically change the prevailing assumptions of both the health care community and the public. The sooner we as a society realize that we cannot have it all and that priorities must be established, second-level allocation will follow. Here again, conventional givens must be challenged, givens that might have operated in times of government plenty, but which are obsolete now in the era of fiscal constraints.

Although macro-allocation decisions are arduous, choices become more painful as they are applied to identifiable individuals. This situation can occur in one of several contexts. First, the individual might be one of many suffering from a specific disease whose treatment has been denied funding under a particular allocation scheme. Under these circumstances, even if it is reasonable to make the decision to withhold scarce resources from a particular use, justifying this to the individual who will suffer is an onerous task. A decision to support no liver or heart transplant facilities would place all individuals at need in a similar position. Although they would not be discriminated against at the individual level, as members of a group they would be denied treatment because society chose to place its priorities elsewhere. Unless the law placed these individuals in a protected class, such policy decisions would most likely hold up under judicial scrutiny.

Perhaps more problematic is the second application at the individual level. Here, a person has a disease whose treatment is funded. However, funding is available only in limited quantities such that not all persons with the disease can be treated. This necessitates what is here referred to as "rationing," which means making a choice among the claims of individuals who are competing for resources limited by public policy. A choice at the macro level has allocated fewer resources than are necessary to treat all individuals affected. If it were government policy to fund 100 liver transplants per year in the United States and 1,000 people required this procedure, 900 individuals would be excluded at this most immediate and wrenching individual level. At this stage, some criteria would have to be established to distinguish, singly, one person from the next, and, collectively, the 100 selected for treatment from the remainder. This decision requires a clinical judgment or some substitute—a lottery, for instance.

It is critical to emphasize that while macro decisions are likely to be made by policymakers, the most difficult decisions, those applying to individuals, would be made largely by clinicians. They would determine, in many cases, who would live through treatment, or die for lack of it, but within the constraints of social policy. Until now in the United States, these constraints have not been clearly articulated or specified to the health providers. The traditional physician-patient relationship and third-party reimbursement, combined with the absence of government budgetary sanctions, provide little incentive for considering as a high priority the economic impact on society of an individual medical choice.

Neonatal care and organ transplantation especially create serious allocation problems, because in these areas, the abstractions of macroallocation must contrast sharply with a micro decision concerning a real human being. As discussed earlier, what appears to be logical when applied to the aggregate often appears harsh or even inhumane at the individual level. Policymakers can talk all they will about the estimated costs of heart or liver transplants or neonatal intensive care programs. With a public that is supportive of high-technology intervention to prolong life at considerable cost and that is sensitive to individual rights, the demand for these expensive medical services will continue to escalate. Once these technologies are available, the momentum in favor of their diffusion will not be stopped without a considerable revision of our basic expectations concerning health care. Any effort by the government to discourage organ transplants will face opposition by physicians who are supportive of such treatment and vehement attack by patients whose survival depends on it. As will be shown in chapter 4, the courts most likely will be hesitant to allow individuals to die for want of a transplant, no matter how costly this may be in the aggregate, because judges are trained to protect the interests of the individual vis-à-vis society.

Even if we are successful in establishing meaningful criteria for allocating acceptable levels of resources to health care, and if we are able to reach agreement as to how these scarce resources are to be distributed within the health sector, the most difficult choices remain. Because the resources available for medical care are certain to be limited, rationing—making choices at the individual level—is unavoidable. All societies ration medicine in some way. Traditionally in the United States, rationing was accomplished through the marketplace—those who could afford health care received it, while those who could not pay for it did not get it. Although ability to pay continues to be one factor in obtaining high-quality care, the rationing that occurs today often takes place in the atmosphere of a media event. The result is a haphazard, inequitable, and inconsistent.

This chapter describes and analyzes the urgent need to design and implement a comprehensive and fair system for allocating public resources at these three levels. It also critically analyzes current allocation methods, especially those such as cost-benefit analysis, which concentrate on economic considerations at the exclusion of broader social ones.

Throughout this discussion of contemporary methods of health care allocation, I argue that a rigorous reevaluation of the basic assumptions behind current policymaking in this area is essential. Only the national government has the capacity to initiate the dialogue essential to developing society-wide priorities and establishing minimal national standards for the distribution of medical care. Although this action should not preclude private and local government initiatives for equity, quality, or cost containment, the expansive scope of the health care issue demands a nationwide commitment to resolving it. This commitment must include a moderation of public expectations as to the capabilities of curative medicine and a realistic appraisal of the difficult trade-offs we, as a society and as individuals, must make in the near future.

Defining Rationing: The Evolution of a Concept

Allocation decisions occur at the aggregate or macro level, while rationing decisions apply to the individual or micro level. Rationing, then, takes place within the context of prior allocation decisions that limit resources. One of the problems in attempting to formulate an argument for the rationing of health care is the absence of any consistent or succinct definition of what the concept of rationing entails.

The term is often used to describe a process of distributing resources differentially. By emphasizing the selectivity of distribution, this use of the term creates the impression that persons are treated unequally in any rationing scheme. Other writers have used the term to refer to constraint on the consumption of medical care by individuals so that the "patient does not receive all the care that he or his physician believes would be of some benefit to him" (Mulley 1983). Meanwhile, the Office of Health Economics (1979:377) questions any use of the term "rationing" in the health care context and suggests that "triage" or "priority selection" be substituted.

Although it is tempting to abandon the term "rationing" and devise a more precise word, I feel that such an approach would do nothing but add to the confusion. Moreover, the complexity of rationing as a concept is useful, because it demonstrates the variety of means through which the distribution of medical care can be effected. Rosenblatt (1981:1403), for instance, distinguishes traditional rationing, which applied to the poor, with new rationing, which applies to all classes. Furthermore, he argues that the term has been broadened to include at least two distinct meanings. First, it refers to the distribution of scarce, high-technology treatment among a class of patients who would benefit. This meaning encompasses efforts to ration organ transplants, neonatal intensive care units and, at this point in its development at least, in vitro fertilization. Second, rationing refers to efforts designed to discourage the overuse of ordinary health care resources such as diagnostic tests, routine surgery, drugs, and hospitalization. These efforts include attempts to change the reimbursement structure and health care delivery system in order to keep down the overall costs of health care. Although Rosenblatt's first definition is closest to my use of the term in succeeding chapters, the analysis here is kept intentionally broad.

In this broad sense, rationing has always been a part of medical decision making. Figure 3.1 presents a spectrum of ways in which health care can be rationed. Whether imposed by a market system in which price determines who has access and who has not, a triage system where care is distributed on the basis of need as defined largely by the medical community, or a queue system in which time and the waiting process become the major rationing device, medical resources always have been distributed according to criteria prone to varying

Figure 3.1
Forms of Rationing: A Continuum of Government Involvement

	1 Physician Discretion	2 Competitive Marketplace	3 Insurance Marketplace	4 Socialized Insurance	5 Implicit Rationing	6 Explicit Rationing	7 Controlled Rationing
Form	*Criteria Used*				*Effects on Health Care*		
1. *Physician Discretion*	—medical benefit to patient —medical risk to patient —social class or mental capacity				—reinforces technological imperative —increases costs with no constraint on major access points —reinforces differential access		
2. *Competitive Marketplace*	—ability to pay				—creates tiered access system —leads to elaborate charity system		
3. *Insurance Marketplace*	—ability to pay for insurance —group membership —employment				—encourages use of resources —escalates demand and costs of health care —spreads risk and thus expands access		
4. *Socialized Insurance* (i.e., Medicaid)	—entitlement				—covers persons lacking adequate private insurance —increases role of government in medical decision making —increases cost to public —creates new tiered system of public v. private sector patients		

5. *Implicit Rationing*	—the queue —limited manpower and facilities —medical benefits to patient with consideration of social costs	—imposes shortage of some health care —increases role of government in regulation and budgeting —limits access to specialists —reinforces tiered system —shifts emphasis toward social benefits and costs
6. *Explicit Rationing*	—triage —medical benefit to patient with emphasis on social costs and benefits —strict allocation	—limits high-cost care with dubious benefits —makes peer review mandatory —imposes cost containment measures —imposes regulation of private as well as public sector —bureaucratizes rationing
7. *Controlled Rationing*	—equity in access to primary care —social benefit over specific patient benefits —cost to society	—eliminates private health care sector —fully bureaucratizes medical decision making —limits discretion of patient, physician, and other health providers —imposes strict regulation and control of all facets of medicine —eliminates tiered system

degrees of subjectivity. In almost all instances, rationing criteria arise from a particular value context that results in an inequitable distribution of resources based on social as well as strictly medical considerations.

In addition to illustrating the range of rationing options for health care, figure 3.1 introduces yet another complexity in defining the concept. Some forms of rationing infer or necessitate government involvement, either direct or indirect, while others fail to distinguish between private and public sector choices. This distinction, in fact, is very critical to a clarification of how current health care options differ from those in the past. The less explicit forms of rationing, toward the left of the continuum, are no longer sufficient to resolve health care dilemmas. As a result, we are now witnessing a trend toward the right side of the spectrum which may eventually culminate in a central role for the government in the rationing of increasingly scarce medical resources. Although explicit rationing under the authority of the government is but one form of rationing, many forces concurrently appear to be moving American society in that direction. As cogently summarized by David Mechanic:

As people have learned to have high and more unrealistic expectations of medicine, demands for care for a variety of conditions, both major and minor, have accelerated. No nation that follows a sane public policy would facilitate the fulfillment of all perceptions of need that a demanding public might be willing to make. As in every other area of life, resources must be rationed. (1977:63)

The relevant question today is not if we ought to ration health care, but rather who ought to have prime responsibility for doing so. Physicians have always rationed medicine when resources available for treatment were scarce. Despite their acceptance of the technological imperative and their ethical codes emphasizing benefit to the patient, doctors must allocate intensive care resources, for instance, on the basis of the patient's prognosis (Detsky et al. 1981). Because the demand for ICU beds often outstrips availability, physicians must allocate them to patients who are most likely to benefit and deny such care to patients with the least favorable prognoses. As noted above, all such medical decisions can be colored by social as well as medical factors. In addition to the functional outcome for the patient, itself always uncertain, the preference of the patient as well as the patient's potential contributions to society are frequently considered (Avorn 1984). As a result, fewer resources are expended on the elderly and those persons with a poorer prognosis, impaired abilities, or an unwillingness to fulfill expected social roles (Mulley 1983:306). Because advanced age often reduces the probability of full recovery and heightens the risks of intervention, rationing by age has been common. Traditional rationing also has a clear social class bias.

Although the rationing of medical care conflicts with the widely accepted social norm that any expenditure is justified in preserving an individual life, the impact of macro-allocation decisions ultimately is greatest at the individual level. Within the context of the explosion of health care costs and the growing expectations and demands of the public for expensive technologies, the human relationships in medicine, particularly those between patient and physician, have become more institutionalized. Moreover, the high cost of many new medical technologies is likely to make their use prohibitive for patients who might benefit and who, in some instances, need the technology to survive. As a result, it is even more crucial that the criteria for making both allocation and rationing decisions be clarified and carefully monitored to ensure that all members of society are served equally well by the health care system.

Given the enormity of the problems and the scope of the task presented in making contemporary health care policy, the increased involvement of the government is not unexpected. Only the public sector has the capacity to reorder spending priorities and mobilize the public to moderate its unrealistic expectations. Unfortunately, too often in the past the public institutions have played the opposite role, substantially raising public expectations. With or without intent, those persons who argue that if left alone the competitive market forces will resolve these problems obscure their complexity and ignore the historical context behind our present situation. Although Joseph Califano (1986:82) undoubtedly is right that an "alert, informed world of business purchasers is one ingredient to the creation of an efficient health care delivery system," he dismisses too easily the essential role of the government in efforts to create such a system. Although the efforts must be shared between the private and public sectors, I agree with Schramm that "only the government can act to redistribute opportunities for care in an equitable fashion and invest in public goods and services" (1984:731). Even if the marketplace operated perfectly in distributing resources, the prime beneficiaries of the reordering of health care priorities would be members of future generations, who have no means of influencing today's marketplace. Although the need for cooperation between the public and private sectors cannot be overstated, the initiative must come from those persons who supposedly represent the best interests of the nation as a whole. The vigor with which public officials attack health care dilemmas and work to avert the emerging crisis will serve as a test of their commitment. Rationing decisions are difficult and politically unpopular, but they will continue to be made with or without government participation and leadership. Evans is correct when he states: "Of all the resource-shortage crises this nation is expected to confront in the future, the problem of resource distribution is likely to be most acute and problematic in medicine" (1983:2208). One might add that we are fast approaching the point at which the future is now.

The Allocation and Rationing of Medicine in the United States

Until recent decades, the allocation of medical resources was primarily a function of the market system. Although the open market was modified by licensing and other types of regulation, effectively the production and distribution of health care was determined by market forces. Brown (1983) summarizes the emergence of nonprofit and for-profit hospitals in light of the emerging categorizing of patients based on their financial means, and he traces the social forces that shifted hospital care from the poor to the middle class. By the 1930s, private hospital care was rationed by price and generally available only to those persons who could afford to pay their own way. Conversely, public hospital care was rationed to the poor on the basis of rigid "means" tests. The result of this market allocation scheme was a dual or tiered system that produced inequalities in distribution as well as severe financial instability for hospitals. More importantly, the escalating cost of private hospital care forced many working and middle class people whose modest means disqualified them for public hospital care to forgo needed treatment.

The response of the market to this situation was to socialize the financial risks of hospitalization by spreading them among many insurance policyholders. Insurance enabled policyholders to obtain expensive medical care when needed without becoming impoverished. Hospitals benefited because their insured patients represented a growing market for their services and a stable source of revenues. Group plans flourished in the 1940s as labor unions pressured employers for nontaxable fringe benefits in the form of health protection. Commercial insurance companies followed Blue Cross hospital insurance plans into this lucrative new market. By 1960, 130 million people were covered by private medical insurance programs.

Although insurance coverage afforded widespread and substantially expanded access to hospital care, a significant minority of the population failed to be served by the new market situation. The lower middle class and the poor could seldom obtain adequate insurance coverage. Also, the greater need of the elderly for health care made them bad insurance risks, thus pricing all but the most wealthy out of the market. In 1962, approximately half of all persons over the age of 65 had no insurance for hospital care, double the proportion among persons under 65 (Brown 1983:260). Because of their greater need for hospital care, many elderly persons were without health insurance protection.

Health insurance, then, drastically changed the market system and did contribute effectively to socializing the financial risk of needing costly medical care for a large segment of American society. Increasingly expensive medical care was distributed to more people, although not without attendant costs. Maldistribution across income levels remained a problem, however, and health insurance also contributed to a shift in emphasis from preventive care and ambulatory services to the more expensive curative care and inpatient hospital services. Also, as noted in chapter 1, because third parties were absorbing the costs, the personal financial incentive to limit the use of medical resources was eliminated, thus forcing up demand for ever-more-costly services. This, in turn, produced a need in the marketplace to contain costs, and resulted in a series of cost-sharing methods which required the insured to weigh their need for the care against out-of-pocket costs. Increasingly high deductibles and co-payments tended to reallocate medical care towards those individuals who were best able to afford to pay the differences.

In response to the obvious inequities of this modified market system, the government entered the marketplace in order first to correct geographical maldistribution of hospital beds caused by hospitals' moving to more wealthy suburban areas, and second to subsidize the hospital care market so that all persons could participate in it. The Hill-Burton Act of 1946 was the major vehicle for addressing the first objective. Over $4 billion in federal grants and loans for construction and modernization of medical facilities was distributed between 1947 and 1974 and matched by an additional $10.4 billion in state and local funds. Although this program failed to equalize the availability or quality of hospital services in urban and rural poverty areas, it was successful in reducing the rural disadvantage by encouraging the construction of many small rural hospitals. The Hill-Burton program's dependence on state and local initiative and matching funds, however, favored communities with sufficient capital and political resources, thus reducing its impact on the overall allocation of hospital services. Also, it failed to stem the movement of private hospitals away from urban core areas and resulted in the construction of unneeded facilities.

The second and more substantial entry of the government into the medical marketplace was the attempt to subsidize health care for the poor and elderly. After initial interest in a national health insurance plan in the 1930s dissipated, and the welfare-linked Kerr-Mills program proved unsatisfactory to the elderly particularly, the compromise Medicare/Medicaid legislation became policy in 1965. As noted earlier, Medicare/Medicaid reduced the grossest inequities that were commonplace before its inception. Unfortunately, these programs also contributed to the rapid escalation of health care costs. Also, because of a series of cost containment measures, they have reinstituted a tiered system of health care distribution similar, ironically, to that which existed early in the century. Although the quality of health care for most segments of society has improved dramatically during this century, access to this quality care continues to vary across social class lines.

Finally, all these major changes in the marketplace notwithstanding,

the emphasis in American medicine continues to be on curative medicine and on expansion of biomedical technology. During all of the
changes as to who shares the risk and who pays, allocation at the
second level, i.e., the priorities within health care, has changed very
little. As noted by Brown:

The gilded age of hospitals encouraged rapid expansion of the total supply
of hospital beds and the acquisition of advanced medical technology. But it
also created serious fiscal problems for many hospitals, contributed substantially to the rapid increase in total health care costs, and encouraged the
expansion of resources for expensive, high technology care. Some of those
resources might have gone for less expensive and more needed ambulatory
care facilities and resources. (1983:271–272)

By modifying who pays, and how, we have been partially successful
in assuring the access of all persons to the health care system. However,
instead of reversing or even revising the public preference for specialized and technology-based curative medicine, these changes have
solidified these preferences. The socializing of health care payments
through private insurance and the subsidizing of care for persons
otherwise unable to participate have removed the price constraints of
the medical marketplace of the past which, although inequitable, func-
tioned effectively. In the absence of any private market mechanism to
allocate and ration scarce resources, the burden falls increasingly on
the public sector to take a forceful role in making these decisions.
Unfortunately, public efforts to date have failed to establish adequate
rationing and allocation policy and, thereby, have exacerbated the
health care crisis.

Trends in Health Care Delivery: Rationing and Allocation Ramifications

One of the major trends in American medicine is the rapid growth of
for-profit, investor-owned medical conglomerates such as the Hospital
Corporation of America and Humana, Inc. Profit-making companies
currently own or manage more than 20 percent of hospitals and vastly
larger proportions of other health-related facilities such as nursing
homes. Increasingly, they are branching into affiliated areas such as
ambulatory clinics, health maintenance organizations, and hospital
supply firms. Other chains are emerging that specialize in services such

as sports medicine, alcohol and drug treatment, physical therapy, and cardiac care. Although Humana received a great deal of publicity from the artificial heart program, it has more quietly opened approximately 200 neighborhood MedFirst facilities and launched Humana Care Plus, an insurance plan that guarantees to employers that their premiums will rise no faster than the Consumer Price Index for at least four years, even though health care costs in general are rising at twice the CPI. This plan encourages enrollees to use Humana facilities by lowering the deductibles if they do so.

Not surprisingly, many doctors view the encroachment of corporate medicine as a threat to their interests and those of their patients. Increasingly, doctors are becoming employees and, in the process, losing the control they once enjoyed over the health care system. General practitioners especially fear that for-profit clinics and hospital satellites will draw patients away from their private practices. Evidence suggests that some patients, indeed, are abandoning their family physicians for the accessibility and lower costs of clinics that are often conveniently located in shopping centers (Fuerst 1985). Critics of for-profit medicine argue that the profit motive is a poor incentive to providing medical care. For Relman (1984), "industrialized" medicine exaggerates the dual system of health care by skimming off a community's paying patients, thus depriving nonprofit institutions of needed revenues and leaving them with most of the nonpaying, indigent patients. Also, Starr (1982) argues that the growth of this medical-industrial complex undermines the traditional physician-patient relationship and replaces emphasis on patient good with emphasis on corporate good. No longer is the physician able to operate as an agent free from the economic considerations imposed by the corporation.

Proponents of this new wave of for-profit medicine counter that the private physician never was free from economic considerations nor from standards set by the health care community. Although corporate medicine might formalize these arrangements, medical decisions have seldom been made in isolation from social and economic realities. Moreover, those supporting for-profit medical services can point out the fact that many of the corporations are composed of groups of previously private physicians who have formed medical partnerships that are economically more rewarding for them. Corporate clinics represent an attractive alternative to private practice, especially for young doctors who do not have an established practice nor the capital necessary to buy into one. Normally, they enjoy good and secure salaries as well as a share of the profits. In many cases, the individual center is owned and operated by a group of doctors who have formed a limited partnership under an arrangement similar to a franchise. A centralized headquarters handles traditional bookkeeping, accounting, and purchasing functions, thereby relieving the physicians of the routine business end of private practice. The participating physicians trade off some degree of their autonomy, then, for a guaranteed salary, a reasonable schedule, and freedom from the burdens of administrating an office.

In spite of the continuing debate over the quality of care provided by for-profit as opposed to nonprofit medicine and the overall impact of these trends on medical practice, it cannot be argued that allocation decisions are moving away from the domain of individual physicians. As employees of the corporation, however, doctors take on an obligation to the stockholders to maximize profits. Although this commitment does not necessarily lead to the neglect of patient welfare, it does seem likely to unduly influence decisions on the margins where patient good is ambiguous and corporate cost and benefit are clear.

These potential conflict situations are even more problematic within the context of the various prepaid arrangements that now abound in which the incentives for doctors to withhold services are evident. The leading form of prepaid plan today is the health maintenance organization, commonly referred to as an HMO. The strength of HMOs is their emphasis on preventive medicine. Because they do away with deductibles and charge low fees, if any, for office visits, in theory HMOs encourage members to get the kind of routine health care— check-ups, innoculations, Pap tests—that can keep health problems from becoming critical. Moreover, by encouraging and promoting primary health care, HMOs are supposed to contribute to the future health of their members, thus keeping down long-range costs to members, to the employer providing coverage, and to the HMO itself.

Unlike the conventional fee-for-service, third-party reimbursement system, however, which encourages doctors to allocate more health care resources, prepaid plans actually tend to discourage the offering of services, because members pay a set fee no matter how much or how little they use the plan. Although this system is likely to increase patient demand, the physician and the organization gain economically by rigorous cost containment. HMOs therefore alter considerably the economic incentives and allocation mechanisms inherent in the conventional health care delivery format.

According to Luft (1983), HMOs create a direct conflict between patients, whose comprehensive coverage leads them to demand more services than they would in a fee-for-service system, and physicians, who have a personal stake in reducing organization outlays for patient care. This is particularly the case in HMO payment schemes that pay physicians a salary and give bonuses if the group performs well. Competing HMO schemes exist that operate on a fee-for-service basis, usually modified to reflect the total budgeted funds available. Still another option is the individual practice association (IPA) format, in which the HMO functions as a health plan that contracts through an intermediary organization with independent, office-based physicians to provide services. At present IPA is the fastest growing type of HMO in the United States (*American Medical News*, August 1, 1986, p. 9). Although the salaried system provides the most explicit incentive structure for physicians to reduce services, informal pressures and organizational norms work to constrain the allocation of resources in all prepaid schemes. As competition among HMOs increases, participating physicians are likely to experience even stronger restraints on their discretion in making medical decisions and to face increasing pressures to limit treatment.

In addition to their influence on the allocation of medical resources through the implicit or explicit expectations they place on participating physicians, prepaid plans also contain costs and allocate resources through the process by which they enroll members. By carefully selecting employee groups that are largely healthy, and by using tactics that attract the most healthy persons from within those groups, HMOs are able to exclude those individuals who are likely to be frequent users of high-cost services, thereby minimizing the cost to those who are enrolled. If the HMO is a for-profit organization, this selection process will ensure higher returns on investment as well. Because most people are healthy and, in general, only a small fraction of a plan's enrollees account for a majority of the costs (McCall and Wai 1981), close screening of prospective enrollees is essential to keeping costs down. By setting variable premium rates that favor young families, through careful location of facilities, and through differential access for certain services, prepaid plans can discourage the sick and elderly from joining or, alternately, make membership so expensive that they are, in effect, excluded. By failing to update the coverage list frequently, thus keeping desired treatments in an experimental category, prepaid health plans can also encourage patients desirous of new and expensive procedures to leave the plan. Even small changes in coverage, if successful in affecting high users, might have a major cost impact with little effect on overall enrollment figures.

Developments in the direction of prepaid, for-profit health care plans clearly represent an insidious form of rationing that in its subtlety obscures the broader ramifications for the allocation of medical resources. By targeting enrollment to healthier groups and encouraging doctors to be penurious with organizational resources, these plans do provide cost effective coverage to members. However, they accomplish this by shifting even more of the cost of caring for the unhealthy to the public sector. Therefore the apparent success of HMOs and other prepaid health plans in lowering costs for society as a whole might be largely illusory. Their increasing role in health care is bound to lead eventually to a situation in which the young and healthy receive good low-cost coverage but the elderly and sick are offered inadequate, expensive coverage at best. According to Luft (1983:335), this situation is the opposite of the risk-pooling implicit in socially desirable insurance. Aggravating the problem is the fact that low-income workers whose employers make considerably smaller, if any, contributions to health insurance are likely to be especially vulnerable to the self-selection mechanisms of these competitive organizations (Taylor and Lawson 1981). Again, I believe this situation illustrates the need for some type of government involvement to protect the interests of those individuals or groups who are excluded, intentionally or not, from the system of coverage.

A final trend in health care delivery with considerable rationing implications is the expanded involvement of corporate employers in medical policymaking. Corporate spending on health insurance has almost doubled since 1980 and now approaches $100 billion annually. Companies that until recently complaisantly paid increased premiums for their employees because the overall costs were small and fully tax deductible are now being faced with excruciating allocation and rationing choices, particularly pertaining to organ transplantation and other high-cost treatments. For instance, after several large outlays, Hewlett-Packard decided no longer to finance any heart, heart-lung, or liver transplants. Like the government, corporations find themselves caught between the urgent need to contain and manage costs, and expectations for comprehensive coverage. To counter the surge in premiums charged by regular insurers, some firms have established self-funded health care plans. Typically, these companies utilize third-party administrators to process claims but decide themselves what medical treatments will be reimbursed (Chapman 1985:40).

Through their decisions whether or not to cover certain procedures, health benefits managers of large corporations are becoming key policymakers in the rationing of medical care. Honeywell Corporation recently formulated a policy on organ transplantation that limits such procedures to patients who are not suffering from any other terminal disease and who are likely to die without the operation. Moreover, it limits coverage to procedures deemed to have reasonable success rates and to medical centers that offer the best combination of performance and price. Also, by negotiating doctor and hospital fees in advance for certain procedures and by exerting pressure on health care providers through their bill-paying intermediaries, corporate managers do influence medical practice. By default, corporations are setting their own standards of what is acceptable medical treatment. In the absence of national standards, and because of the unwillingness of Congress to assume responsibility for setting guidelines and parameters for health care, rationing decisions are being made increasingly in the corporate arena.

In addition to cost considerations, corporations are also concerned about maintaining good employee and public relations. As a result, corporate decisions are influenced by external pressures that transcend either medical or cost criteria. Because of their size and their frequent dominance in local or even regional health care markets, corporations are a major force to be reckoned with in medical allocation and rationing. A critical question, of course, is whether corporations ought to be in effect setting medical decision-making criteria that have broad social ramifications. If not, what alternatives are available at this stage? If so, what mechanisms are available for creating some semblance of order out of the inconsistencies and inequities that are certain to follow?

Current trends toward the consolidation of medical allocation and rationing decisions in the corporate sphere lead to several observations. First, these trends demonstrate that rationing is inherent in medical decision making within the current context of scarce resources. Whether made in the private or public sector, all choices about the distribution of health care resources involve questions of how to allocate them and what criteria to employ. The reality of medical decision making is that allocation and rationing policy is being set increasingly by providers who are responsive to the interests of the organizations they represent. For instance, when the benefits manager of a large corporation decides to reject coverage for liver transplants, he or she has created an allocation policy. Similarly, when a representative of an HMO or other prepaid plan applies membership criteria that exclude prospective transplant recipients, an explicit rationing policy is in effect. In summary, health care policy affecting a large proportion of the public is being made daily in the private sector on largely economic grounds. Not surprisingly, public reaction against this quiet setting of allocation/rationing policy is more subdued than reaction against corresponding attempts by public agencies to openly do primarily the same thing.

Second, and of most relevance to the concerns expressed in this chapter, the allocation/rationing system that emanates from these private sector decisions is piecemeal, fragmented, and rife with inconsistencies. Increasingly, a patient's access to expensive medical treatment such as organ transplantation and in vitro fertilization is based less on the prognosis of the individual patient than on the terms of a coverage policy designed to be cost effective in the aggregate. Decisions that in the past were largely medical ones, where the risk of treatment was weighed against benefits expected to accrue to the patient, now become actuarial ones that center on calculated costs to the corporate employer, to the prepaid group plan enrollees, or to the stockholders of a for-profit health care facility. Although this shift in emphasis is quite understandable in light of the patterns introduced in chapter 1, it remains especially troubling because of the haphazard and patently inequitable way in which the response is made under control of the private sector. Some degree of order, harmony, and fairness clearly needs to be inculcated into the process of making allocative and rationing decisions.

Mechanic (1977) argues that this bureaucratization of medicine is inevitable as we move toward more explicit rationing systems. As the system becomes bureaucratized, control shifts away from the individual physician, first toward colleague control and then toward control by the administrators of the bureaucratic agencies. Concurrently, the role of the physician shifts from that of an entrepreneur, toward that of an expert initial access point into the system, and finally toward that of an administrative official whose duty it is to implement the organization's policy. In the most extreme forms of explicit rationing, the earlier roles disappear. In less extreme schemes they overlap with and at times conflict with the administrative role. The result is that the physician is no longer primarily an agent for the patient. At best the physician must take into account multiple, competing interests that put pressure on him or her to sacrifice potential patient interests in order to satisfy organizational demands.

Importantly, this trend toward bureaucratization is obvious whether the agency is a public one or not. The bureaucratization of medicine threatens the traditional concept of physician responsibility for the best interest of the patient by diluting the personal responsibility of the provider and segmenting responsibility for patient care (Mechanic 1977). By relieving the physician of direct continuing responsibility to a patient, the diffuse organizational structure can too easily lead to an evasion of responsibility by passing blame to others in the organization. Anyone who has ever had to deal with a bureaucratic structure when trying to rectify a problem is acutely aware of the difficulty of finding the person responsible. Where responsibility is unclear, it is easier for a physician to make a decision on the basis of interests other than those of the patient. Furthermore, the detached relationships typical within the bureaucratic context reduce the physicians' personal commitment to patients more commonly found in traditional long-term, one-on-one physician-patient relationships. The psychic reward of doing what is best for the patient, who in turn places trust and confidence in the doctor to act in his or her best interests, is replaced in bureaucratic medicine by rewards for being a good manager or a good member of the bureaucratic team, one who carries his fair load of patients and does not overly commit the organization's resources.

Rationing Medical Resources via Public Relations

A most disturbing form of rationing is the growing reliance on the use of public relations techniques or other private fund-raising activities to secure the funds necessary for expensive medical treatment. Organ and bone marrow transplants, especially those for young children or infants, frequently become causes célèbres for service organizations, fraternal associations, and the mass media. Occasionally, these appeals reach the national media if they happen to be carried by a wire service or get the attention of a notable, but more often they remain local or state stories. The case of the appeal for a liver for Jamie Fiske, discussed in chapter 2, is unusual only in that the president of the United States became personally involved. Service organizations increasingly are called upon for help by individuals unable to afford treatment not covered by insurance policies. Fund-raisers are held and contributions solicited. Similarly, fraternal organizations have established standing funds to pay for the medical treatment of members otherwise unable to raise the necessary "up-front" money that hospitals require for uninsured procedures.

Moreover, there are credible reports that public relations firms exist that will, for a percentage of the funds raised, mount a campaign complete with media tactics and lobbying to public officials. Although some of these appeals have been successful in raising the needed dollars, others have not, instead resulting in considerable disappointment and pain to the potential recipients and their families. A well-designed campaign, however, has good potential for raising substantial funds through powerful emotional appeals, especially if the case is a unique one and competition for funds is limited. It is very difficult, indeed, to resist wanting to help a child obtain a needed bone marrow transplant to save his or her life, particularly if the child is media attractive.

Although one hesitates to criticize any technique that arises from concern for a human being, rationing by public relations is deeply problematic. First, it is deceptive. Although the campaigns frequently play on the themes of equity and justice within the context of the health care system, they can result in inequitable and irrational medical decisions. They introduce a strong element of chance or luck into the decision-making process, because that is often what it takes to strike the public nerve. The public is likely to support the first case enthusiastically, but interest tends to decline as such campaigns become routine. Moreover, persons who are aggressive, educated, and skilled are more likely to participate in these attempts, thus working against those without the temperament and resources necessary to mount a vigorous campaign for funds.

A second problem with public relations rationing is that medical criteria are easily obscured by the dramatic emotional appeals. Persons who are considerably worse medical risks and less likely to survive, but who are the beneficiaries of such public support, may gain access to scarce resources, thus depriving more suitable candidates of the opportunity for treatment. Although one would hope that medical criteria would still define the pool of patients suitable for particular procedures, rationing by public relations appeals is certain to be haphazard and inconsistent. Furthermore, when public opinion conflicts with medical criteria, the health care system is likely to bow to the weight of public pressure, resulting in inefficient uses of limited resources. It is not uncommon for medical decisions not to treat to be reversed by public outcry over the denial.

A third problem with rationing by public relations is the mass media's fascination with the dramatic, the emotional, and the unique. The dramatic cases usually involve high-cost curative medicine. Media attention to such cases reinforces our technological fix mentality, the idea that money will solve the problem, and it boosts the egos of those who have contributed to the appeal to save a life. In the process, the media diverts needed attention from less dramatic but equally worthy cases. Sympathy is easily evoked for the Jamie Fiske who needs a new liver, but not for the corresponding thousands of persons slowly dying of high blood pressure or debilitated by rheumatoid arthritis. Unless one believes there is an unlimited trough of public compassion and willingness to give money to charitable appeals, one is quickly struck with the conclusion that these appeals eventually compete directly with one another. The more successful these highly individualized appeals for funds for high-cost curative procedures, the less response there will be to more abstract appeals in support of preventive medicine or primary care. To the extent that public relations rationing affects the perceptions of public officials, it clearly shapes the allocation of scarce medical resources.

Finally, this media-oriented rationing has a tendency to produce a circus-like atmosphere of press conferences, appearances on talk shows, and the like. Because the prospective patient and family have made a decision to go public, their problem becomes sensationalized, despite the best intentions of those involved. At best, the potential patient is put on public exhibition. At worst, he or she becomes an object to be exploited, the means to someone else's ends—the source of a good human interest story for example, or of a profit for the fund-raising firm. Unfortunately, any effort to generalize the appeal and protect the subject from public scrutiny is likely to reduce the likelihood of public empathy and thus of financial success. Annas (1985:187) contends that this charity or "bake sale" approach is demeaning both to the individual who has to make a public appeal for funds, and to society.

Certainly there is room for public action designed to help those in need. Charitable institutions have played a long and valuable role in American health care. Furthermore, in a free society individuals should be able to use any legal means available to gain access to needed medical treatment. Likewise, service and fraternal organizations traditionally have helped members of their respective communities in time of need. Nothing should be done to discourage the concern that is expressed through these mechanisms. However, as a primary means of rationing medical resources, these private appeals fail. The very presence of public relations rationing raises critical questions regarding the capacity of the health care system, itself, to ration adequately. The emphasis of these appeals on high-technology curative treatment reflects the extent to which the public continues to harbor unrealistic expectations that medicine can heal all if enough money is forthcoming.

The Allocation of Scarce Health Care Resources Through the U.S. Political Process

Public policies relating to the acceptance or rejection of any technology are made within a complex political-social-cultural context which must take into account intense competition among varied interests, public expectations, and the personal biases of a range of decision makers. Certainly, policy regarding medical technology is no exception. According to Dorothy Nelkin (1977:397), three factors are crucial to the allocation of public resources to specific research areas: national objectives; the perceived urgency of specific problems; and the convergence of the political will with technological opportunity. The problem must not only be viewed as urgent, but also must be seen as a matter of public concern, with resulting pressure for immediate resolution through governmental action. Although these perceptions of urgency may be influenced by interest groups, perhaps, writes Nelkin, the "overriding factor shaping priorities for science and technology is the convergence of technological opportunity; that is, the availability of an appropriate technology, with political readiness to accept technological change" (1977:399).

What responsibility, then, does a government have in controlling the use of a technology in order to protect the citizenry, including future generations? It seems that at the least the government, in its role of protector of public health, has a duty to define national goals and provide the mechanisms by which meaningful priorities for society can be established. Assuming a continuing context of scarce resources, three things are necessary: the gathering of extensive data that can help predict possible consequences of courses of action; the development of mechanisms to provide accurate means of continuously monitoring the consequences of the actions taken; and the development of means of coping with consequences judged undesirable. Of all our social institutions, only the national government has the capacity to accomplish these purposes, and then only with considerable commitment and effort.

Stages of Health Policymaking

Policymaking is a dynamic process shaped by the social, political, and technological environment. Although this process is not easily segmented, for analytical purposes it is useful to distinguish among separate stages which together constitute the public policy process. Although there is considerable overlap among the stages, the concentration on particular activities within each stage tends to be relatively consistent. As a result, a variety of schemes have been presented to segment the policy process into chronological stages. One scheme, presented by Brewer and de Leon (1983:18), divides the policy process into six stages: (1) initiation, (2) estimation, (3) selection, (4) implementation, (5) evaluation, and (6) termination. When attempts are made to formulate policy for the allocation of health care, considerable misdirected or premature effort might be avoided if policymakers would focus attention on those stages where immediate action is most essential.

Not surprisingly, most attention until now has been directed toward the more dramatic selection and implementation stages. The selection stage comprises the debate over policy options, the compromise and bargaining activities needed to integrate the various interests, and the making of a final decision. As is often noted, that decision might well be in favor of inaction, which normally reinforces the status quo. The implementation stage includes the development of rules, regulations, and guidelines essential to carrying out the decision; the modification of the decision to reflect operational constraints; the translation of the decision into operational terms; and the establishment of program goals and standards. The more ambiguous the original policy decision, the more discretion accrues to those responsible for implementation. Contrarily, precise definition of rules and obligations reduces this discretion.

Although evaluation and termination are less salient in the policy process, they too are critical elements. Evaluation involves comparison between expected and actual performance levels as measured against established criteria, as well as the assignment of responsibility for discovered discrepancies between expected and actual performance. It is a retrospective activity designed to analyze and strengthen the policy, as well as to reaffirm accountability. Termination occurs when a policy is determined to have failed in meeting its objectives. It involves the determination of costs, benefits, and of the consequences of reducing or eliminating specific programs. Because the policy process is continuous, termination, rather than being a last stage, serves to initiate another round of policymaking. Although program termination is presently infrequent in the area of health policy, continued scarce public resources in combination with politically controversial programs is heightening the importance of this stage in some areas of health care.

It is obvious that meaningful health policy can result only from the accomplishment of the entire policymaking process. However, at the present time, energy must be directed primarily toward the first stages, initiation and estimation. It is futile to engage in later stages of the process until the earlier ones are at least minimally fulfilled. Even worse, misdiagnosis of our problems or failure to define them accurately might aggravate the situation, raising the level of frustration and minimizing future attempts at resolution. We are not even at the point where specific health policy options can be debated meaningfully. Before choices are finalized, substantial effort must be expended on defining the issues, clarifying social priorities, and formulating policy options. Without this groundwork, policies made in the complex and sensitive area of the allocation of health care resources will fail.

Initiating Allocation Policy: Defining the Problem

A basic tenet of this book is that issues in health care always include a significant social dimension. The trends described in chapter 1 expand and intensify that dimension. Although most decision makers hesitate to become embroiled in politically sensitive issues, at the core of the health care crisis are political problems which require political solutions. The simple fact that an issue is a matter of public importance, however, does not guarantee that it will be identified by policymakers as raising a legitimate policy question. Awareness of the existence of a problem in and of itself is not an assurance that an issue will be put on the public agenda. Nelkin (1977:413) argues that the policy importance of any technological innovation depends both on the degree to which it provokes a public response, and on its relationship to organized economic and political interests. According to Cobb and Elder, only those issues which are "commonly perceived by members of the political community as meriting public attention ... and involving matters within the legitimate jurisdiction of existing governmental authority" become part of the public agenda (1972:85).

Despite a near consensus that "the overarching decisions in guiding technology are made by the government, so that public policy is accepted as the primary instrument of collective steering" (Wenk 1981:256), strong opposition to an expanded governmental role in health care has come from several quarters. Ironically, this opposition has itself generated considerable conflict and, to a large extent, heightened the tension that is essential to initiate government action. For Nelkin (1977:408), political demands focus most clearly on issues that are highly visible or dramatic, especially if their potential impact on public health or safety is evident. Health allocation issues are inherently volatile. The proliferation of interest groups with specific demands and the protests confronting technological development politicize the issue substantially. Commercialization of health care services is bound to intensify these divisions.

Granting that health care issues increasingly are part of the government agenda, the initiation stage of the policy process requires that policymakers define the boundaries of the problem and get a sense of its possible importance before determining that it merits further attention. Health care problems compete with other problems for scarce space on the public agenda. Unfortunately, frequently neither the objectives nor the priorities of health policy are clearly articulated, thus making it difficult to ascertain when and if government action is warranted.

In addition to recognizing the problem, the initiation stage requires that the problem context be clarified. Two primary components of problem identification are the relevant contextual and environmental parameters, and the proper time constraints (Brewer and de Leon 1983:42). By cautiously selecting the criteria used to define the problem, and by accounting for external constraints, one can ascertain the seriousness and scope of the problem, its possible effects if left unattended, and the urgency with which it should be addressed.

Determining the contextual parameters entails identifying the groups or individuals who are affected and the extent to which they are likely to respond to the problem. Although this assessment continues throughout the entire policy process, an early analysis of who benefits or is deprived helps define the boundaries of feasible political action, and provides an estimate of the extent of the problem. This information might also help determine the best strategy for confronting the problem. For instance, if it is possible to define the problem tightly, it might be analyzed as a whole. If not, the problem might have to be "disaggregated" into a number of more narrow, discrete, or manageable subproblems. This process of "suboptimation" rests on the assumption that the sum of the solutions or alternatives will resolve the entire problem. There are obvious dangers in this reductionist approach. Boulding (1982:267) warns against wasting our efforts on suboptimization where it leads to finding the best way to do something that should not be done at all. Also, because of the vast array of difficult trade-offs involved, and the complex interaction of health care with a host of cultural and social forces, health policymaking does not appear amenable to subdivision. Instead, it appears to require a more integrated approach.

Time constraints also set the tone for the health policy process and must be assessed early in the initiation stage. The more urgent the problem, the more severe the time constraints. Unfortunately, political institutions tend to postpone action until the problem is a crisis. This creates difficulties because, writes Wenk, "under stress there is a tendency to consider only the most immediate costs and benefits of policy initiatives" (1981:259). Also, decision makers under tight time constraints are liable to make mistakes more often. It is critical to estimate the time frame carefully and to initiate the policy process early enough in the development of an issue to provide adequate leeway for later stages. As the time available to make choices decreases, the opportunities to search for alternatives and to conduct analyses are minimized. This realization reinforces the necessity of initiating the policy process as early as possible and not waiting until the problem reaches crisis proportions.

Setting Policy Objectives

Concurrent with defining the context of a policy, it is necessary to specify what the policy objectives are and what values ought to be pursued. The importance of this enterprise is spelled out by Brewer and deLeon:

The initiation stage provides an important opportunity to address and define policy objectives or goals directly. The objectives will determine what priorities are assigned, and what policies are selected, provide guidelines for the implementation of the chosen programs, and determine the criteria for program evaluation. Thus, the determination of policy objectives is fundamental to the policy task. That objectives are too often left vague or ambiguous—or even not considered at all—may explain why so many programs flounder, as if they had no clear direction or purpose. Without clear objectives, they do not. (1983:48)

Although setting health policy goals and objectives is difficult, especially in the early phases of initiation, it is critical. Before any commitment of resources is made, major energies should be directed toward setting priorities based on clearly stated policy objectives.

At its foundation, much of the controversy surrounding the distribution of medical technologies and services arises from conflicting goals or values. Some of the competing values which influence public policy to varying degrees in all societies are individual freedom and choice; social or public good; scientific and technological progress; quality of life; human dignity; efficiency; social stability; and differing concepts of justice, themselves based on goals of equity, entitlement, or need. Public reactions to specific innovations as well as to health care in general will vary substantially depending on which social values predominate.

Although there is considerable skepticism over the capacity of a pluralistic society to reach a consensus on long-term goals in any area as sensitive and divisive as health care, it is critical that we try. Although admitting that the task is correctly viewed as overwhelming, Carey contends that we must "design and pursue integrated national goals" regarding science and technology problems that are "outpacing the quality and intensity" of our current responses "by widening margins" (1982:13). The President's Commission concludes that successful genetic programs require "concrete goals and specific procedural guidelines that are founded on sound ethical and public policy principles" (1983:42). Lowrance criticizes the current tendency to define risk and set priorities without first designating "preferred societal goals" (1982:110). Another observer explains that the "task of forging political consensus about major national strategies" must be of "high priority in all quarters of the interested public" (Rettig 1982:23). Wenk (1981:256) reminds us that technology is interwoven with human culture and social institutions, and that our goals are critically affected by a combination of those forces. It is a prerequisite for social policy to make the goals explicit. In a pluralistic society, it is critical that the objectives of all relevant participants be given consideration at an early stage. What are the specific goals of the interest groups on various sides of the issue? These pragmatic political questions are important, although too often, perhaps, they become too important.

My contention that the goals and priorities we establish concerning the allocation of health care resources must be national in scope reflects both the extent to which health care is funded at the federal level, and the nationwide ramifications of allocation and rationing policy, which transcend state, regional, or local boundaries. The abortion issue demonstrates the difficulty of maintaining simultaneously a decentralized policymaking apparatus and an equitable distribution of rights and obligations. Just as clearly, the failure of attempts to establish a national policy on abortion suggests that centralization, by itself, is no guarantee of success in framing adequate policy on morally sensitive issues in a pluralistic society. Although local standards might be useful in delineating the parameters of certain policies, the fundamental questions raised by health care issues must be dealt with at the national level. As noted by Spilhaus, "now is the time to revive ideas of how to plan for large national objectives that transcend local and state interest, and that look far beyond present immediacies" (1972:714).

This emphasis on the need to develop a national consensus on broad goals and social priorities regarding health policy does not preclude states having leeway to interpret and implement policy flexibly. In many substantive areas today, federalism gives the states some discretion in implementing national policy. Frequently, the states are given considerable leeway within broad guidelines designed to assure minimal levels of compliance. This latitude might result in conflicting programs, but it also performs the function of dispersing pressure which would otherwise overload the national government. Rettig (1982:23) suggests that the federal government's capacity for centralized policy formulation will perhaps be taxed beyond its limits if it attempts to respond to the full scope of demands. Although some decentralization in the execution of national goals and priorities appears advantageous, health policy objectives must be defined at the national level based on fundamental social values.

Although the need for integrated and clearly articulated policy objectives to deal with the issues in health care is stressed here, it also must be acknowledged that their formulation will be difficult given the excruciatingly complex cultural, social, and political context of medicine. In a pluralistic society, there are many conceivably legitimate, but contradictory, goals, especially on issues as fundamental as the allocation of health care. Furthermore, because these issues are not amenable to bargaining and compromise, attaining a rational balance among the competing goals is a formidable task. As noted earlier, however, the arduous scope of this task should not deter society from attempting to establish goal priorities.

After the objectives have been specified and some consensual foundations are established, policy options can be formulated. Although the possibilities introduced at this stage will be tentative and subject to alteration, the initial development of feasible options must be performed in conjunction with identifying the problem and determining policy objectives. There are few areas in which it is more crucial to scrutinize options at an early stage in the process than in the area of the allocation and rationing of health care resources. In part, this is because considerable dialogue over the advisability of different courses of action is needed as early as possible. It is also due to the fact that new medical techniques and practices are dependent on a series of research and development decisions that precede them, in some cases by decades. For instance, policy decisions made years ago that supported artificial heart research are just now being analyzed more carefully. In pursuit of the objective of reducing heart disease, alternatives to a mechanical heart were unfortunately not seriously considered when the long-term financial commitment was made to invest in the development of another technological fix. Also, attempts at an objective and rigorous evaluation appeared to lack resolve for finding against the artificial heart program (Jonsen 1986). This raises considerable questions concerning the second stage of health policymaking: assessment.

Estimation and Assessment

Once a broad public discussion and debate over policy objectives and options is accomplished, systematic investigation of the problem and a thorough assessment of each idea for addressing it is critical. Within the social context of health care, the estimation stage of policymaking must focus upon the probable consequences of each possible course of action or nonaction. What benefits and costs does each option imply for society? for specific groups? for individuals? Accurate estimates here require a sharpening and refinement of the problem and a narrowing of the range of plausible solutions. Remaining options are ordered according to the criteria established in the initial stage. Although there are never enough resources or time to conduct a definitive analysis or to eliminate all uncertainty, any effort devoted to the assessment of each policy option will help clarify the decision context later and ensure that critical decisions need not be made on the basis of intuition alone.

Technology Assessment. The Organization for Economic Cooperation and Development notes that biotechnology is an especially good example of an area that "requires a science policy designed to provide an ongoing process of technological assessment" (1981:113). Evans (1983:2047) argues that careful assessment can increase the efficiency of the health care delivery system, but in order to do so the methods by which allocation and rationing decisions are made must be improved considerably. Hanft agrees that too little attention is directed toward the consequences of biomedical innovations and warns that once "given the Good Housekeeping seal of the community," it is difficult to restrain the use of a new technique in the health services system, "even when efficacy and costs have not been established" (Powledge and Dach 1977:23). Despite these endorsements, much debate has surrounded technology assessment (TA) over the last decade. Part of the confusion is due to the absence of a single definition of what TA entails. A considerable extent of the disagreement over TA, then, arises from questions of methodology. How broad should the assessment be? Should it have a primarily technical content, or focus on social consequences? How much weight should the various factors be given?

If TA is to be useful in health care policymaking, it must take into consideration a broad spectrum of factors. Milbrath argues for the importance of conducting value analyses before decisions are made. After identifying as fully as possible all values likely to be affected, they can be "weighted according to the importance assigned them by the people" (1986:28). Coates defines technology assessment as "the systematic study of the effects on society that may occur when a technology is introduced, extended, or modified, with special emphasis on the impacts that are unintended, indirect, and delayed" (1971:225). This definition refers to two aspects of TA which are crucial to its full effectiveness. Most obvious is the broad concern with effects on society. More subtle is the emphasis on second-order consequences: those which are unintended, indirect, or delayed. Any assessment of medical technologies or proposed programs to be built around them must focus on both of these concerns as well as on the strictly technical questions of safety and efficacy, which unfortunately too often receive predominant attention.

To this end, Patricia Harris, Secretary of HHS, announced in 1980 that all new health care technologies would have to be evaluated on the basis of their social consequences, as well as their safety and efficacy, before their wide distribution would be financed. Assessment was to include consideration of the potential need for the innovation, the legal and ethical issues concerning its adoption and use, relevant constraints on the availability of the innovation, and effectiveness in terms of economic as well as social costs and benefits.

Technology assessment is frequently assumed to be largely descriptive, but given the many value judgments made at each stage of the analysis, it contains prescriptive components as well. Lawrence Tribe (1973a:627) contends that by emphasizing impacts and outcomes, technology assessment becomes yet another exercise in "instrumental rationality" where policy decisions are viewed simply as the product of trade-offs among existing interests and values in the community. Simply broadening the range of factors considered by expanding the spectrum of affected interests, including social costs and benefits, and by extending the time frame will not resolve the underlying problems of the instrumental mode of analysis. Moreover, he contends that the policy-analytic mode itself is flawed due to its focus on outcomes at the expense of questions of process. Although Tribe does not dismiss technology assessment entirely, he suggests that emphasis should be placed on determining what our most important needs and values ought to be, rather than accepting them as givens. This is in agreement with the emphasis throughout this book on the necessity for clarifying the needs, priorities, and goals of our society before pushing to make policy.

Another controversy involving technology assessment revolves around its political dimension. Harvey Brooks argues that there are no objective or scientific bases upon which final choices about the use of technology can be made. Instead, the "choices themselves are political, depending upon a complex interplay or bargaining process among conflicting economic, political and ideological interests and values" (1973:251). The National Academy of Sciences (1975:3) suggests that a modification of assessment methodology is necessary in order to consider our "deeply ingrained feelings" about the nature of human beings, their freedom, integrity, dignity, and beliefs, which are clearly operative in medical areas. Although Brooks (1976:251) admits that technology assessment can lead people to rethink their own preferences by revealing the relative costs of the options available, he views it as too ready a means of legitimizing political consensus through its supposedly value-free analysis. For Victor Ferkiss the difficulties involved in technology assessment are compounded when technology is judged within the context of "political and social goals which are themselves subject to controversy" (1978:4).

There is also considerable debate over the practicality of forecasting the consequences of technology. Drucker, for instance, contends that assessment designed to predict the remote effects of new technologies is impossible, because the "future impact of technology is almost always beyond anybody's imagination" (1981:251). The dismal record of social and economic experts especially in foreseeing technological impact exists because the consequences of technology are far more difficult to predict than other developments, since its effects result from the convergence of a number of factors, only a few of which are technological. Baltimore (1983:53), too, is bothered by "premature efforts to draw arbitrary lines on what is appropriate research" and contends that such attempts may serve us poorly in the future. The "dilemma of control" for Collingridge (1980) is that social consequences cannot be predicted early in the life of a technology, when control is possible. By the time the undesirable consequences are discovered, the technology is so much a part of the whole economic and social fabric that control is costly and slow at best. He urges that any decisions be reversible, corrigible, and flexible.

The rising expectations of the public, fueled by reports in the media of rapid advances in biomedical technology, are producing a situation where adequate estimation and assessment of new techniques early in the development process is critical. Vastly shortened lag times between basic research and widespread availability of new technologies further accentuate this need. Although current estimation techniques, including technology assessment, are flawed as mechanisms for evaluating the medical policy options constantly being thrust upon us, with major modifications their use now is preferable to waiting until all of their weaknesses have been eliminated. Health care problems are becoming more, not less, complex, and the long-term uncertainties make the search for a perfect estimation technique futile.

Forecasting the Effects of Medical Policy. The end stage renal disease program provides an excellent example of failure to predict with accuracy the long-term impact of government policy on the demand for and use of a developing medical technology. As a result of this failure, a very costly commitment was made by Congress to the sufferers from kidney disease, to the exclusion of other similar diseases. This macroallocation decision was justified, or at least rationalized, on the basis of predictions of future costs that were grossly in error because of an underestimation of the broader impact the program itself would have on medical decisions made at the individual level. The end stage renal disease program serves as a prime illustration of the need to improve our forecasting methods. More importantly, it demonstrates that estimation must be separated from the directly political forces that often make it nothing but a pro forma legitimizing technique in which the projections are designed to corroborate a decision already made.

At the base of forecasting is data acquisition. According to Wenk we must establish a systematic process through which "pitfalls and crises could be avoided" (1981:266). Central to this effort must be the inclusion in our decision-making process of the capacity to use information presently available to forecast consequences with sophistication and elegance, and to contemplate what might occur, especially in terms of those futures we wish to avoid. Kass argues that policy-makers must "face up to reasonable projections of future accomplishments, consider whether they are cause for social concern, and see whether or not the principles *now* enunciated and the practices *now* established are adequate to deal with any such concerns" (1981:459). Although we can never know with certainty what will happen, much less how soon, uncertainty is not the same as ignorance, because our present knowledge can suggest that some events are more likely than others.

In addition to the need for more extensive data on the efficacy and safety of new medical innovations prior to their diffusion, it is essential that the methodological assumptions of epidemiology and other analytical frameworks be thoroughly reevaluated. Not only have many technologies and procedures been put into widespread use before their effectiveness and safety were established—for instance CAT scans and bypass surgery—but also the benefits of widely used treatments have been exaggerated by questionable statistical inferences.

Recent revelations that apparent advances in the treatment of lung cancer are nothing but statistical illusions demonstrate this problem (Feinstein et al. 1985). Researchers found no statistically significant difference in the survival rates of patients treated for lung cancer over the last 30 years, despite the introduction of sophisticated diagnostic tools such as CAT scans, nuclear scans, and ultrasound during that period. Data that show that one-half of all patients now survive for five years as compared with one-third in the 1950s are misleading in making it appear that treatment has been more successful. In fact, the improvement is spurious; it results from the introduction of diagnostic tests that spot the disease sooner than was before possible. Because their cancer was detected earlier, more recent patients could be followed longer, producing the illusion that they lived longer. Even though the real odds of dying of lung cancer are the same now as they were a generation ago, the model wrongly implied a substantial reduction in the chances of dying within five years. The researchers concluded that while they had expected newer cancer treatments to have improved survival rates, it actually appeared likely that these therapies have helped some patients but harmed others, so that their opposing effects on different patients have counterbalanced one another.

One of the researchers, Daniel Sosin, notes that this false confidence in a treatment could affect physicians' decisions as they attempt to weigh the benefits of chemotherapy or surgical therapy against the risks they pose for a particular patient. Overestimating the benefits on the basis of false inferences concerning survival rates might lead physicians to accept greater risks, at substantial personal and societal cost. Within a context where providers are trained to use all treatments that are of any benefit to the patient despite the cost, accurate data on patient benefit and risk are essential. In the case of lung cancer treatment, it appears that considerable resources have been wasted with little, if any, impact on health—resources that could have been better directed elsewhere. A critical question is how many additional widely used treatments for cancer and other diseases are in fact ineffectual.

It is extremely important, then, that we turn a critical eye upon biomedical innovations, because low barriers to entry in this area of technology inevitably increase the dangers of carelessness and abuse. These hazards can be reduced only through adequate planning and continued monitoring of their development. Although concerned that "latent forces are often unperceived by analysts and modellers," Caldwell submits that "futurology and the modelling of possible futures should enable this society to foresee the course of its direction more clearly than was ever possible in the past" (1983:29).

In a similar vein, Lowrance (1982:112) sees a current challenge facing society to develop ways to keep priorities clear and to concentrate decision-making attention on problems which affect large numbers of people in important ways. He concludes that bodies responsible for appraising public risk must answer the following questions regarding their assessment strategies:

1. Are risks, benefits and costs characterized as explicitly as possible?
2. Are uncertainties and intangibles acknowledged and, where possible, estimated?
3. Are programs oriented to agreed-upon societal goals?
4. Do procedures guarantee that high-quality technical evidence is made available and used as the basis for decision?
5. Are risks examined in a properly comparative context along with benefits and costs?
6. Are precautions taken to prevent minor hazards from displacing larger ones on the protection agenda? (1982:124)

Some of the most critical of these questions, and by far the most controversial, center on the mechanisms for measuring, weighing, and evaluating the costs and benefits of various courses of action. Nowhere is the debate more heated than over the use of cost-benefit analysis in making allocation and rationing decisions in medicine.

Cost-Benefit Analysis in Health Policy

The allocation of scarce medical resources is certain to be conducted within the context of cost-benefit analysis (CBA) or some variation of it. Although the consideration of the costs and benefits of a potential policy are inherent in the making of any political decision, CBA as a formal approach was developed in the 1960s to aid in the allocation of public monies for river irrigation projects. Since that time, it has come to be used in almost all areas of public policy evaluation. Despite its widespread use, CBA elicits much controversy, particularly when applied to programs in which the costs and benefits cannot be reduced to dollars and where intangibles outweigh those benefits which can be measured accurately. Health care policy is clearly an area where CBA can be used only with considerable caution.

Although the specifics of each CBA model vary and the assumptions often differ from one application to the next, the basic intent of CBA is to explicate the relevant costs and benefits of a project, and to compute a benefit/cost ratio. If the expected benefits exceed the costs, the project is feasible on economic grounds. Conversely, if costs are greater than benefits, the project should not be funded. A natural extension of this methodology is comparing programs on the basis of their benefit/cost ratios and establishing priorities from most to least justified. Although in theory CBA is straightforward, in practice it is extremely difficult to calculate these values, especially across a set of disparate programs. Questions remain as to what costs and what benefits should be included in a model, how they can be reduced to common units, and who should ultimately make the value judgments inherent in the final policy decision.

Procedures of Cost-Benefit Analysis

Due to the need in cost-benefit analysis for expressing both costs and benefits in the same unit, generally monetary, there is a tendency to include in the analysis only those factors which can be readily translated and for which adequate data are available. Once these data have been collected, the information is used in a formula from which several values are computed. The first of these is *net present value*, or the mathematical difference between the present sums of benefits and costs. The second is the *benefit/cost ratio*, which is simply the division of present benefits by present costs.

In CBA, it is crucial that all future benefits and costs be translated into present value, since many benefits will be spread over future years. The *discount rate* is an adjustment factor used to express future benefits in terms of their present value. This is based on the assumption that individuals prefer consumption today to the same amount of consumption in the future. The present value, then, is the price that people would be willing to pay today for a benefit in the future. Theoretically, it denotes how many dollars must be set aside today for *x* dollars of future benefits. In practice, however, selection of the discount rate is arbitrary, a common figure being 6 or 7 percent. A 6 percent rate means that in order to realize $1.00 worth of future benefits, we must set aside $1.06 today. The higher the discount rate, the greater the emphasis placed on the present. When a lower discount rate is used, future costs and benefits are treated as more equivalent to present ones and are therefore more pertinent to the analysis. Obviously, a high discount rate will affect the benefit/cost ratio unfavorably in the analysis of preventive health care programs, where many benefits occur in the future, while costs are largely in the present.

Conley notes three methods of comparing costs and benefits:

1. comparison of program with alternative of no program.
2. comparison of the differential costs and benefits of various options, and
3. comparison of programs with CBA of each program carried out against alternative of no program and then compared with each other. (1973:243)

The first technique has limited application for policymaking since it makes no determination as to what program might be most efficient. Instead, it simply indicates whether a single program is worthwhile in cost-benefit terms. Until now, many cost-benefit studies for health care programs have been of this type. The second method of comparing costs and benefits is termed "cost effectiveness." This technique compares the costs of providing the same benefit in different ways. Given the goal of reducing disease, which program gives the most return per dollar spent? Although this method produces data as to whether one program is superior to another, it does not make an overall determination of whether either program is worthwhile. The third method determines not only those programs that are economically desirable, but also which of the desirable programs gives the greatest return.

Problems of Cost-Benefit Analysis

No matter what approach is taken, the problem of measurement haunts CBA, especially when comparing disparate programs. Many benefits, especially such intangibles as psychological benefits, cannot be expressed in terms that are directly comparable, much less in dollar terms. Also, there are many second-order costs and benefits which tend to be ignored because data is either sparse or unavailable. Moreover, instruments for measuring nonmonetary social benefits and costs are primitive at best. On the positive side, however, measurement is one area where improvement is likely as more attention is placed on the importance of variables now obscured.

Given the problems, both conceptual and operational, of CBA, it is not surprising that controversy surrounds its continued use. Opponents are especially critical of the tendency of CBA to obscure the moral issues and emphasize the quantification of values. As stated by Caplan, "those who believe in a basic right of all persons to adequate health care will not be much moved by talk of cost, benefit, or social good" (1983:97). Also, because medical technologies are subject to constant change and refinement, they are particularly elusive targets for CBA. In the least, CBA requires subordination of complex moral problems to the task of computing costs and benefits for each possibility. Until now, according to Altman and Blendon (1979:1), new biomedical technologies have been introduced when clinicians believed they would benefit the patient, irrespective of cost. The emphasis on cost effectiveness is altering substantially this traditional mode of operation. Avorn (1984) sees discrimination against the elderly as but one dangerous result of using CBA for the control of health care costs.

Taking a more moderate position, Swint and associates argue that, although use of CBA should not be taken to imply that economic consequences are the only criteria for program approval, "CBA provides decision-makers with information designed to improve their ability to make rational decisions, i.e., it functions as one source of information that they must combine with ethical, sociopolitical, and other (intangible) information for new evaluation" (1979:464). In strong support of CBA, Conley argues

Benefit-cost considerations are crucial to decision making. No decision on the use of resources should ever be made without some estimate, even if crude and subjective, of benefits and costs over time. Ultimately, benefit-cost considerations are the basis for determining whether a particular project should be adopted, how large it should be, and the composition of the resources that are utilized (1973:241).

Although CBA is ingrained in the American policy process, these problems suggest that the approach must be used with caution, especially in comparing health programs that have divergent goals and dimensions. It is especially dangerous when comparing health care programs with other programs whose benefits might be more immediate and which therefore will appear preferable, although in the long run, they are not. CBA appears to be a useful technique for providing information on the costs and benefits of competing programs only if the limits of its conclusions are made clear. In order for CBA to contribute meaningfully to policymaking, measuring instruments must be refined, renewed emphasis must be placed on quantifying major social and psychological costs and benefits, assumptions and their implications must be explicated, and new efforts must be made to anticipate second-order costs and benefits. Even then, the final decision in each case ought to reflect the actual needs, values, and preferences of the people affected by a program and include consideration of other decision-making principles such as equity, justice, and fairness.

There is no doubt that future health policy decisions will be increasingly dependant on CBA, despite the inherent limitations and special problems in applying it to biomedical technologies. As noted by Nelson and associates, because "the continuation and the possible extension of such programs can only be accomplished with further commitments of scarce medical resources, it is inevitable that the issue of returns on this investment relative to alternative uses of the necessary resources must be addressed" (1978:160). Although it is clear from extensive data that many current programs can be justified on the CBA basis, ultimately the choice of goals and selection of priorities involves consideration of a wide variety of social costs and benefits that cannot adequately be measured by the current cost-benefit approach.

The time frame for calculating costs and benefits must also be expanded to account for those benefits which might accrue in the future, as well as second-order or irreversible costs which might arise. Although this is extremely difficult under the cost-benefit formulas currently in use, it is not impossible. More effort to include intangibles, increased use of supporting data to refine assumptions, and delineation of the benefits accruing to a wide range of individuals should strengthen the applicability of cost-benefit analysis to health policies. Given the state of program evaluation and scrutiny at present, there appears to be no other choice but to work on thoroughly revising cost-benefit models to better reflect and anticipate the complex but subtle benefits and costs inherent in the allocation of health care resources.

Problems of Current Allocation Policy Approaches

One dilemma in health care is how the government can contain costs in the public sector without exaggerating the potential inequities inherent in any distribution system. As noted earlier, cost containment measures in the Medicare/Medicaid programs clearly are contributing to the development of a multitiered system. If limits are placed on reimbursement of physicians and hospitals for publicly supported patients, not surprisingly the quality of care will deteriorate. Moreover, if the reimbursement schedules are set artificially low, well below the current market prices in the private sector, at least two different classes of health care will develop: one for the elderly and poor dependent on public support, and the other for the working middle class and others with private insurance coverage. Conversely, without rigid cost constraints on public spending, which constitutes over 40 percent of total health care expenditures in the United States, escalation of costs will continue unabated. The dilemma is the direct contrast between the goals of equity and cost control.

Obviously, it is easier for the government to exert effective control over public spending than to regulate spending in the private sector. Placing rigid cost controls only over public health care spending, however, would solidify the tiered system. Avoiding this dilemma necessitates either abandoning efforts to constrain costs in the public sector, extending these controls uniformly to the private sector as well, or creating a system that encourages cost limits in both sectors without sacrificing equity. The first solution is not practical unless society is willing to make health the ultimate objective and spend unlimited resources for it.

The second solution to this dilemma has proven largely unworkable in the United States both legally and politically. There is also evidence from Britain that the National Health Service itself has spawned an active private insurance sector to serve those persons unwilling to live within the constraints of the public sector. Even in New Zealand, perhaps the most egalitarian of democratic societies, there is a clear trend toward a dual system of health care. In the United States, the political tradition of liberal individualism and the capitalist mode of economic life make state control of medicine unlikely. The bureaucracy required to monitor and regulate the health care industry would be massive and technically complex. Problems with Medicare's diagnosis-related groups (DRGs) exemplify these difficulties. Furthermore, there is little evidence that equity could be served by this approach, especially in light of the likely opposition by health care providers to this magnitude of government intervention. Industry attempts to debilitate or at least soften cost control efforts until now demonstrate the impracticality of the second approach.

The third approach assumes that equity remains an important goal, despite the emphasis on controlling costs. Equity, in turn, can be assured only if the ground rules in the private and public funding sectors are identical. As soon as they diverge, imbalance will result. However, neither of the other possibilities for resolving cost problems can succeed, for the reasons stated above. They are simple approaches, and the complexity of the health care problem requires a multifaceted solution.

Schramm (1984:731) questions whether the complex distributional problems that plague health care policy can be solved by democratic governments, which by design and tradition are responsive to individual as well as collective interests. Can workable allocation schemes and rationing criteria be established that enhance the collective good, yet protect vital individual interests? This seems increasingly unlikely in light of the continually expanding expectations of the public. As noted earlier, demand for medical resources becomes urgent and virtually unlimited when disease strikes loved ones, despite the frequent irrationality of such demands when viewed in the abstract and impersonal aggregate. Writes Schramm, "We have been prepared to spend infinitely on the individual in the past, thus it seems we must continue to do so in the future. We seem incapable of making the level of hospital spending conform to our emerging sense that it must be related to our ability to pay" (1984:730).

Moreover, interest groups are certain to challenge any allocation decisions which adversely affect their members. In a free society, such groups, through lobbying, public relations, and litigation, are capable of weakening or negating efforts to restrain health care, even if restraint is clearly in the interests of the society as a whole. Also, since a liberal society allows individuals the freedom to select their own concept of the good life and to live it with minimal government interference, rationing policy that intervenes in the lifestyle choices of individuals is highly problematic.

As a society, the United States has been hesitant to institute health policies that imply limits on resources committed to an individual. Cost containment measures that attempt to set limits on individual care are widely attacked as counter to the goals of health care. Meanwhile, the right to health care is proselytized in the press and fought over in the courts. According to some observers (Miller and Miller 1986), our inability to make hard choices and set limits to health care results from this view that the individual claim to medical resources ought to be predominant. Schramm sees the status quo as leading to a "tyranny of our own making" through which we will "impoverish ourselves and successive generations by indulging in too much medicine" (1984:732). Market solutions are bound to fail because they serve to reaffirm individual claims to resources and to favor acute care for individuals, regardless of prognosis, over those measures which would improve the health of the community as a whole. Although Schramm contends that the government can assert the collective best interest over individual self-interest, within the liberal tradition, democratic institutions seem to face paralysis when abrogation of individual rights is imminent. Although I agree with his assertion that we must use our democratic institutions to stem the tide and regulate our overindulgence in medical care for the individual at all costs, there is little evidence that our institutions are either willing or capable of executing such a change from above.

Health care is a prime illustration of an area in which there is a major imbalance in the distribution of expected costs and benefits across society. The escalation of health care costs, for instance, does benefit health care providers, particularly the for-profit sector which has flourished in recent years in part because of the inflation of health costs. One reason why the government has been so slow to respond to this emerging crisis concerns the distribution of benefits and costs. Although the benefits of the expanding health dollar are concentrated in a small but powerful segment of the economy, its costs are diffused across many patients and third-party payers. As long as these costs were held within manageable bounds, the incentive for controlling inflation was much less than the alternate concern for shifting the costs. Many attempts by Congress to inhibit cost escalation have been aggressively opposed by a health care industry that profits from the status quo.

Only recently have insurance companies exhibited concern over the long-term dangers of the unbridled escalation of health care costs. Historically, they have, by and large, simply paid the costs and then passed them on to policyholders in the form of higher premiums. Because of tax incentives, themselves the products of successful lobbying by health care providers and employers, health insurance continues to be heavily subsidized by taxpayers. Although this policy has proved attractive to all parties, including consumers, as illustrated in chapter 1 it continues to fuel cost escalation and institutionalize inequities between the middle class professionals and union workers who enjoy comprehensive coverage as an untaxed fringe benefit, and those groups without comparable coverage. Soaring insurance premiums, however, are causing reevaluation on the part of all parties. Employers can no longer afford to provide comprehensive coverage to their employees. Employees are dissatisfied with the growing share of premiums they must pay and with the less complete coverage they enjoy. Finally, insurance companies are beginning to realize that costs can no longer simply be shifted to policyholders without grave long-term consequences.

Preventive v. Curative Medicine: Ideological Perspectives

An interesting paradox is apparent when the preventive medicine/curative medicine distinction is placed within the context of the prevailing ideological dichotomy between conservatism and liberalism. Although liberals most often are found embracing the concept of preventive medicine and arguing that more resources ought to be directed toward that end, at the base it is curative, not preventive, medicine that is more egalitarian. Ironically, preventive medicine is clearly utilitarian in that it emphasizes the societal good accruing from preventive measures, even if these measures are taken at the expense of limiting individual lifestyle choices. Not surprisingly, preventive medicine is frequently justified on directly utilitarian grounds. The contention is that preventive medicine maximizes benefits to society and, in the long run, minimizes the costs of health care. Although there are benefits to individuals as well in preventive health measures, there are also constraints, usually explicit, on behavior.

Contrary to what is often asserted, liberals are forced to defend curative medicine if they are to remain true to their egalitarian principles. Provision of curative medicine for all persons is the only way to provide anything approaching equity in health care. An egalitarian must reject a situation where individuals are denied high-cost curative treatment because they failed to comply with good preventive practices. For instance, while a conservative utilitarian might argue that a person who smokes in spite of the known health risks should not have access to significant curative measures, the liberal is forced to acknowledge the smoker's legitimate claim upon society, because persons with greater needs are entitled to those goods essential to satisfy them. It is utilitarians who can argue persuasively that preventive medicine is preferable because it most efficiently allocates scarce medical resources. At best, liberals must limit their support for preventive medicine to those selected instances that extend equity.

In arguing that a just policy must work always to the advantage of the least well off, the liberal philosopher John Rawls, for instance, would seem to be forced to support curative measures, even at great expense, if the sickest—the least well off—are to benefit. Moreover, preventive measures could be viewed as negating Rawls' first principle, that liberty must be maximized for everyone in a society. If liberty includes the freedom to choose one's own lifestyle, Rawls would have difficulty supporting preventive measures which restrain this choice.

Similarly, conservatives who argue for the continued emphasis on high-technology curative medicine to prolong life, whether for neonatal intensive care to save a Baby Doe or for terminal patients, find themselves in a quandary. This quandary is becoming increasingly serious because the costs of curative medicine are borne by third-party payers. For this to be possible, resources must be shifted from those persons with the fewest needs but the most resources to those with the greatest needs. Certainly, a libertarian such as Robert Nozick must have trouble with the idea of active government involvement in the redistribution of medical resources, particularly if they go to people who suffer because of their own unhealthy lifestyles.

In the end, it is the utilitarian framework which is most naturally attuned to preventive medicine. Curative medicine has less utility for society as a whole, because it means that scarce resources are consumed by a small proportion of the population at a substantial cost to society. The greater number benefit more from preventive health measures, including many that are not medical, such as improved sanitation, housing, and, particularly, education. Many, though not all, preventive health care programs are cost effective, despite the clear bias against them created by the discount rates frequently used in cost-benefit analysis.

Equity: The Neglected Component

Even though the current emphasis in health care policymaking revolves around questions of cost containment, equity and quality continue to be major considerations that should not be obscured. In American culture, the assumptions that quality care should be available to the entire population and that individuals should not needlessly suffer for wont of medical care are well established. Although far from fully egalitarian in scope, this concept of the right to health care makes it unsettling at best for us to dismiss arguments for equity in the allocation of medical resources. Although the discrepancy between the theory and the practice of equity considerations remains wide, it is unlikely that equity can be neglected as a value to be pursued in designing acceptable health policy. For this reason, any policy that depends exclusively on cost effectiveness or cost-benefit rationales without considerations of equity, or, to a lesser extent, of quality, will fail to resolve our health care problems and is likely, in the long run at least, to intensify them.

An affluent society such as the United States should be able to provide good primary health care for all citizens, or at least for all citizens who make a minimal effort to reduce unwarranted health risks in their lives. Obviously, defining what this guaranteed primary health care should be depends on the resources available nationwide for health care. This, in turn, depends on the two types of decisions emphasized in this book: how much money society is willing or capable of committing to health care, and what our priorities are for distribution of these funds so as to provide an equitable base of primary care for all citizens. Only after these decisions are made can we make reasonable choices as to how much we are willing to raise the level of health care. In other words, once we have met the goal of providing access to primary care on as equitable as possible a basis, any remaining funds should be used to expand the base and pursue ambitious life-extending programs. It is probable, however, given the trends discussed in chapter 1, that such funding would be limited at best.

Ethical Bases for Cost Containment

Veatch (1986:33) points out that patients are not treated fairly if too few *or* too many resources are committed to them. He analyzes how each of four ethical principles might justify the allocation of resources to contain costs. Two of the principles are patient-centered and relate only indirectly to societal concerns, while two others operate explicitly at the social level. The patient-oriented principles include "patient-centered beneficence" and "autonomy." The beneficence principle, that one's actions ought to benefit the patient, could reduce treatment in those cases where well-meaning physicians may conclude wrongly that extensive care is required when in fact some of that care does more harm than good. Overdependence on the technological imperative by care givers may obscure the objective welfare of the patient. Under some circumstances, for instance if an intervention offers a slight increase in survival probability at the cost of great suffering, the beneficence principle might require nonintervention. The artificial heart given to Barney Clark clearly raises the question of patient-centered beneficence as do, to a lesser extent, many other high-technology rescue attempts.

The principle of autonomy specifies that the patient's right to self-determination should be respected. Although autonomy requires letting patients refuse treatment, it does not require that they have access to care beyond some accepted standard. Even if care has been determined to be in the patient's best interests, autonomy allows the patients to make their own decisions based on their evaluation of the consequences as they perceive them. Without doubt, the decisions of individuals ultimately are shaped by societal values as well as by their perceptions of the welfare of their families. The growing popularity of "living wills" that express autonomy by rejecting certain life-extending technologies is a response to greater recent awareness of quality-of-life concerns. The autonomy principle forces us to look explicitly at the expectations each individual has for health care.

In addition to patient-centered beneficence and autonomy, Veatch (1986:35) offers social-oriented principles that are also relevant to allocation decisions. The utilitarian notion of "full beneficence" requires that decision makers maximize the net good for society. Of course this is a critical ethical principle for efforts to allocate medical resources through cost-benefit or cost effectiveness analysis. Veatch (1986:35) argues that while this principle has major implications for national and local decision makers, there may be good reasons not to allow this principle to be overriding. As discussed earlier in this chapter, basing allocation solely upon supposed maximum benefits to society would be hazardous because of comparative measurement problems and the inability to ensure that benefits and costs would be distributed throughout the population fairly. The criteria for determining social benefit are rooted in the value system of the policymakers and offer no inherent protection for those in society who are least well off. Consideration of Veatch's fourth principle, "justice," would force the policymaker to look beyond the aggregate and consider the equity or fairness of the allocation scheme. Of all Veatch's principles, however, justice is the most problematic, because there is little agreement as to what it entails. Although there is no likelihood of anything approaching a consensus concerning how to achieve the most fair distribution of health care resources in the United States, agreement must be reached on how to establish the ground rules for making allocation decisions even in the absence of this consensus.

Allocation: Problems of Compliance

It is certain that any arguments for establishing allocation and rationing priorities through the public policy process will encounter stiff opposition. For instance, some persons suggest that the health care crisis is largely an artifact of quantification techniques such as cost-benefit analysis that have become vehicles for "generating a crisis atmosphere in medicine" (Caplan 1983:97). Other observers suggest that by shifting societal priorities, we would have more than sufficient funds to resolve health care funding problems; the illusory crisis could be dissolved by a transfusion of dollars from the defense budget: a transformation of missiles into medicine. These critics contend that the only crisis in health care is the one imposed by a government that is unwilling or unable to establish the proper spending priorities. A reordering of these priorities such that health care receives special emphasis would provide adequate funds to handle the problems of health care allocation. Finally, some observers (Ricardo-Campbell 1982) believe that the major problem in health care today is overregulation. If the competitive market were left free to operate on its own, they argue, medical care dilemmas would dissipate.

Despite the attractiveness of these arguments, they fail to reflect social or political reality. The health care problem is a genuine one that is getting progressively worse. Whether or not one defines the problem as a "crisis," the future of health care in the United States is bleak unless substantial changes are made. Suggesting that these problems are an artifact of cost-benefit analysis or any other analytical approach misrepresents the clear trends in overall expenditures for health care as well as the means by which the monies are distributed. Nowhere is the scope of these problems more obvious than in organ transplantation and neonatal care.

Contentions that the solutions lie solely in shifting funds from other areas of public spending to health care bely two factors. First, whether or not one approves, there is little possibility that national defense funds soon will be transferred to social programs. Even if they were, health care would have to compete for funds with other areas. Under current budgetary deficit conditions, cuts, not increases, in health care spending as a proportion of the federal budget are likely. Assuming the improbable did happen and the government decided to reverse defense and health care priorities, history indicates that the appropriation of additional funds for medicine would be likely to exacerbate rather than resolve the problems. Because health care needs and demands are virtually unlimited and funding sources are finite, shifting higher proportions of the GNP or the federal budget to medical ends simply serves to postpone that inevitable point at which constraints must be imposed.

Although the government alone has the means to initiate and coordinate necessary action, it cannot succeed without the explicit support of health care providers and the consumer public. Unfortunately, neither the patients nor the physicians are doing much to limit increased costs or to improve the rationality of the health care system, nor are they even asking the difficult questions about the value of existing patterns in medicine (Mechanic 1981:4). As discussed in chapter 1, the current structure of third-party reimbursement creates a powerful bias for the allocation of more health care resources than would be demanded if patients bore a larger proportion of the costs for the benefits accrued (Newhouse et al. 1981). In other words, consumers of health care currently assess their own medical needs without considering the full price. Because needs largely define demand, there is an inherent bias in the system towards heightened allocation of resources. Although a large proportion of the public agrees that cost containment in health care is essential, a substantially smaller proportion are willing to sacrifice benefits they presently hold in order to reduce overall costs to society. Few persons seem willing to make drastic lifestyle changes out of responsibility for reducing the overall cost of health care in the United States. They expect the cost to themselves to be reduced at the expense of others, or they suppose that somehow the government can bear these costs.

Even more critical than explicit consumer public support for resource allocation and rationing is the cooperation of the health care profession. As argued earlier, no health program can be successful without at least the tacit support of physicians, hospitals, and other health care providers. Physicians, particularly, are key decision makers on the demand side of medicine: they serve as gatekeepers for access to treatment regimens, technologies, and drugs. Writes Dyer, "Physicians are logical agents of rationing because they appear to have direct control over health care dollars" (1986:5). Redisch (1978) contends that large capital expenditures often are made as a result of physician advocacy. Mulley (1983:300) finds that relatively subjective decisions by physicians about patients' needs determine the demand for expensive intensive care treatment and tend to become institutionalized in the need formulas of hospitals and planning agencies. Staff doctors, for instance, encourage the use of intensive care units because they place far more emphasis on the availability of such facilities for their patients when the need arises than on maintaining a minimal occupancy rate in ICU beds. But as more ICU beds become available, patients with less severe diseases are likely to be admitted, despite questions of effectiveness (Strauss et al. 1986). Also, the combined impact of fee-for-service payments and third-party reimbursement creates a natural incentive for physicians to respond aggressively to the perceived needs of the patients.

Interestingly, in the area of ICU use, there are clear instances of resource rationing in favor of patients whose critical condition is directly self-imposed. According to Mulley, the most common diagnosis among patients under 50 in ICUs is respiratory failure secondary to a drug overdose. Although the overdose is frequently intentional, "rarely under these circumstances do physicians consider the increment in resource costs necessary to provide intensive care. Resources are not withheld from these patients except under unusual circumstances" (1983:295). Medically, the reason for this is that drug overdose represents an acute reversible problem that promises a high probability of recovery with ICU intervention and a very low one without it. Conversely, individuals with chronic, irreversible diseases face a low survival rate with or without the ICU and often are denied such care on the principle of allocating the greater proportion of available resources to those individuals with a realistic chance of survival (Turnbull et al. 1979). The most common reason for ICU admission across all age groups is the need for monitoring and prompt response to any complication that might occur (Thibault et al. 1980). Coronary care units often are used as a precautionary device, even though the probability of complications requiring major intervention is low. Mulley (1983:299) sees the most logical place for rationing intensive care resources in this routine use of ICUs.

Finally, any attempts by the government to require physicians to ration medical care on the grounds of societal rather than patient good is bound to conflict with professional ethics and the traditional patient-physician relationship. Pellegrino (1986) argues that attempts to make the physician the designated guardian or gatekeeper of society's resources are morally unsound and pragmatically suspect. According to Aaron and Schwartz (1984), this approach would require a far-reaching attitude change for those many physicians who believe it unprofessional, if not immoral, to consider costs in deciding what actions to take on behalf of patients. Loewy (1980:697) concludes that economic considerations as they affect either the patient, the hospital, or society are "not germane to ethical medical practice" and that it is dangerous to introduce such extraneous factors into medical decisions. Dyer (1986:6) answers "an emphatic 'No' " to the question of whether or not the physician should be society's agent in reducing health costs. Rationing decisions should not be made by doctors at the bedside, because their primary responsibility is to the patient, not to society: "To ask conscientious physicians to bear the responsibility for lowering the cost of medical care is to create a conflict of interest that threatens to alter the nature of the doctor-patient relationship and the nature of the medical profession itself" (Dyer 1986:6). For these reasons, the majority of the medical profession in the United States is unlikely to develop norms that require or actively encourage rationing (Schuck 1981).

Despite these caveats, the medical profession increasingly will find itself in the difficult position of responding to government initiatives and, eventually, public pressures to effectuate difficult allocation and rationing decisions. Physicians always have made rationing decisions on a case-by-case basis at the bedside or in the hospital administrator's office, but not under governmental pressure in a systematic institutionalized manner. Their central commitment has been to the patient, not to society, and the current shift toward public allocation is a clear threat to traditional medical ethics. Harrison Rogers, in his address as outgoing president of the AMA, sees this reflected in a "very serious movement" toward maintaining a business ethic in the practice of medicine rather than a professional ethic that protects patients:

Almost every force being exerted on doctors today is pushing them away from the professional aspects of what they do, and toward the business aspects. Governmental DRG programs, reductions made in Medicare benefits and payments, restrictions on private plans, preadmission certification, second opinion requirements, requirements for outpatient and ambulatory care—all of those and many others tend to make the doctor think first about the financial aspects of the needed services, and whether the patient or a governmental or private third party will be willing or able to pay for them. (1986).

Lundberg (1983:2224) asks rhetorically how long physicians can continue to make such difficult policy judgments in response to short-term pressures of the moment. Can this piecemeal rationing process continue to dominate, in light of the extensive social investment riding on each decision?

In contrast, Hiatt (1975) argues that the medical profession must take responsibility for evaluating expensive new medical technologies and procedures prior to their being made available to consumers. Because of their crucial role as the point of access to health care, doctors must regulate the supply of medical services as a means of cost control. No longer do the health care providers automatically have a claim to all the societal resources they believe might benefit their patients, nor should they be able to make allocation decisions without an awareness of the complex ramifications for the health care system as a whole. As uncomfortable as this change is for the medical profession, it is well underway in American society. Moreover, this shift is apparent apart from any efforts at government involvement in the allocation of medical care. It is most directly evident in trends toward corporate health care, health maintenance organizations, and the increased allocation role of benefits managers for large U.S. employers.

Although Veatch contends that the general public, not clinicians, ought to make allocation decisions, he points out that "if cost containment is not on the clinician's agenda, it would have to be on someone else's" (1986:38). Knaus (1986) argues that physicians must be involved in both allocation and rationing decisions. Because physicians have to make the crucial rationing decisions, it is particularly important that they be involved in the prior allocation decisions which "virtually always precede rationing decisions." According to John Ashley:

Rationing is painful. Rationing does reduce costs by obviating the demand for allocation of resources. As our society demands that we avoid these costs, physicians should be intimately involved in the allocation and rationing decisions made both at the system and the hospital level. (1986)

There are indications that the most scarce resource in the health care system in the future will not be money directly, or even expensive equipment, but rather, specialized personnel. Recently, the acute shortage of intensive care nurses has caused sudden decreases in the availability of intensive care beds and some types of surgery. Cullen (1981) surveyed ICU directors and found that 75 percent viewed nurses as the single most constrained resource. Similarly, highly trained nurses for transplant operations, although sufficient in most locales under present surgical loads, will be in short supply once transplant facilities multiply as encouraged by present public policy.

Although the shortage of nurses and other highly specialized support personnel is in part a function of limited budgets as reflected in low salaries, it also has roots in the conflict between the traditional role of nursing as primary care and the accelerating movement toward specialized, machine dependent medicine. Within this allocation context, it often is less difficult to secure initial funding for the purchase of expensive medical technologies than it is to pay continuing costs for the personnel required to use and maintain the equipment. This approach is shortsighted and results in situations where access to onsite equipment is denied or delayed because of staffing shortages. This underuse of existing technology is especially frustrating because it represents a waste of substantial investments in equipment whose purchase consumed funds which could have been put to more productive use. As long as capital outlay takes priority over the more mundane and routine operation of medical facilities, shortages of highly trained and motivated support personnel will intensify. Substantially more attention must be directed toward this problem in allocating medical resources.

Revising Public Expectations: The Key to Allocation Policy

The discussion of allocation problems here illustrates the complexity of health care and the difficulty of resolving its inherent conflicts. Any attempt to impose an all-encompassing allocation and rationing scheme on the public is bound to fail on these grounds alone no matter how well planned and implemented it is. The complexity of the problems and the high stakes for a broad array of participants preclude institutionalized solutions imposed from above. The success of any effort to construct meaningful allocation and rationing policy hinges on our ability to modify the expectations and demands of both the providers and users of health care. Although there are ways through which policymakers can influence the incentive structure and thus moderate expectations, in the end it is the consumers and providers themselves who must realize that they are the keys to resolving the burgeoning health crisis.

According to Knowles (1977), the next major advance in health care will result from the assumption of individual responsibility for one's own health. This will require a major revision in the population's perceptions of medicine. Although the public has been conditioned to expect dramatic improvements in health to accrue from breakthroughs in medical research, primarily because of successes in controlling infectious diseases, the greatest health gains of the future promise to come not from medical research but from individual efforts to be healthy. Observers point to the need for mass education to encourage individual health responsibility and persuade the public to moderate demands. As appealing as this approach appears initially, it is improbable that such efforts will be readily rewarded by vastly improved health for the population.

Although Etzioni sees some persuasiveness in these arguments for individual responsibility, he rejects the idea of centering a national health policy on "exhorting Americans to mobilize their individual willpower in order to change to more healthful personal habits" (1978). First, viewing health as an individual responsibility overestimates the magnitude of health benefits that will accrue from changes in lifestyle. In areas other than cigarette smoking, diet, and alcohol abuse, the evidence regarding the adverse impact of lifestyle choices on health is uncertain, speculative, and interlaced with moralistic undertones. According to Etzioni, some forms of self-help, including weight control regimens and exercise, might in fact cause harm to some participants (1978:66). Also, some individuals tend to become overly concerned about minor or nonexistent health problems when focus is placed on individual responsibility, therefore overloading the health care system. Etzioni (1978) concludes that if we mobilize individuals to modify their behavior, we must limit ourselves to changes whose benefit is clearly demonstrated, and in some cases risk inadvertent harm. Although his arguments are well taken, Etzioni would seem to place too much of the burden of proof on proposed lifestyle changes. For instance, although the causal link between exercise and better health has yet to be demonstrated conclusively, and it might in isolated cases actually lead to harm, individuals can be encouraged to exercise in moderation on the basis of statistical evidence of benefit to their health. Effort certainly should not be wasted on mobilizing major changes in lifestyle based solely on speculation, but such efforts should not have to await the degree of verification Etzioni demands. Using such strict criteria of verification, few medical innovations of any type would be introduced.

Any changes in individual attitudes and behavior can only come about within the framework of the social constraints which exist in any society. One cannot underestimate the role of society in shaping the conditions within which individuals make personal choices, including those of personal lifestyle. In a society that emphasizes self-gratification, materialistic values, and immediate pleasure, behavior changes necessary to improve health may be especially unpleasant and unsatisfying and thereby require considerable self-denial. Conversely, a healthy lifestyle might mean forgoing habits that are enjoyable to many people and largely viewed as critical components of free choice. Some people obviously enjoy eating unhealthy foods, drinking alcohol, engaging in promiscuous sex, driving too fast, taking drugs, and smoking. Modifying these habits will not be easy, particularly where society supports them.

According to Etzioni (1978:69), the level of individual strength and wise conduct necessary to modify lifestyle are dependent on social conditions, and in a mass society people are vulnerable to mass persuasion and exploitation. Rather than minimizing the possibility of modifying personal lifestyles, however, as Etzioni implies, this vulnerability would seem to facilitate such changes, though only if there were a strong commitment toward that end in the community. Individual behavior is influenced heavily by what patterns the community approves or disapproves, promotes or discourages and condemns. In other words, the choice of the individual will be conditioned heavily by what is considered acceptable by society. In a society in which the public is bombarded with commercial messages extolling the rewards of cigarettes, alcohol, soft drinks, and high-fat foods, and where the social pressure to drink, smoke, and enjoy instant sexual gratification is reinforced constantly by the media, it is unlikely that many persons will have the strength to fully withstand the onslaught.

Without a doubt, the pressures in contemporary American society do not favor a massive modification of lifestyle where the prime motivation for behavior becomes long-term health instead of immediate pleasure. The consumers' preferences as well as capacity to choose are shaped by the market. Change in individual lifestyle choices, then, is dependent on the capacity of society to reevaluate its goals and priorities and to shift away from the overarching purpose of production and consumption toward one of balance, moderation, and health. Perhaps, given the strength of the former values and the institutions that are built upon them, change is not possible. If this is true, a health care crisis of immense proportions is inevitable, because without a modification of societal values regarding individual responsibility for health there is little incentive for change in personal lifestyle. Under these circumstances, the emphasis will continue to be directed toward curative, technological solutions to health problems, an approach which is ever more elusive.

This analysis points to the need for a collective, centralized initiative to shift the emphasis toward healthy lifestyles. Although individuals have some degree of freedom in such choices, the greater capacity to curb unhealthy habits and evolve healthy ones lies at the societal level. According to Etzioni, "As far as health policy follows, those who call on individuals to act wisely should spend more of their time addressing themselves to the existing sources of power which shape society, be more concerned with environment, workers and consumer protection, and, more deeply, with the nature of the societal project" (1978:73). Because it is society's scarce resources that are being allocated, it seems only fair that society be held ultimately responsible for altering the goals which influence individual behavior. At a minimum, this requires placing the goal of health at least on a par with that of enjoyment. To do this, the incentive structure operating within society must be radically revised to better reward the healthful lifestyle choices of individual members. A major part of this effort must be aimed at reducing the expectations of the public regarding the availability of health care resources and thereby reducing their unrealistic demand for unlimited use of curative medicine. Society must realize the necessity for limits and end the fatuous assumption of unlimited resources.

4

The Role of Government Institutions

Although the key to impeding the emerging health care crisis and stemming our dependence on high-technology medicine is the alteration of public expectations, any allocation/rationing policy will be produced by the political institutions. Despite the important role that the private sector plays in defining the boundaries of health care, a role that is accentuated by for-profit medicine and the influence of corporate benefits managers, the most crucial factor is the extent to which the courts, legislatures, and administrative agents are willing and capable of facing the difficult issues and making decisions that will avert the crisis. The government alone cannot alter the health care system, nor should it, but it ought to take responsibility for framing the dialogue and moderating the demands of the public and the interests of the health care community. Unfortunately, U.S. political institutions seem unable or unwilling to take seriously this responsibility. This chapter analyzes the characteristics of our political institutions which restrain optimism that such action will be forthcoming before it becomes too late.

The Courts and Medical Decision Making

Health law emanates from three sources: common law, statutory law, and administrative law and regulation. Common law is the tradition of civil law that originates from individual case decisions in federal, state, or local courts. Common law precedents may vary from state to state because there is no national system. Two types of civil law are contracts and torts. Contract cases center on allegations that one party has breached an agreement by failing to fulfill an obligation to the other party. In torts, one party asserts that the wrongful conduct of the other party has caused harm, and compensation for the harm is sought. Statutory law is law written by legislative bodies. One subset of it is criminal law, which imposes prescribed sanctions for illegal behavior; criminal law varies from one state to the next, despite certain basic patterns. The final source of health law is the myriad of rules and regulations established by administrative agencies at the state and federal level. These regulations are written to implement the broad statutory mandates of the legislatures or Congress and are often very detailed.

Although there are administrative channels for challenging these rules and regulations, the courts can be called upon to decide whether or not a person has violated statutory or administrative law. Likewise, the courts can rule on the constitutionality of a statutory law or an administrative regulation and negate those actions they feel are unconstitutional. For instance, in 1983 a federal district court negated the Department of Health and Human Services' Baby Doe regulations that provided for an informer's hotline. The courts seem especially willing to hear challenges to regulations concerning public health care.

There are legal aspects to virtually every facet of health care. Whether ruling on the constitutionality of public health statutes, resolving questions of informed consent, defining death, or adjudicating conflicts over health care, the courts play an integral part in medical decision making. In Christoffel's words,

Lawyers have become so involved in practically all aspects of health and health care that they could be considered a new category of health professional. It has become almost routine for lawyers to be involved as advisers in matters ranging from termination of treatment to approval of experimental protocols. (1982:6–7)

Not surprisingly, hospitals now retain legal counsel, either a law firm on retainer or staff counsel, to advise hospital administrators on legal matters. More and more medical decisions are made today within this legal context and under a threat of litigation, perceived or real. In some instances, there is a likelihood that legal considerations have overridden strictly medical ones. More often, the boundaries between the legal and medical indications have become obscured.

Physicians are finding themselves, all too commonly, facing a dilemma. On the one hand, increased pressure to contain costs is being exerted by administrators and payers. On the other hand, the constant threat of liability for medical treatment or nontreatment exists whenever cost appears to have been even considered in making the decision. The courts are likely to rule against decisions to remove life-sustaining care if there is any indication that the decision was even marginally motivated by an attempt to save an institution or a provider money (Johnson 1984:224). Moreover, such dilemmas are bound to increase as the arsenal of life-extending technologies grows.

Aaron and Schwartz (1984:131) state that among the consequences of budget limits, an increase in litigation is the most predictable. Fueled by the contingency fee system where plaintiffs have little to lose even if their suit fails, court challenges are bound to quickly meet any attempts to ration medicine. Some persons denied life-saving treatment, no matter how uneconomical and questionable in efficacy it may be, are certain to file a claim. Aaron and Schwartz comment, "Because of the characteristics of the U.S. tort system, we anticipate that individual and class action suits would be brought by, and on behalf of, many patients denied some potentially beneficial therapy" (1984:132). Because the courts are designed to decide each case on the merits of that case and not on public policy grounds, I anticipate that many of these suits will be successful and that some courts will order life-saving treatment. This has already occurred in a Washington State court's ruling that a man whose life depends upon it has the right to a liver transplant, and that the third-party payer has a duty to pay for the transplant. Pozgar (1983:xii) contends a person will almost always be able to find a sympathetic court to order lifesaving treatment despite the severe burden it places on society and the poor medical risk it might represent.

The Controversy Over Malpractice Suits

Some observers term the rapid expansion of malpractice suits an epidemic. In 1986 alone, 32 state legislatures passed some form of tort reform in response to this declared crisis. According to a special AMA report released in January 1985, the number of malpractice suits, the size of jury awards for damages, and, as a result, the cost of malpractice insurance are all mounting. Although the causes of these increases are many, they are attributable in part to the impersonal complexity of the health care system, heightened consumer awareness and attention to patient rights, and the high consumer expectations about the medical profession that lead to the assumption that if something goes wrong, it must be someone's fault. To some extent, these increases are also tied to advanced medical technologies which under the best of circumstances are high risk. For example, Overcast, Merrikin, and Evans (1985) discuss potential liability suits arising from heart transplantation. The number of malpractice claims filed has increased three-fold in the last decade. One out of five physicians faced a suit in 1984, as compared to one out of eight as recently as 1979. Moreover, the jury awards in particular instances are reaching previously unimaginable figures. In 1982, for instance, there were over 250 jury verdicts in excess of $1 million, some as high as $12 million. The average award in some states is over $100,000.

Not surprisingly, these trends in malpractice awards have drastically raised malpractice insurance premiums, by as much as 400 to 600 percent over the last decade. Although family practitioners' premiums average out to under $10,000 per year, fees for some of the surgical specialties, such as orthopedic surgery and obstetrics, might average $50,000 nationwide, and as high as $100,000 in some states. These increased insurance costs are passed on to health care consumers and to taxpayers. Moreover, these increases affect not only immediate costs but also future costs. For example, as fees for routine gynecological exams escalate—fees which are generally not covered by third-party payers—many women forgo such exams. Thus, many treatable problems (i.e., cervical and breast cancer, and diseases that may lead to infertility) are left to worsen until extensive and expensive treatment is required. This sequence also applies to general routine check-ups. AMA studies predict that rising insurance premiums may add as much as $7 billion to the U.S. health care bill by 1988, up from the estimated $3.6 billion they added in 1984.

In addition to the direct impact of increased malpractice insurance rates on the cost of medical care, these rates have an even more profound indirect effect by encouraging physicians and hospitals to resort to defensive medicine practices. These practices are designed either to avert a lawsuit, or should a suit be filed, to provide appropriate documentation that a wide range of tests and treatments has been used in caring for the plaintiff (Tancredi and Barondess 1980:37). Many diagnostic and therapeutic measures which are of marginal or no benefit to the patient are now used by health care providers to protect themselves from being found liable. Ironically, in some cases, as in unnecessary exposure to x-ray radiation, fetal monitoring, or unwarranted caesarean deliveries, defensive measures might expose patients to the risk of adverse outcomes from the procedures themselves.

Medical malpractice torts are designed to perform two functions: to deter medical negligence and to compensate victims who are injured. There is substantial debate over the extent to which either of these functions are adequately met by the current system. Although the threat of malpractice suits undoubtedly causes physicians and hospitals to exercise more caution in treating patients, it has been blamed for promoting a great deal of "uneconomic and undesirable" behavior (Havighurst 1985:18). Defensive medicine has been defined as "any waste of resources (net excess of costs over benefits) that results from physicians changing their practice patterns in response to the threat of liability" (Danzon 1985:12). The proliferation of diagnostic tests, many of which are of questionable effectiveness, results in pressure on physicians to utilize them, often for legal rather than medical reasons. By practicing defensive medicine and ordering all available tests, the physician might protect himself from a lawsuit. This approach increases the cost of health care, however, frequently with little or no benefit to the patients.

The actual monetary cost of defensive medicine is difficult to estimate. Undoubtedly, unnecessary testing and overutilization of health care resources do occur and are related to the desire of providers to protect themselves from accusations of negligence. Even though litigation often results in acquittal and many cases never even make it to court, the impact of a suit on a physician's reputation and practice can be devastating. In his highly critical attack on malpractice lawyers, DeVito (1984) contends that it is common practice to name several physicians as well as hospitals in a single lawsuit, solely to exploit them and obtain what counsel hopes may be indicting information against a targeted physician. Moreover, few doctors relish the aggravation of becoming a party to a lawsuit, no matter how frivolous it might be. As a result, they will use all resources at their disposal to minimize the chances of legal action. Not surprisingly, the AMA has been calling for penalties for bringing frivolous cases to court.

Although Danzon (1985:12) agrees that the threat of liability might lead to waste, she argues that it also leads to good medicine. Moreover, primary blame for overutilization of resources must be directed toward the third-party retrospective reimbursement system, which shifts the cost away from the individual patient. For Danzon, prospective payment or capitation-based reimbursement, where the total budget is preset or negotiated, would do far more to reduce overuse of health care than the abolition of liability for malpractice, the negative effects of which she believes have been exaggerated. Danzon would place more emphasis on determining the number of injuries avoided because of the threat of liability. Although other forms of quality control such as licensure and peer review are useful, she maintains that "the advantage of the tort system is that it provides a continual, ongoing system of 'regulation by incentives.' And it does not rely on enforcement by the medical profession which, like any other profession, is notoriously reluctant to police its own members" (1985:13).

Still, Danzon supports major reforms of the current malpractice system. Awards should be limited, she believes, to economic loss only, including loss of earning capacity, reasonable medical expenses, and rehabilitation costs. This would eliminate the large awards which primarily reflect highly speculative compensation for pain and suffering. Because malpractice torts basically represent a form of compulsory insurance that we are all required to buy when we buy health care, they should more closely resemble insurance people buy voluntarily. When given the choice, most persons do not buy insurance against pain and suffering. Furthermore, damage awards should be based on a standardized schedule, because individualization of awards encourages excess expenditure on litigation and is inefficient. According to Danzon, payment by a schedule based on age and severity of injury would be preferable to the single ceiling or cap which some states have enacted, because it would account for those variations, which can be considerable. Periodic payments to be made through an annuity or trust fund could be established at the time of settlement and would revert to the defendant in the event of an early death of the patient, less a reasonable payment to the estate.

In order to strengthen the deterrent effect of malpractice torts, Danzon suggests that an uninsurable fine could be levied on the physician or hospital in cases of severe injury due to gross negligence. This would replace the existing punitive damage award but would be paid to the state, not the plaintiff, to defray the public costs of the courts. In this way a defendant found guilty would be unable to pass on the costs to health care consumers. Externalization of costs would be further reduced by Danzon's recommendation that payments made under public aid programs should be reduced by the amount of the tort award. Not only would this eliminate double compensation, it would also transfer costs of injuries from the public to the specific parties responsible.

Another area of contention in malpractice torts concerns the standard of care required of health care personnel. Tort law presently enforces a standard of care drawn from "customary practice." Negligence can be proven if the physician deviates from the norm of the profession. According to Aaron and Schwartz:

Within the present medical system the provision of aggressive care for the terminally ill . . . allows courts to apply absolutist standards under which the failure to provide care that has any prospect for even small medical benefit is grounds for court intervention or a judgment of malpractice. (1984:124)

Surveys show that many doctors who realize that aggressive treatment is often pointless nevertheless carry it out because of pressure from the family, the fear of malpractice suits, or the threat of court intervention on behalf of the patient.

In an era of allocation of scarce medical resources, however, the customary practice standard may be attacked because it leads to the inefficient use of resources. According to Havighurst (1985:18), this standard is unrealistic because it is derived from a market in which third parties unquestionably pay the bills and health providers seek not only safety for their patients, but also protection against lawsuits. He argues that by holding the physician potentially liable if he fails to utilize all available procedures, malpractice torts restrict opportunities for reasonable economizing and force the public to bear unnecessarily high health care costs.

The current standards which emerge from fee-for-service medicine must be moderated if efforts towards cost effective modes of health care delivery such as health maintenence organizations (HMOs) are to succeed in reducing inefficient practice.. The courts should realize that the highest quality care is not always worth the substantial cost and that trade-offs must be made. If a physician can show that performing or omitting a procedure is justified after weighing the costs, risks, and benefits, this should be recognized as an acceptable standard of care and a proper defense. According to Havighurst (1985:17), this recognition would weaken the premise that the same high standards should prevail under all circumstances and would shift emphasis instead toward raising standards where they are unacceptably low. The assumption that there is only one right way to treat patients is less and less valid in light of the complexity of medical decision making today. Continued requirements by the courts for a customary practice standard will strain the health care system considerably at a time when we are realizing the need to make essential though difficult decisions to refrain from using all available resources in every case.

Some observers suggest that the courts should be willing to recognize contracts between health consumers and providers that bind them to a different standard than customary practice. Havighurst (1983) argues that courts should be receptive to a variety of private initiatives that redefine the rights and responsibilities associated with medical injuries. The new competitive health care environment, he feels, gives consumers new opportunities for an informed choice of health plans and leverage for bargaining with providers. Under this system, tort law would govern only in the absence of a negotiated agreement or, conversely, would be adjudicated within the boundaries established in the contract. Danzon (1985:14) agrees that courts should honor previous contracts that call for binding arbitration when injury arises. Many HMOs are taking that approach in order to reduce insurance costs.

No matter what reforms are established, it is unlikely that courts will discontinue recognition of malpractice torts or severely limit damage awards. Juries appear willing to award almost unlimited damages for pain and suffering without consideration of who pays or of the cumulative impact of these individual awards on the health care system. Ongoing efforts by over half of the state legislatures to set ceilings on awards might be successful, but unless they are consistent across all fifty states, they will add confusion to the current situation and may cause a redistribution of health care providers to the more friendly states, those setting lower caps on damages. Also, state legislation limiting pain and suffering damages and contingency fees have been challenged in the courts. Limits on contingency fees, such that an attorney may get a third of the first $50,000 but a scaled-down percentage of anything over (perhaps only 10 percent of everything over $200,000) would reduce the attorneys' incentives for demanding large awards and might lead them more often to encourage their clients to settle out of court. Caps or limits might, however, have just the opposite effect on the defendants in such cases. Knowing that there are set limits on their potential losses if found guilty, and that the lawyers they will face are less likely to be pursuing large punitive damage awards, defendants may prefer to take their chances in court—thus increasing the case load.

Direct Court Intervention in Medical Decisions

For many reasons, then, the courts are fast becoming embroiled in the controversies surrounding the allocation of health care resources. In a litigious society such as ours, it is not surprising that policy decisions concerning an area as sensitive and personally consequential as health care ultimately find their way into the courts. It is likely that no significant health care regulations or legislation will go unchallenged in the courts. Moreover, torts for malpractice and other causes of action, together with contractual disputes over an array of new health care arrangements, will proliferate, assuring the courts a continuing role in setting health care policy. This section discusses the involvement of the courts in several specific areas.

The Courts and Reproduction. As noted above, one of the most difficult rationing situations involves treatment of newborns with birth defects. The Baby Doe case received much publicity and government activity when the Reagan administration attempted to intrude into the medical decision-making process and define the moral claims of such newborns to lifesaving technologies and treatment, without concern for the costs or the parent-physician decision. Neonatal care choices are bound to become more difficult as technologies offer the means to save these lives, if we as a society choose to pay the escalating costs.

As in the Baby Doe case, it is inevitable that the courts will play a central role in attempts to resolve these sensitive issues.

Treatment of newborns with birth defects is but one aspect of a complex of issues surrounding the emerging technologies in one of the most sensitive areas of human existence—reproduction. Reproductive issues raise fundamental value conflicts over the meanings of human life and death, meanings addressed by the basic tenets of a variety of religious and secular ethical frameworks. Societies do not often debate fundamental definitions, but when they do, volatile controversy results. The rapid pace of technological change has created these value conflicts over a very short time span, whereas values themselves normally change gradually over generations through a socialization process. Although there is no doubt that these issues are difficult to deal with politically, thus explaining the tendency of public officials to avoid them when possible, the rapid advances in technology make it mandatory that such issues at least be discussed within the political context.

Table 4.1 lists specific areas in which the courts are now involved in reproduction issues. In almost all of these areas, including neonatal care, the courts are heavily reliant on medical/biological data in framing their decisions. As with abortion (Blank 1984), there is considerable danger, however, when the court relies too heavily on a medical rationale. For instance, the courts' traditional emphasis on the irreversible nature of sterilization as a basis for rejecting its involuntary imposition is undermined by the development of safe and effective reversible techniques such as removal silicone plugs and subdermal implants such as NORPLANT. Although some courts that have ruled against involuntary sterilization of mentally retarded persons or convicted sex offenders have noted that such procedures might be reversible, most conclude, as did Justice Douglas in *Skinner* v. *Oklahoma* (1942), that "the power to sterilize, if exercised, may have subtle, far-reaching and devastating effects.... There is no redemption for the individual whom the law touches. Any experiment which the state conducts is to his irreparable injury. He is forever deprived of a basic liberty."

Will the widespread diffusion of reversible techniques in the near future change the courts' perception of sterilization and overcome the reluctance of many courts to order its imposition? If so, what is a

Table 4.1
Reproduction as an Area of Judicial Decision Making

Preconception Torts
  Sterilization (consent questions)
  Contraception (accessibility)
  Medical malpractice
  Products liability
  Radiation injuries
  Workplace hazards
  Industrial liability

Wrongful Conception and Wrongful Pregnancy
  Failed sterilization
  Failed contraception
  Misdiagnosis or failure to diagnose pregnancy
  Unsuccessful abortion

Conception Stage
  Artificial insemination
  In vitro fertilization
  Embryo transfer
  Cryopreservation
  Surrogate motherhood

Prenatal Stage
  Abortion (accessibility, age, and other qualifications)
  Viability question
  Fetus as patient

Neonatal
  Intensive care
  Neonatal euthanasia
  Torts for wrongful birth
  Torts for wrongful life

reasonable probability of reversibility the courts will accept: 80 percent, 90 percent, 100 percent? Is there any more real likelihood of reversal of a technically reversible procedure ordered by the court than of more conventional procedures, and who decides if and when to effectuate the reversal? In other words, innovations in sterilization procedures will force the courts to reevaluate their previous rulings on the unconstitutionality of compulsory sterilization programs, because the courts' basic stated rationale, irreversibility, is no longer valid.

Ensuring an Adequate Fetal Environment: Court Action. It is clear from the discussion in chapter 2 that the well-being of the fetus is inextricably bound to the actions of the mother. Although the courts are largely cognizant of traditional maternal rights and have been hesitant to constrain those rights, they have shown a willingness to overrule maternal autonomy where the woman's actions represent probable danger to the life or health of the developing fetus. As scientific evidence corroborates the deleterious effects of certain maternal behaviors, the trend in the courts toward finding a cause of action against a pregnant women for conduct injurious to her unborn child is bound to escalate.

Until recently, decisions concerning the behavior of the pregnant woman were largely left to the woman and her physician under the assumption that both parties had the best interest of the fetus in mind. The advent of a new era in knowledge of and technology for the fetus, along with the new medical field of neonatology, has considerably weakened that assumption, however. Fletcher (1983:308) credits the development of neonatal intensive care units with leading to a new imperative to use available therapy and a heightened concern for the interest of the premature newborn.

Because of their fear of liability, hospitals and physicians are turning increasingly to the courts for decisions that they made independently in the recent past. This trend is illustrated by the case of a woman who refused to have a caesarean section despite its recommendation by the medical staff due to fetal distress (Bowes and Selgestad 1981). When the woman refused, the hospital's attorney petitioned the juvenile court for an order to proceed with a caesarean against the patient's wishes. Within two hours the judge and attorneys representing the mother and the fetus met in the patient's hospital room and a hearing was conducted. The court ruled that necessary medical treatment, including surgery, could be administered against the will of the mother. Although in this case the mother relented and complied with the court order, if she had not, surgery would have been conducted against her will for the benefit of the fetus. Bowes and Selgestad conclude that although the courts might not always be willing or able to intervene because of time constraints, there is a need for hospital staffs to "discuss and plan for the eventuality of situations of disputed fetal versus maternal rights" (1981:214). Such situations are certain to multiply in the near future, especially if rationing of scarce medical resources shifts emphasis to preventive approaches that require lifestyle changes.

Court pressure on the mother to utilize available fetal therapies is bound to grow also as experimental techniques become routine therapeutic procedures (Blank 1986). Although fetal surgery and therapy are now at a primitive level and immediate concern focuses on possible harm to the fetus and the mother, rapid advances in instrumentation, technique, and skills will soon lower the risks to fetus and mother and expand substantially the options available for intervening in utero to surgically correct fetal defects. Once this occurs, women as a whole are likely to accept or demand therapy for their unborn children with medical problems. Major dilemmas will arise, however, when a pregnant woman, for whatever reason, refuses consent.

The failure of a woman to consent to fetal therapy is likely to lead to state intervention, primarily through court action. According to Fletcher, "as long as the experimental stage of fetal therapy persists, the obligation of parents to participate is not compelling. However, if the therapy becomes standard practice, the obligation to accept it for the fetus becomes much stronger" (1983:300). Robertson comes to a similar but even stronger conclusion regarding maternal duty:

When prenatal surgical techniques are still experimental, the mother and physician have no duty to use them. When the procedures are medically established, the question of whether they may choose to use them vanishes. It becomes good medicine and proper parental behavior to employ them. In such cases the benefit to the fetus from the intervention clearly outweighs the risks of the intervention. (1982:351)

Parents in our society are legally, as well as morally, obligated to foster the well-being of their children and protect them as much as possible from imminent dangers. As demonstrated in chapter 2, some of the most serious dangers to developing humans take place during the fetal stage. As knowledge of fetal development expands and new techniques are developed to ameliorate or reduce these dangers, our sense of moral obligation toward the treatable fetus will increase.

This trend is reinforced by the social recognition of the fetus as a human being at earlier and earlier stages as new technologies allow us to view, study, and eventually help the fetus prenatally. The bonding process between parents and fetus will occur far before birth, as soon as the parents are able to see the fetus move, discover the sex of the fetus, or realize the fetus has a correctable problem. Writes Fletcher, "The more living persons actually see the fetus by ultrasound or any future method to be developed, the more human and valuable the fetus will become" (1983:307). Individual parents, as well as society in general, are likely to elevate the moral status of the fetus. In turn, the courts will continue their movement toward recognizing the legal status of the fetus at earlier and earlier stages of development. This trend, of course, clashes headlong with the Supreme Court's decision in *Roe* v. *Wade* that women have the constitutionally guaranteed right to abortion until the end of the second trimester. In the not-so-remote future the Court must resolve the logical inconsistency of holding a woman responsible for harming her fetus but not for terminating its existence.

Boycotts by Health Care Providers: A New Area of Court Involvement

As allocation of health care resources tightens and cost containment measures designed to reduce government spending expand, the probability of boycotts by health providers against government policies is heightened. The introduction of diagnosis-related groups (DRGs) by the federal government for Medicare and Medicaid reimbursement and even more drastic constraints in state reimbursement formulas have led to a widening gap between the market price of health services and the price that these governments will pay. In an effort to obtain higher fees, health care groups in several states have threatened to boycott Medicaid programs.

In February 1983, a boycott by the Michigan State Medical Society of patients financed by Michigan Medicaid was challenged under federal antitrust law. The Federal Trade Commission (FTC) affirmed an administrative judge's decision that the medical society's action violated section 5 of the FTC Act by conspiring to boycott patients and thus unreasonably restrain trade. The FTC held that the Sherman Antitrust Act applied equally to boycotts against private parties and against the state, and it rejected the Noerr-Pennington defense that the boycott was actually an attempt to influence public officials to increase payment and was therefore not in violation of the Sherman Act.

Raup (1985) contends that the FTC's action here conflicts with a recent Supreme Court ruling (*NAACP* v. *Claiborne Hardware Co.*, 1982) which held that the First Amendment prohibited Mississippi from imposing tort liability on the organizers of a nonviolent boycott of white-owned business by black citizens attempting to influence the government to end de jure segregation. Despite the Court's predilection for not penalizing attempts to influence the government, in health care matters it may be less tolerant. At least one court has found in favor of patients denied Medicaid-funded care because of a boycott who were forced to pay for the care the state otherwise would have paid for (*DeGregorio* v. *Segal*, 1978). The court agreed that they had been injured by the boycott and could initiate antitrust action against the providers.

Obviously, Medicaid programs are not required to pay market prices for services used by the patients they cover. The market power that the state holds because it pays over 40 percent of health costs is reinforced by coercive state laws which limit the ability of health care providers to refuse treatment of state-supported patients. To some degree, then, the state can exploit providers by paying less than the competitive price. However, when providers are denied a normal profit for treating Medicaid patients, it is natural that they will use all available mechanisms to place pressure on the government to raise their reimbursement schedules. As noted in chapter 1, the unfortunate result is the emergence of a two-tiered system of health care under which those on government funding are unable to obtain adequate health care, because providers see it as in their best interests not to deal with Medicaid patients.

Until recently, caps on Medicaid payment, where they existed, still allowed reasonable reimbursement levels. However, the trend in the last several years toward severely limiting or freezing state reimbursement for many procedures such as kidney dialysis has led more and more providers to refuse to handle Medicaid patients. As the proportion of providers refusing to treat such patients increases, one of two things can happen: the states may increase reimbursement rates to an acceptable level, or they may accelerate efforts to coerce providers into caring for state-supported patients. In Massachusetts and Connecticut, for instance, nursing homes are prohibited by law from discriminating against Medicaid patients. Raup notes, "New Jersey has gone a step further: It requires all nursing homes to reserve a certain number of beds for Medicaid patients as a condition of operating in the state" (1985:28). The tactic applied to nursing homes can be used against any provider licensed by the state.

The providers, for their part, have united in many states to bring political pressure to bear on state legislatures and administrative agencies. The threat of boycott is being used increasingly to dramatize the bargaining power of physicians and other providers. Although the primary target of these boycotts is the state, the boycott can be carried out only by refusing treatment to Medicaid patients, with whom the providers have no particular grievance. As such, it is a secondary boycott, because it induces the Medicaid beneficiaries to put pressure on the state to raise its reimbursement rates so that they have access to health care services. The Medicaid patients, not the state, however, represent the injured parties in the boycott (*DeGregorio v. Segal*, 1978).

The courts' entry into the health care system through their regulation of health provider groups demonstrates the intricate relationships between the public and private health care spheres. It also demonstrates the scope of state power in regulating the health care industry, should states choose to exercise it. The limited court action so far, though far from conclusive, implies that even if the government were to cut Medicaid/Medicare reimbursement rates considerably, it has means available to enforce compliance from the medical community as a whole even though it may be powerless to force any single physician to treat government-supported patients. Although there is substantial risk of further entrenching a tiered health care system under such circumstances, the courts appear willing to accept vigorous legislative action in this area.

Do the Courts Have the Capacity to Make Medical Policy Decisions?

The discussion above substantiates the assumption that the courts will continue to be major participants in medical decision making. Increasingly, they will be asked to resolve not only specific rationing cases, but also the broader constitutional questions raised by the distribution of scarce medical resources. As in the past, eventually the public will turn to the courts to resolve these dilemmas and establish the parameters of individual rights. According to Youngblood and Folse (1981:53), the courts are distinguishable from other governing entities in the primary status they accord to the role of reason and principle, a trait that specially qualifies them for articulating and protecting individual rights.

The courts face severe problems, however, in resolving issues raised by the introduction of sophisticated medical technologies. First, there is the general controversy over whether or not courts ought to be making public policy (to debate the prior question of whether or not they actually do make social policy seems academic). A second, more specific question concerns the competency of the courts to make policy in the traditionally private and increasingly technical area of medicine. Before evaluating the latter question of technical competency, the debate over the role of courts in setting public policy is described briefly.

The Courts and Policymaking. In spite of the ongoing debate over whether the courts ought to actively make social policy or should demonstrate various degrees of restraint (Halpern and Lamb 1982; McDowell 1982), the involvement of the courts in making policy is widespread. Courts administer law and public policy in addition to adjudicating controversies. Despite disclaimers, they always have. Although to some extent the courts have been forced into policymaking by other governmental institutions and by society as a whole and have reacted to other branches of government by striking down their actions, Gambitta, May, and Foster remark that "occasionally, yet with increased frequency, federal courts have devised independently and mandated unilaterally detailed positive rules, standards and formulae prescribing governmental behavior and establishing official state policy" (1981:10). Courts do construct legal rules and social remedies that have consequences extending far beyond the original litigants and the specific dispute. One need only look at the broad impact of *Roe* v. *Wade*, or at the recent wrongful life torts and the pressures they exert on physicians to utilize prenatal diagnostic techniques to see social consequences extending beyond the original litigation (Blank 1986). Moreover, as Gambitta, May, and Foster (1981:14) cogently note, anticipated litigation becomes a necessary component in the calculus of policy formation, because virtually every public policy at some point must meet the test of litigation.

Critics of an active court role argue that inherent limitations on judicial policymaking preclude such a role in issues concerning medical technology. For Schoenberg (1979), anything with as few legal precedents and as politically controversial as the defining of "life" and "death" should be left to t¹ determination of the elected representatives of the people. More specifically, because the judicial process is passive and retrospective, it is viewed by some as too slow to react to rapid technological progress. Horowitz (1977:257) contends that the judicial process is a poor format for weighing the alternatives and calculating the social costs of each new development. The courts are ill-equipped to gauge the future. Additionally, the adjudication process itself works against policymaking. For Horowitz (1977:33), adjudication is focused, piecemeal, and makes no provision for policy review. Elliot L. Seagall, president of the American Society of Law and Medicine, is quoted by Arehart-Treichel as contending that the "U.S. legal system is one generation behind the medical science" (1980:156).

Also, because the primary function of the court is to resolve conflicts centering on the rights and obligations of the parties before it, individual cases are decided supposedly on evidence produced by the parties to each case, and not on the grounds of public policy considerations. Although particular decisions might have important policy implications, Green notes that the courts "generally refrain from deciding individual cases on the bases of deliberately establishing public-policy controls" (1976:171). In those instances where judicial decisions have consequences beyond the immediate parties to the case, according to Nakamura and Smallwood there are often "serious difficulties in communicating new legal requirements to populations that are not yet within the jurisdiction of courts" (1980:107). As a result, decisions are episodic, unpredictable, and often inconsistent. Case-by-case adjudication across a wide variety of state and federal courts adds to the confusion. Judge David Bazelon concludes:

Regulation through the common law has many drawbacks. It has a substantial impact on science, technology, and the economy generally. It "regulates" and constrains just as surely as an agency does. . . . It also imposes extremely high costs in damages, insurance, and attorneys' fees. Moreover, judicial regulation cannot provide the consistency, rationality, or political responsiveness offered by a consciously designed and clearly articulated legislative solution. A courtroom is not the place to decide such complex and controversial issues of fact and policy. And judges are not the appropriate persons to decide them. (1983:19)

Proponents of an active role for the courts counter that, especially in sensitive policy areas, the courts have a role to play (Miller 1982). For instance, the same constraints alleged to prevent the courts from making policy in the health domain were present when civil rights were at issue, but the courts initiated substantial policy changes in that area. The American common law tradition allows for judicial innovation and social change when other branches of government bog down. The expanding concept of fundamental rights, especially as it relates to privacy and self-determination in health care matters, and the notion of compelling state interest plainly demonstrate the conceivable justification for court influence on health care policy.

Tribe (1973:98) suggests that at the expressive and symbolic levels, the law has a potential role as a catalyst for needed changes in the system. The law dramatizes injustices and channels executive as well as legislative attention toward areas needing more systematic reform or comprehensive regulation. Although the law reflects public values, it also induces cultural and moral change through alterations in legal doctrine. Despite the fragmented, oblique, and at times contradictory policy implications of judicial decisions, it appears likely that the most critical health issues ultimately will reach the Supreme Court for resolution. Contrarily, despite the indications that the courts are being cast into these issues by default, it is unlikely that as now constituted they are truly willing to play a critical role in setting societal priorities and goals regarding the allocation of medical resources, or capable of doing so. New technological developments promise to complicate rather than resolve the constellation of constitutional, political, and social problems facing them.

Despite the limitations of the courts, they are at this stage unmistakably involved in the resolution of individual uses of health care technology. According to May (1981:120), state courts are pressing deeper into the business of the medical community, taking away the authority of the medical profession to make its decisions free from outside control. The courts are heavily involved in governing the delivery and quality of medical services through their action on statutes that set policies, create control agencies, and generally influence medical practice. Moreover, they influence health care policy through their rulings in medical malpractice lawsuits and in the way they set down standards for the practice of medicine in deciding these suits. May (1981:122) contends that the courts' dissolution in recent years of the locality rule (which allowed for consideration of less stringent locally defined standards of care) has led to greater patient rights and higher expectations of health care delivery. Ironically, it has also broadened deference to the expert testimony of the national medical community at the expense of the individual physician, and forced the courts to become embroiled in an increasingly complex, professionalized, and expert-dominated set of policy issues.

The Courts and Medical "Fact." One of the obvious difficulties emerging from the increased technical complexity of issues brought about by medical advances is the need for the courts to secure and understand the medical "facts." Although there is little systematic analysis of the problems arising from the entrance of the courts into areas that necessitate substantial technical knowledge, there is a growing concern among political observers over the inability of the courts to respond to scientific testimony and to make decisions based on scientific evidence (Rist and Anson 1977). Certainly these trends raise questions concerning the extent to which judges have the ability to make responsible policy in areas in which scientific judgment and interpretation are of the essence. Also, there are broader questions as to how well the courts use scientific terms and concepts in reaching their conclusions.

In his detailed critique of the courts' involvement in social policymaking, Horowitz (1977:31) concludes that judges not only lack information themselves, but may also lack the experience and skill necessary to interpret such information if they receive it. Judges are generalists, not specialists. One consequence of the "generalist dominance" in the courts, according to Horowitz, is that in the "interstices where expertise is lacking, the generalist fills the gaps with his own 'generalized normative axioms'" (1977:25). The lack of attention to important facts is, therefore, a characteristic of the judicial process, and critics such as Horowitz call for either enhancement of judicial capacity to handle scientific data and to foresee the consequence of court action, or restraint on the part of the courts so as to avoid making policy in those fields where institutional capacity is most limited.

Matheny and Williams (1981:349) add that the adversary system itself works against adequate use of biological evidence, and that disputes about medical policy are ill-served by an adversary system. Some means must be devised to ensure that scientific testimony is properly used. Still, the courts must be prepared to deal with inconclusive evidence, because these problems are ever more critical and demand resolution. For Rosen,

A basic problem for the Supreme Court is not whether it will allow fact situations to influence its interpretation of the Constitution, but whether it will in adjudicating any given issue accept a statement of the relevant facts prepared by a lower court or instead set forth its own understanding of the facts. (1972:11)

Other observers are less willing to conclude that the courts are incapable of integrating scientific data into their decisions. Youngblood and Folse (1981:30), although agreeing with many of Horowitz's criticisms, note that court decisions must be based on the Constitution and not on the theories of social scientists and others. They dispute the contention that judges cannot deal with scientific findings and argue that there is ample opportunity for specialists to contribute in the courts. In addition to the considerable staff and research resources available to judges, the adversary process can work to provide the judge with the relevant information. Amicus curiae briefs and substantive specialization in some courts assure that judges are not necessarily novices.

Youngblood and Folse contend, however, that in spite of the capacity the courts do have to integrate scientific findings into their decisions, they should not attempt merely to balance the evidence. Judges should make decisions on their "commonsense understanding of human nature" and their "sense of fairness operating within the confines of principle," not solely on the basis of "the facts" in a technical sense. They strongly reject Horowitz's prescriptions that court techniques be reformulated to handle scientific testimony, or that the courts avoid policymaking in technical fields. For Youngblood and Folse, neither prescription is compatible with the traditional role of the courts, and either course of action would ultimately threaten their legitimacy as governing bodies. They state: "Were a court to approach its task by identifying and balancing the social costs and benefits of various outcomes, it would be doing something other than articulating or preserving rights.... The court would no longer be operating within the confines of principle" (1981:58). Judicial decisions, then, should not be based on assessment of the social costs and benefits of alternative outcomes even if the courts have the capacity to make such assessments. These authors reject any attempts to alter judicial decision making to sharpen the focus on policy consequences.

Although major transformations of the judicial process might be seen as overkill, critical adjustments in the way courts deal with biological evidence are essential. Steps must be taken to ensure that when the courts use biological evidence as part of their rationale for a ruling, they are fully aware of the ramifications. The courts are put in a difficult position when they base decisions on biological testimony, especially when they fail to recognize or understand the extent to which technological advances are altering biological "fact." Medical controversies, according to Yellin, have an "inherently hybrid technical and legal character" and "present issues that can be resolved by neither purely technical nor purely legal analysis" (1981:491). Such issues force the courts to deal not only with new forms of information, but also with new methods of analysis for understanding causality which are totally alien to the language and mode of analysis of the legal profession. It is not surprising, therefore, that these new demands on the courts are producing severe strain.

Summary: The Courts and Rationing

As decisions are made by the government and other third-party payers to ration medical technologies on the basis of competing notions of the collective good, individuals will turn to those agencies which traditionally have established individual rights vis-á-vis the collective good: the courts. They will ask the courts to redress what they consider unjust or unfair allocation and rationing schemes. Any rationing formula is bound to be challenged in the courts. Furthermore, if it becomes apparent that rationing decisions are based on social as well as medical criteria for valuing human lives differentially, the public will be moved to protest and will increasingly turn to the courts.

To this end, the courts are likely to become the arena of difficult debates regarding the constitutionality of government attempts to influence individual lifestyle decisions, traditionally private matters. Has the 55-year-old chronic drinker who has been denied a $250,000 life-saving liver transplant been denied a constitutional right to live? Do all persons have an unmitigated claim to health care even if their health problems are the direct product of their own behavior? These issues are raised by the current attention given to the ills of cigarette smoking, alcohol-related deaths, AIDS, genital herpes, and to the effects of a sedentary lifestyle. It will be up to the courts to decide whether or not people have an obligation to care for themselves in a manner that will maximize good health. Evans notes that "unfortunately a vast majority of the population fails to fulfill its end of the 'social contract' and chooses to engage in practices and behavior known to be detrimental to their health" (1983:2210). To what extent will the courts dismiss the implicit indictment against these persons or, conversely, will they agree that those individuals who have done the most to preserve their health be the first to benefit from available resources? The courts, as primary guarantors of individual rights, will undoubtedly have a fundamental role in such policymaking. When the question becomes who is entitled to treatment, procedures certain to be scrutinized closely are major organ transplantations, coronary artery bypass surgery, neonatal intensive care, and terminal patient care.

In summary, the rationing of medical technologies is likely to become more common in the near future. The courts already are heavily involved in medical decision making. Because the courts have been traditionally the arbiter and definer of individual rights, they will continue to be called upon to resolve the conflicts over rights that emerge from allocation and rationing policies. Such determination by the courts will depend to some extent on medical criteria and on state-of-the-art medical science.

Legislative and Executive Action in the Allocation and Rationing of Health Care

A significant proportion of allocation and rationing decisions are now being made in the courts largely by default, because of nonaction by legislative bodies. This situation occurs because the courts, unlike the legislatures, have little control over their agenda. The courts' case load is determined externally. Any person or group with the skill and resources necessary to file suit can do so, and the court must respond. As a result, many critical health care decisions are being made by those government appointees least able to evade the issues or ignore the conflicts now emerging—judges who are "untrained in the scientific and economic nuances of what is at stake" (Florio 1985:43).

By contrast, the legislatures do have control over the policy agenda, at least to the extent that they can delay consideration of an issue until political pressures become so strong that they are forced to take action. Even if a bill is introduced in a legislature, there are many ways to deny it full consideration. It can be left to die in a committee or subcommittee. It can be killed, in effect, by the leadership, if they assign it to a committee that they know to be unsympathetic to the bill. Through these tactics, potentially embarrassing or highly controversial measures can be quietly stricken from the public agenda until external momentum forces action.

Congress: Minimal Action

As noted in chapter 1, health care issues often are not amenable to the conventional legislative process, which relies on bargaining, compromise, and negotiation strategies. As Coates asserts, "cut and fit accommodation and incremental change, the traditional strategies of government, are increasingly ineffective, if not sterile modes of operation" (1978:33). Furthermore, as a deliberative body, Congress is extremely slow both in recognizing policy problems and in acting upon them. For Allan Shick (1977:10), the "legislative process is weighted against quick and comprehensive responses" and encourages negotiation and compromise to build majorities at each stage. The result is piecemeal and often contradictory legislation which reflects the lack of consensus or bitter conflict over the issues.

Reinforcing the inherent congressional bias against quick and comprehensive responses to problems is what Green describes as the tendency of legislatures to "refrain from enacting regulatory laws until there is an obvious need for legislation" (1973:388). Congress fails to direct attention to issues that are not pressing, because it is too busy with urgent problems. This results in a vicious circle of priority-setting, since problems that are ignored as they develop eventually do become crises. Therefore, it is improbable that Congress, as presently structured, has the wherewithall to initiate action on policy issues where urgency is more remote.

Recent congressional response to the impending crisis in the Medicare trust fund exemplifies this incapacity. Although it is generally agreed that the trust fund will go bankrupt in the 1990s unless swift action is taken to restructure the Medicare system, response by Congress has been too slow and insufficient in scope to avert this disaster. Current cost containment measures might postpone bankruptcy, but the core problems of Medicare within the context of demographic and technological trends have not been addressed, because politically they are very risky. Cost containment as a theory is politically popular today. However, cutting specific benefits, particularly those for the elderly, is career-threatening for most public officials. Despite the need for prompt and comprehensive restructuring of Medicare, the congressional process makes it unlikely that sufficient action will be forthcoming. This is understandable in a legislative body for whom attention to immediate problems is the norm. The severe Medicare funding crisis is at least six or eight years down the road. Unfortunately, in politics, that is the remote future: one must win at least several more elections by promising action on more immediate concerns in order even to be around long enough to deal with such a far-off matter. Thus, attention is concentrated on the present or the near future.

Another characteristic of Congress which diminishes its capacity to make anticipatory health policy is the internal fragmentation of decision-making power. Although the rationale behind the committee system is to divide labor and thereby maximize skill and minimize the overall workload, Tribe concludes that "the existing system of specialized committees, riddled with rivalries and fragmented by jurisdictional division, cannot be relied upon to provide the focus without which public concern is just so much undirected energy" (1973a:609). The present committee system fails to address matters that cut across its divisions, and it leads to duplication of effort as numerous committees stake claims to jurisdiction on important issues. Moreover, it retards the policymaking process without assurance that relevant policy interdependencies will be considered (Shick 1977:14). Since health allocation issues tend to combine what in the past were perceived to be separate issues, and to multiply the number of interests which demand consideration, the process is frustrated.

Specialization in Congress has also led to a situation where few members are well-informed about any one specific issue. Voting is often in response to cue-giving by those colleagues considered experts (Matthews and Stimson 1975), or the result of logrolling or vote tradeoffs. Seldom are more than a handful of members familiar with any particular piece of technical legislation. Jasper concludes that in Congress, "there is a very thin base of knowledge and very limited resources for solving these problems in an intelligent and thoughtful fashion" (1974:152). Schoenberg adds that "legislators are frequently unsophisticated about science and do not understand the fundamental issues involved in the application of new discoveries" (1979:93). Hearings are characterized by low attendance, and congressmen tend to be responsive to selective testimony, often from those who have a high stake on either side of the issue.

Although these problems persist, Congress has attempted to alleviate them. Congress created the Office of Technology Assessment (OTA) in 1972 to increase its ability to analyze technological developments. Despite its intention, the OTA has been criticized for dissipating its energies on routine tasks for congressional committees while failing in its ostensible goal of providing "an early warning system for Congress" (Boffey 1976a:213). Although the recent work of the OTA in infertility prevention and in biotechnology demonstrates a broadened perspective, these criticisms illustrate the difficulties of moving beyond the immediate parochial concerns of congressional leaders to establish a prospective, future-oriented approach to policymaking, even when a new office is created for that particular purpose.

In 1986, Congress proposed establishment of the Biomedical Ethics Board, composed of six senators and six representatives, with an equal number of members from each party. Part of the task of this board will be to appoint and oversee a Biomedical Ethics Advisory Committee, to include fourteen members from a wide array of backgrounds, including ethics, law, and the social sciences, as well as the lay public. A total of $7.5 million was requested to fund this body for three years. It will be interesting to see if the Biomedical Ethics Board, once underway, will have a genuine role to play.

As long as there is no widespread public demand for a comprehensive revision of health care policy, Congress is unlikely to undertake it. The demands of powerful interest groups frequently are met through piecemeal legislation which is often inconsistent and counterproductive. While the health care establishment is unable to achieve all of its goals, in part because of the lack of a consensus among its many components, it has been largely successful in keeping change to a minimum. The absence of a strong counterdemand for change by the public, who are largely satisfied with the status quo, means that the most salient pressure on congressmen comes from groups opposed to a restructuring of health care. As a result, the lack of vigorous, future-oriented deliberation on these issues by public officials who desire reelection should not be surprising.

The Bureaucracy of Health Care

The massive scope and complexity of the federal bureaucracy, combined with the fragmentation caused by its jurisdictional boundaries, have produced overlapping and confusing lines of authority. Figure 4.1 presents a representative list of the agencies involved in making health policy. Given the historical development of these agencies and their competition for influence and at times survival, there is nothing approaching a single locus of power for health policymaking. There is no coordinating mechanism to ensure that policy is consistent or to eliminate the duplication and confusion that result when more than one agency makes policy in the same substantive area. An unfortunate by-product of these overlapping jurisdictions is that agencies do not always cooperate fully with one another or coordinate their efforts. Comprehensive and future-oriented policy is unlikely to be produced as long as this competition exists.

Another problem inherent to bureaucracies that minimizes their objectivity and causes them to lose sight of broader public responsi-

Figure 4.1

Selected Federal Health Policy and Financing Agencies

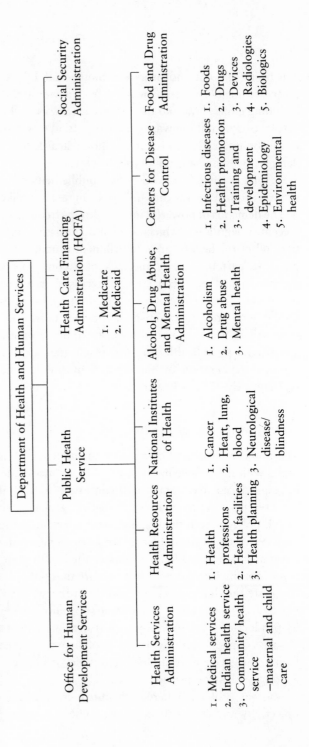

–migrant health
–national health service corps

4. Allergy/infectious diseases
5. Metabolic/digestive diseases
6. Environmental health
7. Dental services
8. General medical services

6. Occupational safety and health

Other Actors in Public Health in Federal Government
1. Veterans Administration
2. Department of Defense
3. Department of Agriculture
4. Department of Housing and Urban Development
5. Department of Labor (OSHA)
6. Environmental Protection Agency

bilities is their dependence on special interest group support. According to Freeman, "the larger diffuse goals of public interest easily become contracted to mean the goals of self-interested clients who are organized, constantly on the job defining problems, providing information, and seeking advantage" (1974:160). Given the paramount role of special interests in the existing bureaucratic system and the fragmentation across agencies, it seems that if the government is to make objective and comprehensive health policy, an agency must be created which is free from dominance by interest groups and yet allows for widespread public access. However, this appears unlikely within the current institutional context, where the growth and survival of a public agency depends upon its success in establishing routine relationships with its clients. Like Congress, the federal bureaucracy, at least as it now operates, appears incapable of dealing with the complex and controversial problems of allocating and rationing scarce medical resources.

Some recent developments in the executive branch appear to be a move toward a more active government involvement in biomedical issues. Within the Department of Health and Human Services (HHS), the Office of Health Technology Assessment was established to coordinate analysis and testing by agencies; to determine safety, efficacy, and cost effectiveness of new and existing biomedical technologies; and to assist in determining which mechanisms should be used to promote, inhibit, or control the use of these technologies. Also within HHS, the National Institutes of Health (NIH) created an Office for the Medical Applications of Technology. NIH also has attempted to broaden the roles of its various national advisory councils in an effort to enlarge the contribution of public representatives to the development of research policies and priorities. It has continued to come under attack, however, for a decision-making process dominated by the medical elite (Martson 1978).

Another feature of the American political system which shapes health policy is its decentralized nature, both in structure and function. The authority to make health policy is dispersed across an array of governmental units from the national to the local level and among the branches at each level. The cumulative impact of both federalism and the separation of powers drastically reduces the possibility of establishing a single, comprehensive approach to the allocation and rationing of health resources. Because the motivations and needs of policymakers in each political jurisdiction vary, each jurisdiction is jealous of the power it has and works hard to retain it. Given this context, it is understandable that health policy in the United States continues to be haphazard and irregular.

State Legislatures and Health Policy

Although most attention concerning the allocation of health care resources focuses on the national government, the state legislatures are constitutionally responsible for the public health. Congressional action is usually a response to already existing state legislation and serves primarily to set minimum national standards and/or provide federal matching funds to encourage state action of a particular type. Federal court decisions have also been made in reaction to state statutes, either declaring specific legislation unconstitutional or liberalizing and standardizing state action. Although the role of the federal government in health policy has expanded, particularly since adoption of the massive Medicare and Medicaid programs in the mid-1960s, most public health legislation continues to be made within the fifty states. The result has been considerable inconsistency from state to state, and a highly fragmented health policy across the nation. While this decentralized approach to health policy has some advantages and many defenders, a rational allocation policy is not among its strengths.

Constraints are placed on Congress in dealing with sensitive and volatile health issues, but the state legislatures face even more difficulties. Serving on most state legislatures continues to be a part-time vocation with low compensation and relatively short tenure. The high turnover rate ensures that power in the states is likely to be concentrated in the hands of the few legislators who return on a regular basis and in interest groups whose lobbyists usually maintain a long tenure. In addition to the amateur nature of many state legislatures, the sessions of most are limited in length, often by the state constitution. About thirty-five legislatures now meet annually and several states have removed restrictions on length, but most still limit sessions to sixty or ninety days. Most of this time is usually spent on budget and revenue matters, leaving little time to consider substantive legislation.

Contributing to the inability of state legislatures to draft innovative health policy, especially that of a highly technical nature, is the paucity of professional staff. As noted earlier, Congress relies heavily on professional staff to research and write legislation. State legislators and legislative committees rarely enjoy a similar luxury. There is a clear trend in the larger states toward professional staffing, but most states lack even minimally adequate staffs. Some states have established joint standing committees or interim committees that meet when the whole body is out of session. Despite this, committees in the state legislatures do not usually play as pivotal a role as their counterparts in Congress. This reinforces the ability of lobbyists to exert strong influence over specific state legislation and permits the state's executive office more flexibility and influence in drafting legislation. It also contributes to the lack of cohesive and comprehensive health policy.

The larger, more affluent states, such as California and Texas, have a difficult time dealing with the surging costs of health care. The smaller, less affluent states—particularly those with dispersed populations, such as Idaho and North Dakota—simply do not have the financial bases necessary to fund the same levels of medical care for their respective citizenries. This means that the health care available to the residents of one state might not be available to their friends or relatives in a neighboring state. This situation raises the question of the patent unfairness of a decentralized system of medical allocation. De facto rationing of health care resources does exist across state boundaries, in spite of the mistaken assumption that all citizens have equal claims to health care.

Ironically, recent cutbacks in federal funding of categorical health-related grants and cost containment measures in Medicare and Medicaid place more of the burden for payment on the separate states, thereby accentuating the variation from state to state. Some states have taken on the added responsibility of picking up the federal government's share of Medicaid that has been cut, while others have failed to do so. This, in turn, has increased state-to-state discrepancies in health care coverage for the indigent, the costs of which have in large measure been passed on by the states to the counties. In many states, the financial footing of counties is often precarious, because their tax-raising potential is restricted by state law. Several large medical bills for indigent residents might be enough to place many a county in dire financial straits. Yet it seems untenable that the decision whether or not to pay for intensive care for a particular infant or to fund an organ transplant should be made by county commissioners, who are put in the position of making rationing decisions while balancing their limited budgets. This has led counties in some states to establish contingency funds to purchase insurance to cover such cases. Cooperation of this type will contribute to rational policy, but it is highly tenuous and dependent on the continued mutual benefit of the participating counties. Ultimately, relegating the funding of health care for indigents to the counties will place the final decisions in the courts.

The problems experienced by the states, however, have not precluded some innovative initiatives. For instance, in 1982 Massachusetts passed legislation that mandated that hospitals slow their growth in spending by adhering to a strict predetermined formula. It was estimated that over a five-year period, expenditures would be reduced by 35 to 40 percent (Aaron and Schwartz 1984:115). In March, 1987, Virginia became the first state to establish a separate compensation program for badly brain-damaged babies (*American Medical News*, March 13, 1987, p. 1). California, too, has by necessity shown leadership in its efforts to control state MediCal costs by requiring hospitals to bid for a contract under which the hospital provides all services to MediCal patients at a flat daily rate. States also retain substantial authority to regulate hospitals and insurance companies, as well as the conduct of health professionals, through licensing and accrediting boards. Generally, state public health regulations will be upheld by the courts if it can reasonably be shown that they are necessary to protect and promote the public's health, safety, and general welfare, and that they are reasonably drawn to accomplish that end (Christoffel 1982:61).

The lack of a national allocation and rationing policy also raises the possibility of serious interstate controversies regarding state responsibilities for reimbursement. Several cases have arisen recently where patients were transported from one state to another for emergency treatment. This is bound to become more common where regional centers such as the Children's Hospital in Denver are responsible for delivering highly specialized services such as neonatal intensive care. Which state pays for expensive specialized care of an indigent patient: the state where the treatment is given, or the patient's state of residence? If it is to be the state in which the specialized facility exists, should prior approval of the relevant health agency be required? States grant reciprocity in other areas; perhaps disputes over health care costs could be settled similarly, but the high costs involved might preclude such arrangements.

The Proliferation of Health Care Industry Regulations

It has been estimated that 25 percent of hospital costs are attributable to meeting the regulatory requirements imposed by an array of local, state, and national governments and agencies (Pozgar 1983:xi). Many of these regulations duplicate one another, and some are in conflict. A study by the Hospital Association of New York State found that New York hospitals must deal with approximately 164 regulatory agencies or associations, 96 of which are state controlled. These regulations pertain to admitting procedures, patient safety, use and control of drugs, hospital planning, minimum standards of care, and so forth. In addition to government regulations and guidelines, voluntary medical associations such as the AMA and the Joint Commission on Accreditation of Hospitals set minimum requirements. Although many of these regulations are critical to the provision of quality health care, the paperwork they demand and the confusion they cause could be minimized through a consolidation of jurisdictions.

Caution is advised before placing substantial faith in any health care legislation designed to limit public expenditures. Any system devised by the legislature can and probably will be circumvented by certain elements in the health care community which see it as in their financial interests to do so. The difficulty of designing a system that minimizes opportunities for evasion by health providers or consumers cannot be overestimated. The problems are similar to those of writing tax laws that close all the loopholes.

An excellent example of American ingenuity in circumventing recent cost containment legislation is the reaction of health care providers to the Medicare diagnosis-related groups (DRGs). The goal of DRGs was to contain hospital costs by setting reimbursement limits on Medicare payments according to schedules based on the average costs in the previous year of some 470 procedures. Prior to the use of DRGs, it was the common practice of many hospitals to extend the stay of Medicare patients beyond the time necessary for medical treatment.

Because the hospitals were being reimbursed by Medicare on a fee-for-service basis, there was no incentive for them to terminate the patient's stay, especially if they had empty hospital beds. This practice not only raised the cost of the health care paid for by Medicare, it also increased the cost to the patient. Prior to the DRG system, the major activity of Medicare fraud and abuse investigators was to identify those care providers whose patients had exceedingly long average stays.

Within the first year of the DRG reimbursement system, the most common type of fraud and abuse had shifted to involve hospitals that were releasing patients too early. Hospitals now have a financial incentive to shorten hospital stays, because they will get the full DRG amount no matter how long the patient remains hospitalized. If the patient's stay is longer than the average, the hospital must absorb the difference. However, if the stay is less than the predetermined average, the hospital keeps the excess. The intent of the law was clearly to eliminate the incentive for lengthening hospital stays unnecessarily. The intent was not to shorten hospital stays to the detriment of the patient's health. Yet there is evidence that the latter situation is not uncommon. Data indicate that the average stay in some hospitals for Medicare patients has been cut dramatically. In some cases, it has dropped from over ten days per stay to an average of three. Obviously, this implies that either these hospitals had been keeping patients on the average over three times as long as necessary for treatment, or that they are now releasing patients far sooner than is warranted medically. In actuality, the truth is probably somewhere in between: before DRGs they abused the system by extending stays, and now they abuse the system by releasing the patients as soon as they possibly can.

Moreover, if patients are being released prematurely, one would expect readmission rates to increase—and they are. Since each admission represents a new DRG payment, there is an incentive for hospitals to release early and then readmit the patient a short time later. Also, because nursing homes and other rehabilitative units are not covered by DRGs, the movement of patients between hospitals and these other units will accelerate. This is especially suspicious in cases where the rehabilitation centers and nursing homes are owned by the same corporation as the hospital, a situation which is becoming more frequent. Unless this pattern is consistent and excessive, however, it is very difficult to prove that abuse has occurred, because of the medical judgment involved.

Technology Assessment Mechanisms and Allocation/Rationing Policy

As noted in chapter 3, assessment of medical technologies has received considerable attention in the last decade both in the public and private sectors. Seymour Perry (1986) estimates that at least 45 organizations are involved in technology assessment, the most prominent of which are the Clinical Efficacy Assessment Project (American College of Physicians); the Diagnostic and Therapeutic Technology Assessment program (AMA); the Medical Necessity and Technology Evaluation and Coverage Programs (Blue Cross/Blue Shield); and the Hospital Technology Service Program (American Hospital Association). In addition, many medical professional societies, health provider organizations, nonprofit health-related organizations, university health institutes, and manufacturers of drugs and medical devices have formal or informal capacities for evaluation and assessment.

Despite the scope of these activities, there is little or no coordination, cooperation, or even exchange of information among the many organizations making these assessment efforts. Moreover, their assessments are usually narrowly focused and rarely entail the collection of primary data. They largely fail to place the specific assessments in the broader context of the national health crisis. This is not surprising, because each organization has a stake in the results of its assessment. Furthermore, none of these organizations has the resources to support necessary research, including clinical trials. Although there appears to be a realization that a more coherent system of medical technology assessment is essential if we are to make rational decisions concerning health care, genuine collaboration between these groups is problematic without a major initiative from the federal government. Given the current and most likely long-term emphasis on cost containment, efforts to strengthen medical technology assessment, even to achieve consensus on its basic objectives and approaches, will be difficult.

Impetus for government involvement in health technology assessment came from a 1976 OTA report which concluded that assessment should be made before costly new medical technologies and procedures were put into general use (OTA 1976). This report called for the establishment of formal mechanisms for accomplishing that task and played a part in the program of the National Institutes of Health designed to develop a consensus on technical issues. The shortlived National Center for Health Care Technology (NCHCT) was an attempt to strengthen and centralize efforts to assess health care technologies. After the center's demise in 1981, the OTA reiterated the importance to the nation of a rational and systematic approach to medical technology assessment (OTA, 1982).

In 1984, Congress enacted legislation signed by the President (Public Law 98–551) which revised the existing National Center for Health Services Research and broadened its mandate for assessing new technology to include not only considerations of safety and efficacy but, as appropriate, cost effectiveness. The new name of the center is the National Center for Health Services Research Assessment/Health Care Technology Assessment (NCHSR/HCTA). This law also established a council to advise the Secretary of HHS and the director of the center about health care technology assessment, and it instituted a council on health care technology under the sponsorship of the National Academy of Sciences (NAS), with partial governmental support.

The latter provision implemented a recommendation by the Institute of Medicine (IOM 1983) that proposed creation of a private/public organization to assess medical technology as part of the institute. In the legislation as passed, the council is charged with promoting technology assessment and identifying obsolete or inappropriately applied health care technologies. It has responsibility for establishing a clearinghouse for information on health care technologies and assessments as well as coordinating and commissioning assessments of specific technologies. HHS is authorized to award the NAS up to $500,000 to cover two-thirds of the costs for planning and establishing the council. Operational funds will match one dollar of federal grant money with at least twice that amount from private sources.

The initiation of the council has been delayed due to the need for sufficient long-term private support, opposition from the AMA, and some initial constitutional problems with the authorizing legislation. In addition to the problem of soliciting funds and cooperation from groups in the private sector concerned with the results of technology assessment, there is the question of the degree of cooperation the council will receive from federal agencies. Without such cooperation, the council will be unable to implement its mandate to establish a clearinghouse. Perry (1986:242) suggests that the brief experience of the NCHCT and other organizations that have attempted to solicit such cooperation is not encouraging. Finally, there remain questions as to whether a council under the aegis of the IOM, and therefore dependent on support by private sector interested parties, could render unbiased assessments.

Another recent privately sponsored effort to establish, in the words of Balfe et al. (1985), "a broad framework for decision making that looks beyond the immediate concerns of today to the issues that will be confronting the health sector into the next century" is the Health Policy Agenda for the American People (HPA). Initiated by the AMA in 1982, it represents the combined effort of 172 private and public organizations working together to provide a broad health care policy framework while simultaneously safeguarding the essential elements of individual decision making. Phase I of the two-phase project produced 159 principles and 41 issues covering a wide spectrum of health concerns (Boyle 1984). During phase II, which began in late 1984, policy proposals consistent with these principles were developed in response to the issues. At a press conference on February 23, 1987, HPA unveiled its report (*American Medical News*, March 6, 1987, p. 1). Among its position statements the report concluded:

Society must come to grips with the moral and ethical questions posed by rapid developments in health care technology—who should have access to this technology, under what circumstances should technology be applied or withdrawn, and the respective roles of providers and patients in reaching these decisions.

Throughout its deliberations, HPA placed emphasis on consensus building across the wide array of groups participating in the project. As with other such efforts in the past, it is questionable whether HPA will have any substantial policy impact.

A clear example of the difficulties inherent in establishing an unbiased national assessment program is the Prospective Payment Assessment Commission (ProPac) that was established by the legislation that imposed a prospective payment system for Medicare. ProPac was included in the legislation because of concern that the Health Care Financing Administration and HHS, in their quest to contain costs, would not pay adequate attention to technological advances if they increased costs. In order to check this perceived bias, ProPac members are appointed by the congressional OTA, even though it also advises HHS in the executive branch.

In congruence with congressional intent, in 1985 ProPac members vowed to take an unbiased approach toward technology assessment. They suggest that adjustments may be required in the financial incentives created by prospective payments to encourage adoption of more costly but quality-enhancing technologies. Presently, the DRG system encourages adoption of cost-reducing technologies, but discourages cost-raising ones. Unbiased assessment, however, will likely result in recommendations to use some technologies which will increase costs, and thus run counter to current efforts to cut the costs of Medicare. Because of this inherent conflict in values, it is probable that recommendations by ProPac to introduce beneficial but costly technologies into the DRG system will be rejected, thereby throwing this entire assessment enterprise into question.

ProPac was also charged by Congress with conducting or sponsoring assessments of medical technology needed to advise the secretary of HHS about reimbursement rates for DRGs. Not surprisingly, little funding for that task has been forthcoming. As a result, ProPac must rely primarily on published literature and existing assessments as it develops recommendations about the incorporation of new medical technologies into the prospective payment system. Although it can emphasize those appraisals that it regards as the most appropriate and fair, the lack of resources to produce original assessments weakens its role in the policymaking process. To the extent that the allocation and ultimately rationing of health care will be based on technology assessment, the lack of coherent and nonpolitical assessment mechanisms will put into question any such efforts.

Alternative Mechanisms: The Public and Health Policy

In part due to the perceived inadequacy of existing legislative and administrative institutions to deal with the issues derived from medical technology, there has been a resurgence of demands for effective participation of potentially affected groups in making policy. Dorothy Nelkin suggests that demands for public scrutiny are inevitable "given the policy importance of many areas of scientific research and the growing concern in the biological sciences with basic life processes" (1980:484). Heightened sensitivity to the social implications of biomedical developments, the expanding role of the federal government in health care funding, and the fear by some that societal decisions are being made largely without adequate public input have produced growing concern over who should make the critical policy decisions that face us.

Charles Weiner (1982:73) sees the central imperative of the "major unresolved national issues" that arise out of the emergence of these technologies to be determining the role the public should play in defining the purposes and goals of these innovations and in establishing the conditions under which they are developed. Certainly, defining the role of the public in decision making is not a new problem nor one unique to biomedical issues. This topic has been debated since the time of Plato and will continue to be the subject of controversy. For Richard Rettig, "Nevertheless, the problem remains of how appropriately to consult the public on issues where scientific and technological considerations loom large" (1982:22).

Because health allocation issues are of public concern, it is not surprising that an often expressed theme is the need for greater public participation in the decision-making process. Comroe (1978:937) concludes that over the long run a well-educated and well-informed public will more often than not make the correct decision. Similarly, Kaplan (1975) argues that we must rely upon the sensibility of the ordinary citizen, not the experts, in resolving the questions of human values raised by biomedical technologies. I argue that no solution will be possible without vigorous public support—support that will not be forthcoming unless the public has substantial input into the policy being made. Whether or not the decisions will be better ones is problematical. The important point is that without such public involvement and support, any policy for rationing medicine will fail.

For Weiner, it is now "clear that the question is not whether the public should participate in scientific and technological affairs that have important social consequences, but how they can participate effectively and intelligently" (1982:82). If the public is to have a positive role, as many observers assume, how can this role best be manifested in decisions concerning the allocation of health care? Moreover, who should be included in the "public" that establishes policies and controls, and how ought these controls be organized and applied? Although it is popular to express a desire for increasing the role of the public, what is the risk in putting too much faith in the public's desire or ability to accept this responsibility?

Although demands for greater public participation and control of technological policy appear to have considerable momentum at present, not all observers are enamored of this trend. Donald Fredrickson (1978:80) a former director of NIH, cautions against the "dangerous illusion" of the infallibility of public control of technology and contends that there are critical limits to "public governance of science." Another danger of making the decision process too participatory is that inordinate attention might be seized by well-organized interests or by those groups able to gain access to public officials and convince them that they speak for the public. According to William Lowrence: "To oppose closed bureaucratic procedures is usually legitimate, but it is a lot harder to devise proceedings that are not only open to the affected polity but that encourage extensive 'public' participation without just opening channels for special-interest lobbying" (1982:116).

Other critics of attempts to expand public control view such control as a means for delaying or blocking technological applications rather than as an objective evaluative mechanism. They fear cooptation by groups opposed to specific applications. Especially in times of high inflation and interest rates, the advantage of broad public participation might be offset by the high costs imposed by delays when large investments are involved. According to the Organization for Economic Cooperation and Development, "inflation has placed a powerful new weapon in the hands of intervenors against the development of large scale technologies" (1981:97).

Many observers, rather than urging expanding public participation, continue to emphasize self-governance by experts, a means of decision making corresponding closely to a model of control by a technocratic elite. For instance, David Price (1978) favors maintenance of the present system of peer review over drastic moves toward wider public involvement in specific technological decisions. His view is based on the assumption, again, that only experts have the knowledge essential to make the complex technical decisions required and that they should therefore bear the responsibility for making policy. But although the role of health experts and planners is crucial, allocation/rationing decisions ultimately reduce to value questions. Value-based decisions that affect the public have to be made with considerable support by that public. That support is more likely when the public views itself as having a role in the process, though this should not negate the contributions of the technocrats in providing the data and methodologies for analyzing the problem. Lappe and Martin (1978) contend that science is a social enterprise, with broad social and moral consequences. As a result, it must be regulated democratically. In addition, possible adverse affects on public health make it crucial that key decisions are made by members of the public and that the public be informed. This last point places responsibility on the experts as well as on the government institutions to educate the public concerning medical policy options.

The debate over who should make health policy persists within the wider context of the role of the public in science and technology in general. On the one hand there are the supporters of a technocratic elite model which reserves to experts the responsibility for making technical decisions. The experts alone, they argue, have the interest and knowledge necessary to make informed decisions on these difficult and complicated problems. To expand public control is to invite trouble because the public is uninformed, uninterested, and ignorant on these matters. Contrarily, proponents of broadened public control contend that the public is as qualified as the experts to make policy decisions on issues that are as much social and moral as they are technical. The extensive social consequences of specific technological applications warrant close public scrutiny.

Although some supporters of public control tend to assume that the entire public ought to be involved in policymaking, it is more reasonable to define the public as composed of more or less specialized, attentive publics. One can hope to expand the attentive public on a particular issue by framing the issue in readily understandable terms and by educating that public about the options and the consequences of each, but it is unrealistic and probably a waste of valuable effort and resources to attempt to integrate the entire public into the health policymaking process in any direct manner. Energies instead should be directed toward ensuring that every person who is concerned about a specific issue area has the opportunity to participate meaningfully. The task, then, is to provide mechanisms through which interested members of the public can become informed and at the same time take on more than a token role in formulating policy choices. Although it is not possible to attain the degree of public awareness and participation essential for the working of the true democratic egalitarian model, it is possible to expand substantially the base of interest and control. This can be accomplished by making existing political institutions more open and responsive to public demands and by designing new mechanisms to maximize public input.

Participatory Mechanisms

The debate over the role of the public in making health policy and the growing demands of various groups for expanded participation has led to renewed concern over the ability of current institutions to assure reasonable levels of public control. It also has raised critical questions of what the most appropriate and effective forms of lay participation in complex technical areas might be, and who should be responsible for protecting the broader public interests. As a result of these pressures, both legislative and administrative bodies have taken steps to accommodate lay perceptions in the policy process. Within government, many attempts have been made to increase citizen input into policy decisions, most with minimal success because of inherent "procedural biases that mitigate against effective implementation" (Nelkin 1977:76).

Despite recent efforts to integrate the public into health policy decisions by expanding public involvement through public hearings, institutional review boards, and an array of ad hoc mechanisms, Rettig states that "political institutions of popular, democratic control are inadequate to guide the scientific and technological enterprise and mediate its effects" (1982:22). Weiner (1982:81) argues that although public interest in development of medical technologies is high, "opportunities for public participation at the decision-making level are still limited and participation is often ineffective" (1982:81). Despite the highly visible adverse effects of medical technology in recent years, there has been little public discussion of the potential consequences of basic health care research or new technologies, nor has there been significant public debate on desirable priorities for allocating and rationing health resources. Although this absence of attention is due in part to the fragmented and specialized nature of public interests, it also reflects institutional gaps.

Before any mechanism can be effective in maximizing public involvement in health care allocation and rationing decisions, there is a need for more effective means of educating the public. The technical nature of many of the issues in medical policy are beyond even the expertise of those not trained in a particular medical specialty. If framed with care, however, even these issues can be understood by a relatively broad attentive public. Also, it is important to distinguish between making technical decisions requiring substantial expertise and establishing broad societal priorities. It seems reasonable that primary attention be placed initially on the latter. Although lay representation on medical review committees might under some circumstances be useful, attention recently has shifted toward creating mechanisms for effective public input on the broader social concerns about the direction of medical research and application in a number of areas.

If attentive publics are to have an informed role, however, they must be reasonably aware of the technical aspects. Charles Weiner (1982:90) sees the experts themselves as crucial initiators of public discussion. Experts have the capacity to anticipate and identify problems related to their work at an early stage and participate with other groups to make choices consistent with more inclusive public value systems. Formation has been proposed of bodies responsible for analyzing technical aspects of major policy problems, developing alternative responses to these problems, making recommendations to policymakers, and providing continuous review and analysis of programs. Presumably, these bodies would produce useful information which could be transmitted also to the attentive public and the policymakers.

Although the present methods of securing input from experts are numerous, they are seldom satisfactory and are often criticized as biased or inadequate. In committee hearings, expert medical witnesses give their testimony in rapid succession, generally to a handful of members. Expert input is also available through ad hoc commissions, task forces, consultants, conferences, and informal solicitation of advice by government officials. Seldom is this testimony systematically conveyed to the public or presented in a form which makes it as accessible as possible to the mass media. Although the Office of Technology Assessment was established by Congress to give internal technical advise, and various mechanisms, including a science advisor, a science advisory council, and an office of science and technology have been introduced in the executive branch, normally their impact has been inconsistent and sporadic and their reports largely unavailable to the public. Also, seldom have these bodies focused on health care technologies.

One of the problems in educating the public about the technical aspects of health issues is the presence of glaring differences of opinion regarding the "facts" among the experts themselves. Rettig (1982:23) sees this lack of elite consensus on "the appropriate response to a number of key policy issues affecting the scientific and technological enterprise" as a critical shortcoming: "Without such consensus, clear signals cannot be given . . . and popular support for agreed-upon policies cannot be generated" (1982:23). In each health policy area, lack of agreement about the scientific evidence relevant to public and official understanding of the issue often heightens debate over use of the technology. Because existing institutions are dependent on expert testimony in some form, when the experts disagree, confusion results. Because those who testify often represent groups that have an obvious stake in the policy decision, it is not surprising that they emphasize the data favorable to their position. The escalating claims of expert opponents often appear to generate enormous confusion in the minds of the public. In response to this situation, the Task Force of the Presidential Advisory Group on Anticipated Advances in Science and Technology proposed a series of experiments to resolve factual disputes and provide a sounder basis for public decisions (Task Force 1976:653).

The most prominent of these proposals is the "science court" which supposedly concentrates solely on clarifying questions of fact, while leaving social value questions to the normal policymaking process. The purpose of the science court is to "create a situation in which adversaries direct their best arguments at each other and at a panel of sophisticated scientific judges rather than at the general public" (Task Force 1976:653). The basic mechanism is an adversary hearing, open to the public and chaired by a distinguished referee. The disinterested judges before whom the arguments are made are experts in scientific areas adjacent to that of the dispute. According to the Task Force, after the adversary proceedings, the judges prepare a report "noting points on which the advocates agree and reaching judgments on disputed statements of fact"; the objective is to describe the current state of the technology and "obtain statements founded on that knowledge, which will provide defensible, credible, technical bases for urgent policy decisions" (1976:653).

Although the science court concept has gained much attention, it has drawn criticism as well. One objection is that facts and values are inseparable when considering public policy issues, and the more controversial the issue, the greater the uncertainty over the facts. In a process that already overemphasizes the technical aspects of the problems, there is fear that a science court will further obscure the political and social dimensions. There is also the possibility that it will accentuate the extremes when the truth might be somewhere in between. Casper (1976:31) questions the need for scientific judges, noting that this assumes that politicians and other citizens are unable to weigh the claims of experts and judge for themselves. A person does not need detailed technical knowledge, he maintains, to make decisions on policy implications and priorities.

Another suggestion for making expert input more useful and more accessible to the public is the proposed restructuring of congressional hearings into formal adversary hearings where a genuine debate format is used. Casper (1976:34) argues that such a format would improve the quality of information available to both the decision makers and the public so that they could arrive at informed judgments. He also favors public forums in which experts would offer insights into social and political as well as technical implications. The biases of the experts would be stated and the broader issues argued through the medium of television, resulting in a "tradition of public dialogue" concerning the implications of new technologies (Caspar 1976:34). In 1979, Edward Kennedy proposed a President's Council on the Health Sciences to establish priorities in the health sciences and critically analyze current policy. This panel would have been composed of nine laypersons, including six members from the general public and three social scientists (President's Commission 1982:86). Like most such proposals, the Health Science Promotion Act of 1979 that would have authorized this council was not, however, passed by Congress.

Administrative channels of participation have received considerable attention in the last decade. "Participatory reforms," according to Dorothy Nelkin, "are mostly intended to expand the information available to the public and to channel information about public preferences to decision-making agencies" (1980:487). Some procedural reforms have also sought to open the administrative process and allow public representatives to take an active part in the development of policies. The Administrative Procedures Act of 1946, for example, requires all federal agencies to publicize proposed regulations in the *Federal Register* and to solicit public comments which are taken into account in drafting the final regulations. The National Research Act of 1974 extended the use of the *Register* as a public forum by requiring the secretary of Health, Education, and Welfare to make public the reports of the National Commission on the Protection of Human Subjects and give reasons if he failed to follow their recommendations in announcing the proposed regulations. According to Nelkin (1980:487), however, it is unlikely that most citizens have the initiative, money, and expertise necessary to seek out and utilize the 60,000-page annual *Federal Register*.

Although other administrative reforms, including the Freedom of Information Act, require agencies to disclose information upon specific request, few members of the public are actually able to gain access. Advisory boards of varying types have become a commonly utilized channel for allowing lay participation in policymaking. In 1975, 45 agencies employed over 1,250 advisory committees with over 22,000 members, although in many cases participants were largely representatives of organized interest groups (Nelkin 1980:488). Recent national commissions have also included some nonscientists while at the same time utilizing open hearings, public opinion surveys, and other mechanisms designed to elicit public opinion. For instance, in a special study on the implications of biomedical research, the National Commission on the Protection of Human Subjects reported the findings of a national panel of 121 consultants, a random national sample of 1,679 adults, and a four-day colloquium of 25 scientists and scholars.

Similarly, the Ethics Advisory Board held 11 public hearings throughout the United States before recommending the lifting of the moratorium on the federal funding of in vitro fertilization research in 1979.

Institutional review boards (IRBs), which are required to monitor all research proposals involving human experimentation considered for federal funds through NIH or the National Science Foundation, have traditionally had few lay members. Recent policy regulations call for the inclusion of greater proportions of lay persons and for the opening of IRB meetings to the general public. Although these changes probably will not result in large infusions of public input, they do facilitate access and participation for a broader spectrum of the public. Weiner (1982), however, contends that lay participation on IRBs is diluted, because lay members seldom vote as a bloc and frequently are swayed by those with technical expertise. Also, although hearings are largely open to the general public, most of those attending and those giving testimony come from groups who have knowledge of the subject at hand and a specific position to argue.

A more innovative attempt to encourage effective public involvement was the Science for Citizens Program authorized by the 1976 National Science Foundation budget. This program was designed to improve public understanding of the issues, encourage scientists to participate in activities aimed at resolving policy issues, and enable nonprofit citizen groups to acquire technical expertise to assist them in dealing with the technical aspects of the issues. In addition to continuing traditional methods of educating and involving the public such as conferences and hearings, this program was to create regional science centers across the nation. Not unexpectedly, Science for Citizens generated strong opposition from those who perceived the program as primarily a means of subsidizing groups that would intervene to block programs that government officials had already authorized (Boffey 1976:349). Although money for the program has been appropriated since 1977, its focus has shifted toward funding research projects that involve science education for citizens and away from the more innovative and controversial original provisions.

A more direct mechanism for public input, and one which has potential mostly at the local level, is the citizen court. As proposed by Sheldon Krimsky (1978), the citizen court is a body governing science policy whose decisions are recognized as authoritative and legitimate.

It is patterned after the Cambridge Experimental Review Board, a panel of nine local nonscientists appointed to advise the mayor of Cambridge, Massachusetts, in 1975 when he feared that the public health might be threatened by proposed recombinant DNA research at Harvard University (Nelkin 1980:489). After three months of open public advisory hearings, this board recommended a draft ordinance to regulate the conduct of this research. In the process, both the nine panel laypersons and the Cambridge public had the opportunity to be educated on both the technical and social aspects of a sophisticated area of research. The President's Commission (1982:12n) notes that between 1977 and 1979, the states of New York and Maryland, and five towns in states ranging from New Jersey to California, followed the Cambridge model. Moreover, a second wave of legislation was enacted in several Boston-area communities in 1981 and 1982 specifically addressed to the commercial uses of DNA technology (Krimsky 1982).

Abrams and Primack (1980) recommend a "critical review and public assessment" procedure to provide the long-range and outside perspective which they believe is necessary for the resolution of controversies in technology. This two-stage approach to problem solving first involves independent scientists who identify problems and suggest alternative solutions through their preparation of a specific technical plan. The second stage of this approach would involve the widespread dissemination of the plan, accompanied by open public discussion and rigorous debate. Etzioni's (1973:55) two-tiered approach might be amenable to Abrams and Primack's proposal. In addition to the creation of a permanent national commission "charged with formulating alternative guidelines for public policy," Etzioni recommends a "myriad of local review boards" which would review individual decisions and attack specific problems. It seems that any of these proposals might be applicable to the problem of ensuring balanced input into health care policy.

According to Jon Miller and associates, (1980:299), issues involving science and technology appear to be susceptible to referenda. In about half of the states, referenda allow groups to bypass the legislature and the normal paths of influence and put a vote directly to the public. Other states have provisions for the legislature to submit laws voluntarily to the electorate for approval, and some states make the referendum process available only to local units of government. Often the result is to oversimplify and dramatize the issue, but, at the same time, referenda do heighten public awareness of problems. The question remains, however, of whether referenda merely place the resolution of technical issues before the least interested and informed persons in society. It has also been questioned whether the public is genuinely educated through this process or simply exposed to the propaganda of competing groups with high stakes in the result. Miller et al. (1980:300) conclude that within the referendum context it is most difficult to stimulate the level of interest and information needed to make a rational decision in most scientific matters. Moreover, voting turnout continues to be low on referenda concerning all but the most poignant and dramatic problems.

Bipartisan Deception and Health Policy

In a recent book on the workings of the Bipartisan Commission on Social Security, Paul Light concludes that there are certain public issues that are best dealt with in secret negotiations outside of the public spotlight (1985). Those issues that involve cutting benefits or raising taxes, rather than distributing the government largess, he terms "dedistributive." Health care policy issues, particularly those concerning Medicare and Medicaid, appear to be prime examples. These issues, he argues, cannot be resolved in the public forum because they elicit insurmountable opposition from powerful interests on many sides. According to Light:

With the public and interest groups firmly opposed to most of the major options in the dedistributive agenda, Congress and the President are well advised to build prenegotiated packages outside the constitutional system, returning to the normal process only at the last minute. (1985)

Light argues that the opportunity for closed-door negotiation must therefore be returned to Congress.

Light advocates that bipartisan commissions act mainly as fronts for secret bargains made between the president and congressional leaders. This process circumvents the need to debate and defend the various alternatives in public. Just as the Commission on Social Security Reform provided the opportunity for a "gang of nine" to build a compromise, wrap it in a bipartisan flag, and ram it through Congress, so Congress might deal with the painful choices concerning health allocation and rationing.

Although this approach might seem at first glance an efficient way to make health care allocation decisions, any efforts to eliminate the public contribution to health policymaking are likely to be counterproductive in the long run. Unlike Social Security, which was explicitly established as a national program and has existed in that form for half a century, health care has a complex mixture of private and public dimensions with extremely elusive jurisdictional boundaries. Even the single federal program of Medicare is not a promising target for the secret bargaining approach. Even major adjustments in Social Security benefits and taxes cannot be compared in scope to the life-and-death stakes involved in specific allocation decisions. Medical allocation policy which establishes priorities about who lives and who dies should not be made in secret negotiation sessions, no matter how efficient they may appear from a decision-making perspective. Even in the absence of efforts to establish policy covertly, an unreasonable share of health care decisions are being made without adequate public input. Legitimizing deception by government leaders under the guise of bipartisan commissions would frustrate, rather than facilitate, progression towards a meaningful and lasting resolution of our problems.

A New Branch: The Council for Long-Range Societal Guidance?

Lester Milbrath (1986) contends that a major failing of our system in dealing with crisis comes from the fact that our government does not have the capability for long-range future planning. Milbrath (1986:12) explains that good judgment includes the ability to think systematically about the future. Since current governmental institutions are too busy with urgent problems and have very little time to consider long-range questions, he recommends the creation of a special unit designed to provide society with a much better understanding of where it is headed and what steps must be taken to get where we want to go.

To this end, Milbrath proposes establishing, as part of the national government, a Council for Long-Range Societal Guidance. The special charge of the council would be to look to the long-range consequences of proposed government actions and provide guidance to leaders and citizens. The council would engage in long-range forecasting and develop possible future scenarios. It would also monitor conditions and changes in society, facilitate social learning, enhance citizen dialogue and thinking about the issues, and make recommendations to public officials based on thorough research and deep thought. Milbrath conceives of the council as composed of thirty generalists who have demonstrated a high capacity for thinking about broad social issues. These generalists, however, would be aided by two or more competing forecasting teams and adequate staffing to ensure an open flow of information and ideas. As a result of the council's efforts, the public interest would be "given a greater chance to become defined by careful, intellectual, holistic, long-term analysis, instead of simplistic, sloganized appeals to short-term interests" (Milbrath 1986:24).

Although the specifics of Milbrath's proposal might or might not be feasible or desirable, the concept of a new governmental mechanism to provide a future-oriented dialogue over health care issues is attractive. As long as the existing institutions fail to give adequate attention to the initiation and estimation stages of the policy process and are unable or unwilling even to set reasonable priorities and goals for health care, resolution of allocation problems is impossible. I agree strongly with Milbrath that "well-deliberated long-range policies offer better solutions than hasty patchwork actions" (1986:33). Unfortunately, as noted throughout this book, fragmented, piecemeal, and simplistic attempts to deal with the complex problems concerning the allocation of health care resources are the norm. The resulting policies continue to fall far short of what is needed as we grapple with continually more difficult decisions.

Alternative Mechanisms: A Summary

The difficult problems inherent in any decision to allocate and ration scarce medical resources require mechanisms designed to provide more adequate public as well as expert input. Although I believe that an ambitious innovation such as Milbrath's council would be the most efficient way of attacking these problems, revised national commissions, with expanded public hearings supplemented by more extensive survey data and widespread dissemination of the conclusions, would seem to be a valuable beginning. Although there are inherent limitations both in the commission approach and in public hearings, they appear to provide an adequate foundation for a broader dialogue over the issues. The President's Commission for the Study of Ethical Problems and its various reports on securing access to medicine represents a beginning in attempting to clarify the basic issues, although as noted by Mendeloff, the commission tended to avoid explaining the ethical justifications for its recommendations. He concludes that "while commissions have useful functions to serve, on hotly controversial issues, they are unlikely to provide the principled guidance that some will expect them to provide" (Mendeloff 1985:89).

Medical policymaking requires mechanisms and a process through which all interests can be represented, including scientists and clinicians, interest groups, and the general public, since all have a role to play and unique characteristics which make their input critical. Experts can provide a technical foundation upon which the public can make an informed choice. Because interest groups provide the basic link, however imperfect, between the public and the decision makers, it is crucial that their input be guaranteed. Finally, the general public must be educated as to the alternatives available as well as the state of medical technology, and ultimately must be called upon to provide input concerning social priorities. Milbrath comments, "A complex public dialogue on these matters will help provide a basis for evaluating new ideas should the time come when peoples' minds are more open" (1986:35–36).

Although it is of some urgency that effective mechanisms be established for ensuring input into decision making by all concerned, it is reasonable that effort first be directed at adapting current channels to the maximum extent possible before rushing to create new ones. I agree with Milbrath (1986:6) that the best strategy at this stage is to consolidate the best of what we have and amend it so that it works better in creating forward-looking public policy.

5

Prospects for the Future: Making the Hard Choices

In order to avert a disaster in health care, difficult allocation and rationing decisions must be made. This will require a continuing emphasis on cost containment, but any resolution of the problem will also necessitate major alterations in the way health care is perceived by Americans. We must replace our haphazard and patchwork means of allocating resources, which is both inequitable and irrational, with a clearcut set of goals and priorities for resource distribution. Although I argue that this will best be accomplished through a shift in emphasis from high-technology, curative medicine to a broad preventive approach, that is an issue that society must decide in its dialogue over goals and priorities. Whatever decisions are made, the trade-offs must be clarified.

A second theme which must be reemphasized here is the need to alter drastically public expectations and demands concerning health care. This, in turn, necessitates a modulation of basic values concerning rights and responsibilities. Although the government has a role to play in educating the public to the problems and in guaranteeing a public forum for dialogue on how to resolve them, government action cannot be successful alone, without accompanying transformations of public expectations and behavior. This chapter describes several of these transformations and analyzes the problems in effecting them within the American value system and health care tradition.

Rationing and Individual Rights to Health Care

One of the difficulties that must be faced in any scheme to ration health care resources in the United States emanates from the emphasis given to individual rights in the liberal value system. Although considerations of the common good or societal good are important in this system, they are largely secondary to the consideration of individual rights. As noted in chapter 1, Americans have come to consistently expect increasing levels of health care as a right or entitlement. Once a new technology has ceased to be experimental, demands for universal access arise within the individual rights context. Although the full theoretical foundations of this approach are complex, one clear basis is the natural rights tradition.

Natural rights theories evolved prior to the eighteenth century as a defense of human liberty and autonomy against the oppressive powers of the state. These theories are founded on the assumption that there is a set of rights so basic to human existence that they are independent of the existing legal principles of any given society. Every human is obliged to respect the natural rights of others—rights that are morally fundamental and inalienable. In his *Second Treatise on Government*, seventeenth-century English philosopher John Locke maintained that the primary job of the state is to secure these rights for its citizens. Natural rights theories are intuitively attractive even though in practice they fail to provide much guidance in decision making, especially in the area of biomedical policy.

There are two basic problems in applying the concept of natural rights to questions raised by medical technologies. First, an inherent problem in the natural rights approach is delineating specifically what the fundamental human rights are. There is some general agreement on this, but the inclusion of or emphasis on specific rights is subjective and varies from one theorist to the next. Most commonly these rights are described only in general terms, as in Locke's "life, liberty, and property," and the priorities among them are often confused or unstated.

A second problem that arises most prominently in health care issues is who qualifies as human; i.e., what characteristics are necessary for human existence? This question is central to any definition of rights and obligations. If, as Norman Bowie and Robert Simon (1977) contend, rights give us basic human dignity and allow us to respect persons as ends in themselves, then the definition of "person" is crucial. It is easy to say that all humans have natural—i.e., "human"—rights, but in practice it has never been that straightforward. Society has always set arbitrary boundaries, whether by age or socioeconomic status, on rights considered basic. For instance, voting is considered a fundamental civil right and a protection of one's interests, yet there is no universal acceptance of the criteria for exercising this fundamental right.

Although there have always been problems in defining those persons entitled to particular rights, within the context of medical technology it is becoming more and more difficult to define human life. For example, the irreversibly comatose patient is biologically alive and thus retains certain rights, but it has been questioned whether such life is a fully human existence and whether a person in that condition should continue to be afforded full human rights (Hardin 1974). One problem with defining "human" at present is that medical technology has so drastically altered the conditions of life that our traditional definitions become meaningless or at least ambiguous. The introduction of the concept of "brain death" has produced great confusion in the political institutions designed to protect rights.

One of the long-standing debates in Western political philosophy is the conflict between these rights on the one hand and the obligations of individuals on the other. One result has been to draw a distinction between what are termed "negative" and "positive" rights. Negative rights are those that impose obligations on others to refrain from interfering with the rights bearer. John Locke, for instance, places almost exclusive reliance on one's obligation to refrain from interfering with another's life, liberty, or property. Each person under such conditions has a sphere of autonomy that others are obliged not to violate, but no one is further obliged to take positive action to provide that person with property, liberty, or life. One is entitled to protection of certain rights but has no claims on others to guarantee them.

By contrast, positive rights are those that impose obligations on others to provide those goods and services necessary for each individual to have at least a minimally decent level of human existence. Joel Feinberg (1973:59) makes the distinction as follows: "A positive right is a right to other persons' positive actions; a negative right is a right to other persons' omissions or forbearances. For every positive right I have, someone else has a duty to do something; for every negative right I have, someone else has a duty to refrain from doing something" (1973:59). Although the necessary level of positive rights is not clearly defined, this concept requires the presence of institutions that assure a minimal level of material well-being, through the redistribution of goods and services if needed. Tom Beauchamp and James Childress (1979:51) suggest that "much confusion in moral discourse about public policies governing biomedicine" can be traced to the failure to distinguish positive rights from negative rights. The negative rights approach envisions the state as a referee among competing interests so that the natural rights of all are protected, while the positive rights approach implies positive action by the state to provide for the welfare of its citizens. Those persons who focus exclusively on negative rights obviously would attack the implementation of positive rights as an unjustified restriction on the liberty of those asked to take positive action to protect the rights of others. However it is approached, the natural rights perspective fails to provide a set of rights upon which everyone would agree.

Controversies concerning each of the four health care areas of focus in this book are intractably linked to society's perceptions of rights. The degree to which society allocates scarce medical resources to transplantation of organs and neonatal intensive care units will reflect closely the extent to which claims by individuals for these services are viewed as legitimate. Large expenditures to extend the lives of a small proportion of persons for relatively short periods will not be justified on the grounds of societal good, but rather on the basis of individual rights to lifesaving procedures. The question turns primarily on the definition of the right to health care as a positive claim on society to provide the necessary technologies for a person to live. In like manner, the allocation of societal resources for technologies aiding reproduction is dependent in large part on views concerning the right of reproduction. Despite inconsistent public policy, one of the most basic sets of rights in American culture relates to freedom to bear children. Until now, however, reproduction has been viewed primarily as a negative right. In other words, with few exceptions, adults have the right to have as many children as they desire. Or, conversely, if they choose not to have children, they have the right to avail themselves of contraception, sterilization, and abortion techniques. In the absence of a compelling state interest that overrides the rights of the person, the individual has a right to reproduce as long as this action harms no one. With the emergence of technology-mediated reproduction, however, the scope of procreative choice is drastically extended.

Reproductive technologies raise the question of whether reproductive autonomy should be logically extended, to become a positive right—a claim upon society to assure, through whatever means possible, the capacity to reproduce. If the right to procreation is interpreted as a positive one, then an infertile person might have a claim to these technologies. Under such circumstances, individuals who are unable to afford those treatments necessary to achieve reproduction could expect society to guarantee access. A woman with blocked fallopian tubes would have a claim to in vitro fertilization. An infertile man would be ensured participation in artificial insemination techniques or access to corrective surgery, if feasible. Once procreative rights are regarded as positive, however, drawing reasonable boundaries becomes difficult. Does a woman who is unable to carry a fetus to term, because of the absence of a uterus or some other condition, have a legitimate claim to a surrogate mother? Wherever the lines are drawn, some individuals are likely to have limited opportunity to have children. The advent of the new technologies of reproduction raises serious questions. Any shifts towards a positive rights perspective will accentuate the already growing demand for these technologies and encourage entrepreneurs to provide a broad variety of these reproductive services.

Finally, few medical issues have greater potential for pitting the rights of two persons against each other than those concerned with the environment for fetal development. Although most cogent in cases of fetal surgery and coerced caesarean sections for the benefit of the fetus, the complete dependence of the developing fetus on the mother creates a web of maternal responsibilities that might counter her own right to autonomy and privacy in reproduction and childbearing. At times she might be legally restrained from performing some action that under other circumstances would be considered a personal choice, for instance smoking cigarettes or drinking alcohol. Although the Supreme Court has recognized that the parent-child relationship is special, entailing constitutional protection of parental discretion, it has also ruled that "the state has a wide range of power for limiting parental freedom and authority in things affecting the child's welfare" (*Prince v. Massachusetts*, 1944). Considerable deference is given to the rights of the mother. However, the state also has an interest in protecting children who are unable to protect themselves, and it has the power to do so under the parens patriae doctrine. Although our society generally presumes that parents will act in the best interest of their child, the law is clear that in addition to parental rights there are corresponding duties to act responsibly in the parenting role. Parental discretion can be limited when it violates the best interest of the child, whether born or unborn.

Full freedom in procreation for a woman includes the capacity to make all decisions during gestation and in giving birth to the child, once she decides to have the child. What she eats, where she works, what type of recreational activity she participates in, and whether she smokes are her decisions alone. However, because a pregnant woman's choices in these disparate areas might adversely affect the fetus, conflicts will arise. John Robertson (1983:437ff) makes a valuable distinction between the woman's right to procreate and her right to bodily integrity during the course of pregnancy. The conflicts here arise in the management of the pregnancy only after the woman has made her decision to conceive and exercised her constitutional choice whether or not to abort the fetus. Only after she decides to forgo her right to abortion and the state chooses to protect the fetus does the woman lose her liberty to act in ways that might adversely affect the fetus. Although a woman is under no obligation to become pregnant or even to allow the fetus to remain, once she has done these things she assumes obligations to the fetus that limit her autonomy (Robertson 1983:437ff).

Problems, then, arise in balancing out negative as well as positive rights and in determining whose rights take precedence in cases of conflict. In addition, any rights must be viewed within a broader social context that includes consideration of other values such as fairness and equity. Although a person might believe he or she has a right to a transplant operation, the realization that expending up to 100 units of blood and many thousands of dollars on an operation that has a low chance of restoring the recipient to a reasonable quality of life diverts resources from many other persons who would benefit more may make such surgery seem unfair. Questions abound in medicine as to what legitimate claim a person has on health care resources. It is clear that the more broadly we define an individual's positive right to these resources, the more constraints we place on the rights of others. Any policy decision to limit the claims of citizens covered by public health care plans risks discriminating against those persons who lack adequate private resources and raises questions of equity.

The central problem in expanding our notions of a positive right to health care is in setting reasonable boundaries. It is one thing to argue that all persons have a right to primary health care. It is quite another to assume that this right encompasses guaranteed access to a full range of curative or rescue technologies. Within the framework of scarce medical resources and virtually unlimited, though extremely expensive, technological intervention possibilities, constraints on what a right to health care entails must be established and enforced, no matter how difficult that might be. Someone has to pay for each person's claim on medical resources. When these costs become prohibitive, rights must be defined more narrowly.

In addition to the need for setting reasonable boundaries of rights to health care, we must reinstitute the notion of individual responsibility for health. Every right ought to carry with it a corresponding obligation to those upon whom the claim is levied. This is especially relevant in attempts to tie allocation and rationing criteria to individual lifestyle choice. It could be argued that in order to claim societal health resources, a person should be expected to act responsibly and not unduly contribute to the risk of ill health. Although people have a right to design their own lifestyle, if they choose to engage in practices and behavior that puts them at high risk, they should be prepared to relinquish their claim on societal health care resources. By not balancing their rights with responsibilities, they would surrender positive extensions of those rights. The concept of responsibility, then, places rights in a social context and allows an observer to set priorities among rights according to the extent to which each interest is affected. In order to determine the rights that are appropriate, each application would have to be analyzed carefully within this more complex and dynamic context. The responsibility of society toward particular individuals or groups would have to be gauged and their freedom of expression and choice be balanced against their broader responsibilities to society.

The distinction between positive and negative rights is clear in cases of unhealthy or high-risk lifestyle choices. The right not to wear seat belts, for instance, must be weighed against the positive right to medical resources if one is injured because seat belts were not used despite the substantial burden such injuries place on society in the aggregate. It is necessary to decide how it is most appropriate for society to preempt rights: either pass mandatory seat belt laws and constrain the right not to wear the belt, or refuse to allocate societal resources to treat persons injured because they failed to take this action.

A preventive approach places restrictions on the negative right—the right not to be interfered with—and justifies state intervention on grounds of avoiding the future health costs associated with this behavior. Obviously, this means that the right of many people to choose whether to wear seat belts or not will be constrained in order to protect the health of the few people who are in an accident and would be injured more seriously if they chose not to take this preventive measure. Although this approach seems most reasonable, perhaps the more direct threat of rationing resources away from those injured while not wearing seat belts is also appropriate. The same approach could be used to penalize persons who fail to take other preventive actions, but only with severe consequences for the concept of positive rights. Using this approach, cigarette smokers could continue to exercise that lifestyle choice, but they would lose their claim upon society for health resources to treat the results of their behavior. The same could be done for voluntary obesity, alcohol consumption, promiscuity, and so forth. Understandably, this approach requires a complete revision of the prevailing notion of rights in the United States. Whereas the conventional notion of rights largely excludes responsibility for personal behavior, this revised concept would shift emphasis heavily toward responsibility. Furthermore, those persons who failed to act responsibly would lose in large portion their claim upon societal health resources.

Individual Responsibility for Health

The debate over the role of individual choice in determining personal health, although now intensifying, is far from new. As noted in chapter 1, the ancient Greeks stressed the effects of behavior on health. According to Plato, individuals have a responsibility to live in a manner that prevents illness. Those who do not have no claim on community resources for treatment. A virtuous citizen lives a life of moderation and exercises strict self-control. Likewise, the Greek physician Galen concluded that persons who allow harm to come to their bodies when there exists knowledge and the possibility of life's action to prevent it are morally culpable.

This view of individual blame for illness remained prevalent until the end of the nineteenth century. Health was assumed to be within the reach of each person, given a modicum of self-control and motivation. Each person was, in great measure, the guardian and preserver of his or her own health. Illness was a state individuals brought upon themselves through ignorance or intemperance of habit. The logical extension of this approach was to blame the victim. Even today, there is an assumption among many persons that the victims of illness or disease are being punished for their own failings. As evidence of the currency of this viewpoint, one need not look beyond the reaction of some fundamentalist religious leaders to AIDS.

Although it is doubtful that the concept of individual responsibility for health was ever fully displaced, in the early twentieth century knowledge about the relationship between poor social conditions and disease, and a resulting heightened social awareness, shifted emphasis toward societal responsibility for public health. There emerged the notion that society, not the individual, has the means to overcome poverty and disease, and the responsibility for maintaining the health of its people. To a large extent, this view developed from the fact that much disease in the latter nineteenth century was caused by inadequate water and sewage systems and by abhorrent working conditions over which individuals had little control. Ironically, this emphasis on social responsibility led to an increased paternalism which assumed that individuals were incapable of controlling their own health. Responsibility for disease prevention measures was placed on patients and their physicians, but public health programs proliferated to ameliorate social conditions deemed unhealthy. Through the 1960s at least, the emphasis was on the social right of the individual to health care. In contrast, individual responsibility for personal health was downplayed and those persons who raised the issue were criticized as lacking a social conscience.

Several seemingly unrelated trends in the last several decades, however, have resulted in a shift back toward an emphasis on individual responsibility for personal health. Because this approach confronts, and indeed threatens, the prevailing belief in individual rights and social responsibility, there has been no shortage of critics who view this pattern as regressive and dangerous. Allegrante and Green (1981) argue that this approach to disease prevention can deteriorate into "victim-blaming" if it becomes too strident and one-sided and fails to recognize the responsibility of society and government to develop and execute public policies that ameliorate conditions which help engender the unhealthful behaviors people adopt. If the so-called voluntary behavior of individuals is the result of socioeconomic and cultural factors, then blaming the individual wrongly evades the real cause, which is rooted in underlying social inequities. At the base of this criticism, then, is the ideological debate over the extent to which lifestyles are determined by individual or societal forces. Veatch admits that while it would be a serious problem if the voluntarist theory led to the abandonment of social responsibility, "important values are affirmed in the view that the human is in some sense responsible for his own medical destiny. that he is not merely the receptacle for external forces" (1980:53).

Despite this ongoing debate, the confluence of several developments is placing defenders of the social responsibility approach in a precarious position. First, the nature of health problems has changed drastically since the era of the public health reform movement. While the control of disease at the turn of the century depended upon economic development and the establishment of environmentally oriented health policies and agencies to fund them, the major health problems today increasingly are based directly on the behavior and living habits of the individual. According to John Knowles:

The idea of individual responsibility has been submerged to individual rights—rights, or demands, to be guaranteed by government and delivered by public and private institutions. The cost of sloth, gluttony, alcoholic intemperance, reckless driving, sexual frenzy, and smoking is now a national, and not just an individual, responsibility. This is justified as individual freedom—but one man's freedom in health is another man's shackle in taxes and insurance premiums. I believe the idea of a "right" to health should be replaced by the idea of an individual moral obligation to preserve one's own health—a public duty if you will. The individual then has the "right" to expect help with information, accessible services of good quality, and minimal financial barriers. (1977:59)

Similarly, Lowrance points out that as the death toll from communicable diseases has lessened, mortality has shifted to degenerative diseases which are attributable either to personal lifestyle or to causative agents in the environment (1982:100). Both of these factors are controllable if we as individuals and as a community are willing to reconsider our current goals of progress, free lifestyle, and the affluent standards of living that accrue from an industrial society, and modify our personal behavior especially concerning what we eat, drink, smoke, and otherwise ingest. At present, an unreasonably high proportion of early deaths result from heart disease and cancer, both tied to some extent to lifestyle. Hamburg (1982) notes that half of the mortality from the ten leading causes of death in the United States is strongly influenced by lifestyle. Behavioral factors contribute to much of our burden of illness, and this is not limited to the adult population. Brunswick and Messeri (1986:56) conclude that "lifestyle factors were observed to have an independent and additive contribution toward increasing morbidity" among urban black youth, both male and female. Furthermore according to Lowrance, "motor vehicles and other accidents kill the most children under 14; for black males between the ages of 15 and 24, homicide is the largest threat; cirrhosis of the liver is the fourth leading cause of death for people between 25 and 64" (1982:101).

Reinforcing this trend toward reevaluating the extent of morbidity and mortality that are directly tied to individual behavior is the current concern over the costs of health care. The insurmountable economic burden of medical care, to which the individual right–societal responsibility approach has contributed, is intensifying pressures to reduce or at least contain costs wherever possible. Because the need for the most expensive medical interventions such as long-term intensive care and organ transplantation is frequently a product of unhealthy individual action, it is likely that individual behavior that contributes to the need for these massive expenditures will be scrutinized more and more closely.

Moreover, because few persons today pay fully for their own medical care—the burden being shared by third-party payers including the government—"illness nowadays is a social event, a social expense" (Harsanyi and Hutton 1981:258). This means that people who try to take care of themselves are helping underwrite the costs incurred by those who fail to do so. Understandably, there is an increasingly vocal demand to shift the monetary burden to those individuals who knowingly take the health risks. Results of this demand can be seen in moves toward lower insurance premiums for nonsmokers, recommendations to raise the tax on alcoholic beverages to pay for alcohol abuse programs, and corporate incentives for participation in physical fitness programs.

Considerable initiative for these actions comes from distaste at having to pay for someone else's bad habits. Kenneth Warner (1983) estimates that the average nonsmoker must pay one hundred dollars in taxes and additional insurance premiums per year to cover the medical costs of smokers. This growing demand for societal action reflects a desire for protection from the costs of calamities others bring upon themselves—in other words, it is a demand for fairness (Wikler 1978). The specter of unbounded increases in health care costs, reflected in skyrocketing medical insurance premiums, fuels the demand that persons engaging in a high risk or unhealthy behavior pay their own way. This individual responsibility model is in direct contrast with the social responsibility model in which the individual is not held personally accountable for the results of his or her actions. Whereas the latter model recoils from placing blame on the victim, the present perspective makes an explicit goal of assigning responsibility, of finding fault in the individual.

James Vaupel (1980:109) warns that much of the enthusiasm about altering lifestyles seems to be founded on a desire for morality rather than health, harkening back to Aristotle's holistic notion of health as the path to virtue. Vaupel (1980:108) contends that while enough is presently known about the impact of personal behavior on health in order to justify efforts to begin developing more effective health and safety education and incentive programs, success hinges on clearer research findings concerning exactly what individuals can do to take better care of themselves.

According to Sher (1983:11), many medical needs are foreseeable and avoidable consequences of individuals' actions. Where the condition requiring care is predictable and avoidable and the person behaves such as to incur the condition, it might be termed "deserved." Although the medical needs created by such irresponsible behavior may not create valid claims on society for aid, it is unlikely that we would deny medical service even to those who have voluntarily brought on their own conditions. "It seems inhumane, and indeed indecent, to let someone suffer or die for lack of easily available treatment," according to Sher (1983:12). Despite this caveat, Sher concludes that when political and economic constraints make the meeting of all health needs impossible, "even those who accept the ideal of freedom may endorse some restrictions on choice to correct for unavoidable distortions of judgment" (Sher 1983:12). One such person is Robert Veatch:

> I reach the conclusion that it is fair, that it is just, if persons in need of health services resulting from true, voluntary risks are treated differently from those in need of the same services for other reasons. In fact, it would be unfair if the two groups were treated equally. (1980:54)

A related matter concerns the disposition of cases involving individuals who have consciously chosen not to purchase health insurance. Although it is irrational in these times not to protect future financial security by purchasing health insurance, many people who can afford such insurance allocate their resources to more immediate and tangible expenditures. Questions arise as to the obligation of society to pay for needed health care for these individuals and the fairness of making others in society assume the risk that they avoided covering. Although it is not realistic to expect people to sacrifice food, clothing, and other necessities to buy medical insurance they may never use, one could argue that health insurance ought to take precedence over video recorders, new automobiles, and so forth. However, as legitimate needs in society have come to encompass a broad array of material goods, any attempts to ensure voluntary participation would fail. This dilemma, of course, could be largely resolved by the creation of a national health insurance plan that would mandate such participation by requiring payment of all wage earners making above some minimum level.

The individual responsibility model becomes especially appropriate in light of the shift toward viewing health care as a positive right, because positive rights are accompanied by more extensive obligations. As noted earlier, while negative rights are correlative only with the negative duty not to interfere with the rights of others, positive rights entail the duty to provide others in society with a minimal level of goods and services. Conversely, the recipient of positive rights has an obligation to other possessors of that right not to waste those goods and services. By transforming the right to health care from a negative to a positive right, considerably more obligations are placed on the recipients of that right.

Furthermore, the nineteenth-century model of social responsibility for health is no longer appropriate because of the aforementioned change in the nature of the health problems confronting us. Preventive health care is no longer a matter of mobilizing resources to overcome unavoidable public hazards such as poor sanitation and water supplies. Most, although certainly not all, health hazards today are avoidable by individual action. The individual responsibility model therefore makes even more sense because the individual alone can now avoid many diseases. Whereas in the past, the major causes of disease were out of the individual's hands, today the individual can make a difference. In an era where social action was necessary to overcome threats to health, it did not make sense to hold the individual responsible. Although society and its agents retain the responsibility to ameliorate where possible the causes of diseases, increasingly individuals can play an important role in their own health. Writes Veatch, "Even for those conditions that do not yet lend themselves to such direct voluntary control, the chronic diseases and even genetic diseases, there exists the possibility of purposive, rational decisions that have an indirect impact on the risk" (1980:52). With that capacity comes a heightened individual responsibility for health, especially within the context of health care as a positive right through which the individual has claims upon society to provide some minimal level of medical care. Although we should not abandon the social responsibility model, it must be tempered with a heavy dose of individual responsibility.

Public Attempts to Alter Lifestyle Choices

Until recently, public incursions into matters of individual lifestyle have been considered far outside the legitimate sphere of government activity and roundly condemned. The evidence here suggests that this perception is weakening, especially where lifestyle can be causally related to health problems. For instance, in 1979 the Surgeon General's report entitled *Healthy People* concluded that the foremost causes of illness lie in individual behavior and could be met most effectively through extensive changes in the lifestyles of most persons. Although this report was hailed by the Carter administration and others as the foundation for a "second public health revolution," it sparked considerable debate over the proper approach to health care (Neubauer and Pratt 1981). In discussing the high incidence of early death in the affluent United States, Vaupel (1980:119) explains that although some health factors are beyond our control, "it does seem plausible that factors—such as health care, unhealthy habits and pollution levels—that can be affected by public policies play a major role" (1980:119). He is especially concerned with the high correlations between infant mortality rates and improper diet and use of drugs by pregnant women.

The government is under substantial pressure from many interests to broaden the scope of its involvement in personal lifestyle determination. Whether out of concern for fairness, paternalism, strict economics, or a blame-the-victim mentality, momentum is increasing for aggressive efforts to effect changes in individual behavior deemed dangerous to health. This is clearly evident for smoking and drinking. Attempts to ban smoking in public places and to remove the drinker from the highways are being approached with near missionary zeal by an array of organized interest groups that are lobbying hard, particularly in state legislatures. Although their motivations and proposed strategies differ, proponents of government involvement effectively utilize impressive data on the social and economic costs of the targeted behavior to buttress their arguments.

Vigorous debate over public involvement in programs designed to reduce morbidity and mortality rates linked to personal behavior is assured, because there is powerful opposition to any constraints on individual behavior, no matter how injurious to that person's health. As noted by Miller, however, "virtually no public health measure of consequence can be cited that does not in some measure, according to someone's view, limit individual freedoms" (1984:553). Within the value context discussed in chapter 1 and its emphasis on personal rights, there are strong ideological presumptions against state action. Civil liberty proponents argue that competent adults have a right to engage in foolish and even self-destructive practices as long as they are not immediate threats to others. From both ideological liberals and conservatives, government intervention is railed against as an unwarranted intrusion upon personal autonomy—as an example of heavy-handed paternalism. For instance, liberal Senator Alan Cranston stated in response to the imposition of motorcycle helmet laws which were shown to dramatically reduce fatalities from motorcycle accidents: "This is an outrageous example of an overbearing, overprotective bureaucracy gratuitously trying to restrict the freedom of choice of the individual" (Moreno and Bayer 1985:39).

Moreno and Bayer (1985:37) contend that these critics of health promotion strategies have seized the ideological high ground and forced the advocates to defend state intervention solely on the basis of economic costs for society accruing from risky personal behavior. They argue that proponents of intervention would be on a more solid ethical ground in asserting the moral primacy of health itself as a social good (Moreno and Bayer 1985:37). The well-being of the members of the community is in itself a legitimate concern of public policy. Certainly health is a critical element of this well-being. Economic arguments alone, they argue, fail to justify ethically aggressive state intervention and can cut both ways. Similarly, Russell (1986:112) argues that while good health has intrinsic value and is worth paying for, by emphasizing cost savings, the most ardent proponents of prevention have put themselves in the untenable position of arguing that a preventive measure is a good investment only because it saves money. With this logic, the burden of proof is placed on the proponents to demonstrate that prevention is invariably the best monetary investment, which it may not be. Although the paucity of conclusive scientific data on the deleterious effects of many lifestyle practices on health and the impracticality of effective enforcement of intrusive social policy buttress the arguments of the opposition, they do not negate the need for vigorous debate over the issue.

Despite the continuing controversy over the role of government in altering personal behavior judged to be unhealthy, there is a wide range of mechanisms through which society might influence lifestyle choices. They range from education on the one hand, to explicit forms of coercion under the authority of law on the other. In between these extremes are a limitless array of positive and negative incentives. Noncoercive measures to encourage healthful lifestyles might include provision of jogging paths and bicycle lanes and access to healthful as opposed to junk foods. Financial incentives such as lowered insurance premium rates, decreased taxes, and other rewards for prudent personal lifestyles easily degenerate into disincentives which, in effect, punish individuals for socially unacceptable practices. Alcohol and cigarette taxes designed to alter personal behavior are one clear form of disincentive. For instance, Warner (1986) estimates that an 8 to 16 cent tax increase per pack of cigarettes would encourage 1 to 2 million young persons and up to 1.5 million adults to quit smoking or not to start, thus preventing hundreds of thousands of premature smoking-related deaths. In most instances, however, such simplistic approaches are inequitable and regressive in that they are hardest on the less wealthy, especially the poor. A more subtle means of enforcing compliance is by establishing standards of duty under the tort system and assigning liability for personal practices that violate court-enforced societal norms. Any policy to change lifestyles will probably depend on some combination of incentives and disincentives—in other words, rewards or punishments—for societally defined acceptable and unacceptable individual action. The principles of the HPA listed in figure 5.1 illustrate some of the participants who should be involved.

One critical question which deserves substantially more attention is how society sets the baseline for incentives and disincentives. There is a latent assumption that the newest technologies somehow ought to set the baseline. Although not surprising, given the strength of the technological imperative in our system, this approach must be reevaluated. As noted throughout this book, the finite resources available for health care can never meet the infinite demands which medical innovations seem to foster. By building an incentive/disincentive structure on the baseline of the newest technologies, there is little to discourage continually escalating use of these innovations. A shift toward the individual responsibility model must include an awareness of any inconsistencies in the incentive/disincentive structure.

The most coercive mechanisms for controlling personal lifestyle choices are regulations that specifically prohibit certain practices under threat of law. The strength of the outcry against mandatory motorcycle helmet laws in the mid-1970s demonstrates the difficulty of framing regulatory policies that are perceived as impinging upon personal choice in the pluralist United States. Similar difficulties in

Figure 5.1
Selected Principles of the Health Policy Agenda for the American People

---

Principle 4–5. Health care providers and purchasers of health care have the mutual responsibility to make the most efficient and effective use of available health care resources; develop and promote safe and healthful life-styles for all Americans; and encourage active participation by individuals in the planning and implementation of their health care.

•   •   •   •

Principle 4–8. Health care professionals and other providers of health services should assume a major responsibility for the preparation and provision of educational information, incentives, and services to individuals and the public to promote health and prevent disease and disability. Representatives of government, industry, labor, and educational and philanthropic organizations should participate in these efforts. Emphasis should be given to preventive services for pregnant women, infants, and children.

Principle 4–9. Individuals have a personal responsibility to seek out and act on information that promotes a healthful life-style for themselves and those for whom they are responsible and should be given incentives for the pursuit of continuation of such conduct.

Principle 4–10. Employers should utilize their unique opportunity and responsibility to promote health and prevent disease and disability by taking every reasonable step to provide a safe and healthful workplace consistent with the nature and inherent risks of the employment activity; fully informing employees, their representatives, and government agencies of workplace practices and personal behavior that enhances the health of their employees.

•   •   •   •

Principle 4–19. When resources are finite, decision mechanisms should be available for the application of equitable criteria to determine that limitations should be imposed on the scope and intensity of care to be provided.

Source: Balfe et al. 1985.

enforcing mandatory seat belt laws and antismoking ordinances suggest that direct government efforts to regulate individual lifestyle, even to promote health and prevent illness, are likely to withstand neither constitutional tests nor public opinion. As noted in chapter 1, Americans value their freedom to select their own lifestyle and tend to react against direct government intervention, whether based upon economic or paternalistic rationales. Ultimately, this persuasion will be devastating unless some limits are set, as difficult a task as that might be.

In our society, education concerning the potentially harmful effects of personal practices on the individual's health is the most acceptable means of altering behavior. Although it is not as explicitly intrusive as other options discussed above, education can be selective and manipulative. Particularly in the United States, with its emphasis on mass persuasion, education efforts seldom are completely neutral nor, perhaps, should they be. The effectiveness of an education campaign, whether it be designed to encourage people to quit smoking, to obtain annual dental checkups, or to buckle up their seat belts, is measured by the extent to which individuals alter behavior. To some degree, every educational campaign has a message to sell—it advocates that a particular responsible choice be made.

Not surprisingly, education efforts are criticized from both sides in the lifestyles debate, although for different reasons. Some advocates of reform cite the minimal effectiveness of education programs as evidence that such efforts are a waste of resources and a subterfuge for inaction. In contrast, opponents argue that education efforts are not neutral either by design or effect. They contend that under the guise of education, individuals are manipulated. At the least, they are given the impression that if they do not change their behavior, they are being irresponsible. In spite of these problems, I believe that the most acceptable means for reducing unhealthy and unsafe personal behavior is education and that such education should come before habits are formed, preferably early in youth. James Vaupel (1980:107) notes, however, that a relatively low priority has been placed on health education in the United States. Well under 1 percent of total health expenditures are allocated to education. Moreover, the quality of existing health education efforts tends to be low and the results discouraging. Still, as explained by Ingelfinger (1980:143), preventive health measures are probably brought about more by education efforts through the media and society as a whole than by the medical profession. According to Ingelfinger, this means that the medical profession should not be expected to play a major role in altering detrimental lifestyles. Presumably, they should not ignore their educational responsibilities, either.

Rationing by Lifestyle

Although education is the most feasible means of promoting healthy personal lifestyles in our society, it alone is unlikely to drastically alter individual behavior because such behavior, no matter how destructive, has broad attraction to many people. Appeals to the individual's own future health as well as to more general social goals will fail to avert the need for expending a large proportion of the health care budget on conditions and diseases that are preventable.

In an age of scarce resources in which medical goods and services are rationed, the debate over lifestyle choice increasingly will focus on the extent to which lifestyle ought to influence rationing decisions. While the ethical controversy over this question will not abate, the economic/policy context necessitates moves toward that end. For Engelhardt:

> It will also be morally acceptable for society, if it pursues expensive life-saving treatment, to exclude persons who through their own choices increase the cost of care.... There is no invidious discrimination against persons in setting a limit to coverage or in precluding coverage if the costs are increased through free choice. (1984:70)

More than any of the other issues surrounding the rationing of medical resources, this aspect of lifestyle promises to be the most poignant. When should lifestyle criteria be expressly entered into the rationing equation? Who is responsible for establishing the criteria? What impact will this selection process have on the practice of medicine? Before examining these questions in depth, a brief survey of the current knowledge concerning lifestyles and health status is presented.

Personal Habits and Health: Alcohol, Cigarettes, and Diet

In their article, "High-Cost Users of Medical Care," Zook and Moore (1980) found that 13 percent of the patients accounted for as much hospital billing as did the other 87 percent. Since only one person in ten enters a hospital in any given year in the United States, these figures suggest that as few as 1.3 percent of the population consumes over half of the hospital resources used in a given year. More importantly for the purposes here, their results demonstrated that adverse lifestyles were noted more often in the medical records of high-cost than low-cost adult patients. "Alcoholism, heavy smoking, and obesity were particularly prominent," according to Zook and Moore (1980:1001). Patients in whom these habits were indicated required greater repeated hospitalization for an illness, thus increasing the "limit cost" of the illness. This small proportion of patients exerts disproportionate leverage on medical resources by repeated use of hospital facilities. The authors suggest: "Preventive incentives through insurance or health taxes on selected hazardous habits (or the commodities that they consume) may deserve careful attention in any debate on national health insurance" (1980:1001).

In a major longitudinal study of 7,000 people in Alameda County, California begun in 1965, researchers found that lifestyle choices are significantly associated with better health and lower death rates when adjusted for age. They found that the healthiest people usually were those who followed all or most of seven personal habits: (1) sleeping at least seven or eight hours per night; (2) eating breakfast; (3) rarely snacking between meals; (4) maintaining a reasonable diet; (5) not smoking; (6) drinking alcohol in moderation or not at all; and (7) often taking part in physical activity. A preliminary report of this research (Belloc and Breslow 1972:419) concluded that while each practice taken alone contributed to better health, those persons who followed all seven practices enjoyed health comparable to that of persons 30 years younger who followed few or none. Moreover, the death rate among men who followed all seven good health practices was only 28 percent that of men who followed three or fewer (Breslow and Enstrom 1980). These earlier findings, except for the contribution of breakfast and eating between meals, were reconfirmed in the final report (Berkman and Breslow 1983).

Three adverse lifestyles were identified as most critical by Zook and Moore and the Alameda study. This section describes the current state of knowledge regarding the impact of each lifestyle on health; discusses the problems inherent in attempts to influence these practices; and finally, analyzes the social implications of any attempts to allocate or ration medicine on the basis of individual lifestyles that necessitate the expenditure of considerable medical resources.

Alcohol-Related Illness

Alcohol is by far the most widely abused chemical in the western world and is implicated in more deaths than any other substance. Its chronic use in large quantities leads to marked deterioration in the user. According to West, "alcoholism and related problems may well embody the nation's most vexing set of health policy issues" (1984:26). Overall, alcohol-related costs impose an enormous burden on society in both economic and noneconomic terms. In its report to Congress, the National Institute on Alcohol Abuse and Alcoholism (NIAAA) estimated that in 1978, 10 million adults and 3.3 million teenagers suffered from alcohol problems (Noble 1978). The economic cost alone of alcohol problems for 1977 was calculated to total $50 billion (HHS 1983:95). A major component of this total was the excessive health care cost of approximately $17 billion, which in 1977 represented about 10 percent of the total U.S. health care expenditure. Assuming this percentage has remained fairly constant over the last decade, approximately $40 billion would have been expended for alcohol-related diseases in 1985. A 1983 Office of Technology Assessment report placed the total cost of alcohol-related problems at $120 billion. Although any estimates are crude, the costs of these problems are massive both to individuals and to society as a whole.

Many studies have demonstrated that heavy drinkers use considerably more medical resources than nondrinkers. Zook and Moore (1980) found that persons with alcohol-related illnesses consistently were found among the high-cost patients. Similarly, Forsythe, Griffiths, and Reiff (1982) concluded that the cost differentials between alcoholics and nonalcoholics are significant. Over a four-year period, alcoholics averaged almost 250 percent more inpatient/outpatient costs than nonalcoholics. Another study concluded that alcohol abusers incur $2,000 in extra medical treatment annually (HHS 1983:93). These figures are not surprising, because alcoholism is associated with an array of chronic medical problems that require continued medical care and repeated readmissions to treatment programs.

Overall mortality rates for abusers of alcohol are approximately two and one-half times those of the general population. Death from alcohol overdoses, alone or in combination with other drugs, accounts for about 10,000 deaths and perhaps 100,000 episodes of medical

Table 5.1
Estimated Deaths Related to Alcohol in the United States

Cause of Death	Number of Deaths (1975)	Percentage Related to Alcohol	Number Related to Alcohol
Alcohol as a direct cause			
Alcoholism	4,897	100	4,897
Alcoholic psychosis	356	100	356
Cirrhosis of the liver	31,623	41–95	12,965–30,042
Total	36,876	41–100	18,218–35,295
Alcohol as an indirect cause Accidents			
Motor vehicle	45,853	30–50	13,756–22,926
Falls	14,896	44	6,614
Fires	6,071	26	1,572
Other	33,026	11	3,666
Homicides	21,310	49–70	10,442–14,917
Suicides	27,063	25–37	6,766–10,013
Total	148,219	29–40	42,816–59,708
Overall Total	185,095	11–100	61,034–95,003

Source: NIAAA 1978:13.

intervention annually. Moreover, suicide, homicide, and automobile and other accidental deaths are considerably higher among heavy drinkers. Approximately 50 percent of the 45,000 or so highway deaths each year are attributed to inebriated drivers or pedestrians. From 1978 through 1984, the total number of alcohol-related traffic deaths ranged from 17,861 to 21,114 per year (Centers for Disease Control 1986:450). In addition, an estimated 10,000 alcohol-related deaths result from falls, fires, and other accidents each year. Although the figures vary substantially, deaths related to alcohol abuse have been estimated by various researchers to approach 100,000 (table 5.1). In any year this represents as many as 11 percent of the total deaths in the United States (Noble 1978).

Because the major focus here is on lifestyle choices and health, attention is directed toward those diseases that have been linked directly to alcohol usage. There is hardly a tissue or a function of the human body that is immune to the damaging effects of large amounts of alcohol. According to Wolf (1984:30)

The mechanisms of alcohol poisoning are both direct and indirect, either damaging cells and tissues of the body or distorting their function in some way so that control of secretions, the behavior of the circulation, and the absorption of nutrients or other aspects of the bodily economy are disrupted. Individual susceptibility to alcohol's effects appears to vary with genetic inheritance, with nutritional state, and in other lesser understood circumstances.

Heavy alcohol consumption has serious deleterious effects on the heart, liver, pancreas, immune and endocrine systems, blood, and brain.

There is no question that brain damage is a major hazard of alcoholism. Some degree of impaired brain function is likely to be found in the majority of diagnosed alcoholics (West 1984:11). Alcohol is also a cause of major mental illnesses, including acute alcoholic dementia and delirium tremens. In addition to diabetes, other endocrine effects are hypogonadism and feminization in the male (Lieber 1982) and suppression of the secretion of growth hormone (Prinz et al. 1980). Heavy alcohol consumption also has deleterious effects on both heart and skeletal muscle manifested by weakness and destruction of the muscle fibers (Slavin et al. 1983). Moreover, alcohol abuse accentuates the deposits of fat and scar tissue that ultimately lead to ischemic heart disease.

Heavy alcohol use has also been linked to lowering the resistance to infection, thereby explaining the heightened rates of mortality from pneumonia among alcoholics. Furthermore, alcohol abuse has been implicated in promoting the development of some forms of cancer, especially of the mouth, pharynx, larynx, esophagus, and liver. To this list, Eckhardt and associates (1981) add the possibility that alcohol abuse promotes cancer of the pancreas, colon, and prostate. Not only do alcoholic patients with cancer have lower survival rates, but also they have heightened probabilities of developing another primary tumor. As discussed in chapter 2, pregnant women who ingest large amounts of alcohol are at high risk of giving birth to children with fetal alcohol syndrome (FAS). The consumption of even small amounts of alcohol by the mother during pregnancy increases the risk of birth defects and is associated with decreased birth weight, increased rates of spontaneous abortion, and increased neonatal mortality.

Cirrhosis of the Liver. Although alcohol abuse is statistically associated with increased risk for the above diseases and conditions, the most direct damage from heavy alcohol consumption is to the digestive system. The entire gastrointestinal tract, the pancreas, and the liver are frequent victims. Of these, the liver is the organ most vulnerable to the injurious effects of chronic alcohol intake. Of the 10 million abusers of alcohol in the United States, an estimated 5 to 15 percent will develop cirrhosis of the liver, one of the leading causes of death in the western world (Lieber 1978). Senior (1983) found that death due to liver disease is the most rapidly increasing cause of death in Canada and that 80 percent of the cases are alcohol related. Although the rate of cirrhosis is declining in the United States, it remains the most common cause of death among alcoholics. Moreover, in some urban areas of the country, liver cirrhosis is the fourth leading cause of death among persons aged 25 to 60, exceeded only by heart and lung disease and cancer (Wooddell 1980:125).

Because it is primarily caused by alcohol consumption, cirrhosis of the liver is largely preventable. Most persons over 30 who die of cirrhosis have a history of drinking, usually at least ten to twenty years of excessive alcohol abuse. Importantly, the progression of the disease appears to be cumulative. When alcohol consumption stops, the liver ceases to deteriorate. Also, if consumption slows, deterioration also slows (Cook 1984:71). In addition to cirrhosis, other liver diseases associated with alcohol abuse are "fatty liver," causing impairment of the liver's ability to metabolize fats, and alcoholic hepatitis, both of which may progress to cirrhosis. An estimated 24 to 50 percent of alcoholics eventually develop hepatitis, perhaps as early as three months after the beginning of excessive alcohol consumption. The estimated mortality associated with alcoholic hepatitis varies from 10 to 40 percent, depending on the patients included (Wooddell 1980:129). In addition to the 30,000 lives lost to liver failure each year, the morbidity caused by these diseases is extensive and costly.

The Policy Issues. The policy impact of cirrhosis of the liver is amplified today because of the possibility of liver transplantation as a means of circumventing the destruction caused by alcohol abuse. As noted in chapter 2, liver transplants are especially controversial because the survival rates are as yet relatively low and the costs are high. They are also controversial because the most frequent medical indication for a liver transplant is liver failure caused by cirrhosis.

To date, there has been little sympathy for alcoholics with liver disease. Of all the habits discussed here, alcohol abuse is perhaps least empathized with by the general public and by medical professionals. Moreover, because of the potential damage from heavy alcohol consumption to other organs and bodily functions, the alcoholic generally represents a poor medical risk. Even if he or she survives the transplant, long-term survival depends also on the fitness of other organ systems, especially the heart, lungs, and pancreas. Many argue that if the root problem, alcohol abuse, is not controlled, there is little sense in giving the alcoholic a healthy liver only to have it too then damaged by alcohol. Why should society expend scarce resources to transplant a new liver into an alcoholic, when these resources could be used elsewhere to treat persons who are better medical risks?

As noted in the introduction to this chapter, there is a clear trend in public opinion towards promoting the right of persons who do not engage in unhealthy lifestyles to be protected from the social and economic burden of those who do. Because alcohol abusers traditionally have been treated with disdain by the public as a whole and because the costs of alcoholism are salient, debate over lifestyle choice and allocation of medical resources is likely to focus on this habit. What is the proper role of the government in reducing alcohol consumption and, therefore, altering the practices of many citizens?

Coercive measures are unlikely to work without a clear shift in attitudes concerning alcohol abuse. Although policies designed to discourage drinking, such as higher taxes on alcohol, the banning of advertising, and tougher drunken driving laws might reduce consumption, the experience with Prohibition illustrates the futility of more coercive intrusions into lifestyle choices in the United States. (While Prohibition failed miserably to legislate morality, and it is usually attacked on those grounds, Cook notes that "the most reliable statistical effects of alcohol abuse—mortality due to cirrhosis of the liver and to acute alcohol overdose—dropped dramatically during the early years of prohibition" [1984:66]. Alcohol consumption declined substantially, especially among the working class.) Certainly, more effective education and prevention efforts are warranted and should be targeted at high-risk populations, particularly the young. Beyond these efforts, the government will have little success unless the use of alcohol becomes socially unfashionable. Given the trends in alcohol consumption which have changed little among adults since 1970 (Cook 1984:72), there is little hope in the foreseeable future of a major attitudinal change.

Although no one would defend alcohol abuse on constitutional grounds, the choice whether to drink or not is viewed by many persons as a basic private decision. Recent evidence that the susceptibility of at least some persons to alcoholism is genetically determined, in combination with the possibility that a genetic marker for that trait may become available, adds another dimension to the issue (Schuckit 1985). Wolf (1984:46) suggests that "those who are genetically susceptible will be able to be identified and exposed to especially enriched and focused educational efforts" (1984:46). Such a policy, I believe, would engender substantial opposition, as would any policy designed to ration medicine so that sufferers from cirrhosis and other alcohol-caused diseases would be denied intensive and expensive treatment. Despite this expected reaction, pressures to ration treatment are currently building because of the increased economic burden of alcohol-related illnesses on society.

Smoking and Health

Imagine an observer who dwells on Halley's comet catching up each 76 years with the happenings to the purportedly intelligent life on this planet. Since the last fly-by in 1910, the planet has suffered two massive wars and a continuous succession of localized armed conflicts, killing tens of millions. Famine—attributable to unchecked population growth, irregular food distribution, and political ineptitude—also has killed a vast number of us. Surprisingly, however, these massive global calamities are rivaled in public health importance by a self-inflicted blight that also effects a staggering number of people.

During the comet's last circuit, one of the most important global killers has been tobacco (Rothman 1986:133).

Although the effects of smoking are not as pronounced physically as those of alcoholism, because a substantially larger proportion of persons partake of the habit, cigarette smoking is the major preventable cause of illness and death in America. Despite some success of the government antismoking campaign over the last two decades, over 50 million Americans continue to smoke. Warner and Murt (1983) estimate that the campaign has encouraged millions of people to quit smoking and millions not to initiate the habit and resulted in the avoidance of more than 200,000 premature deaths between 1964 and 1978. However, these premature deaths prevented constitute only a small fraction of the four million deaths attributable to smoking that occurred in the United States during that period.

Recent studies indicate that almost 10 percent of all medical costs are directly related to smoking (Luce and Schweitzer 1978). Cady (1982:1105) cites estimates that in Massachusetts the annual medical costs of smokers are $520 per person greater than for nonsmokers. This figure is equivalent to a cost of $1.10 per pack of cigarettes smoked in that state each year. According to Cady, "It would be informative for smokers to recognize that other people are paying even more than the cost of the package of cigarettes to subsidize the consequences of their habit" (1982:1105).

It is not surprising in light of these data that smoking represents the one personal habit that has been addressed by the national government. The 1964 Report of the Advisory Committee to the Surgeon General, *Smoking and Health*, concluded: "Cigarette smoking is a health hazard of sufficient importance in the United States to warrant remedial action" (HEW 1864:1). As a result, the Federal Cigarette Labeling and Advertising Act of 1965 required the Secretary of Health, Education, and Welfare to submit regular reports to Congress on the health consequences of smoking, together with legislative recommendations. The Office on Smoking and Health has maintained responsibility for this function and issues regular reports on the status of research. The 1979 *Smoking and Health* listed the following major health problems as being associated with cigarette smoking:

Cardiovascular diseases
Cancer
   Lung cancer
   Cancer of the larynx
   Oral cancer
   Cancer of the esophagus
   Bladder cancer
   Cancer of the kidney
   Cancer of the pancreas
Bronchopulmonary diseases
   Chronic bronchitis
   Emphysema
Peptic ulcer disease
Fetal growth retardation
Perinatal mortality

On the basis of over 30,000 studies involving many millions of individuals, the report concluded that "cigarette smoking is the single most important environmental factor contributing to premature mortality in the United States" (HEW, 1979b:2–9).

The lighted cigarette generates approximately 2,000 compounds, many of which have been identified as toxic and carcinogenic agents. Because of their high concentration in tobacco smoke, carbon monoxide, nicotine, and tars are judged most likely to contribute to the health hazards of smoking. Additionally, compounds considered probable health hazards even in smaller quantities are acrolein, hydrocyanic acid, nitric oxide and nitrogen dioxide in the gas phase, and cresols and phenol in the particulate phase. Suspected contributors to ill health include, among many others, acetone, benzene, formaldehyde, hydrogen sulfide, methyl alcohol, dimenthylamine, DDT, endrin, nickel compounds, and pyridene (HEW 1979b:1–29ff).

The overall mortality rate of male cigarette smokers is 1.7 times that of nonsmokers. The American Cancer Society (1982) estimates that 30 percent of all cancer deaths are associated with smoking. Moreover, as the number of cigarettes smoked increases, mortality rates also increase. Although mortality risk rates for diseases of the lung and various cancers are especially high among smokers, coronary heart disease is the leading killer. Extensive long-term research demonstrates conclusively that smoking is a major risk factor for an array of cardiovascular diseases which continue to be the largest cause of death in the United States. According to the Surgeon General (HEW, 1979b:1–15), cigarette smoking is causally related to coronary heart disease for both men and women. Moreover, cigarette smoking has been found to increase the risk of heart attack recurrence among survivors of cardiac arrest (Hallstrom, Cobb, and Ray 1986). From the perspective of preventive medicine, it is critical that cessation of smoking reduces the risk of morality from coronary heart disease significantly. After ten years off cigarettes, the former smoker's risk approaches that of the lifetime nonsmoker.

Next to chronic heart disease, cancer is the leading cause of death in the United States. More people die from lung cancer than from any other form. Undisputedly, cigarette smoking is a primary cause of lung cancer. The risk of developing lung cancer for individuals who smoke more than two packs of cigarettes a day is approximately 20 times that of nonsmokers. For every preventable death from highway accidents, there are approximately two deaths from lung cancer which could have been avoided if the individual had not smoked. The rates of lung cancer are increasing especially among women, who as a group registered the largest increase in cigarette smoking over the last decade. The risk of lung cancer is magnified with increased smoking as measured by the number of cigarettes smoked per day, the duration of smoking, the age at initiation of smoking, the degree of inhalation, and the tar and nicotine content of the cigarettes smoked. As with heart disease, ex-smokers experience decreasing lung cancer mortality rates which after not smoking for 10 to 15 years approach the rates of nonsmokers.

In addition to its relationship to lung cancer, smoking is a significant causal factor in the development of cancer of the larynx, oral cancer, and cancer of the esophagus. Cigarette smoking is statistically associated with heightened rates of bladder cancer, cancer of the kidney, and cancer of the pancreas. In many cases, cigarette smoking acts both independently and synergistically with other lifestyle factors such as alcohol consumption, obesity, or occupational exposures to heighten the risk of cancer or other diseases.

Although heart disease and cancer are most clearly linked to smoking, cigarette smokers also have a higher prevalence of chronic obstructive lung diseases. Cigarette smoking is the single most important cause of chronic bronchitis and emphysema, which together rank second only to coronary heart disease as a cause of Social Security-compensated disability. Although air pollution and occupational exposures are important contributors and may act synergistically with smoking, cigarette smoking is far more consequential in producing respiratory disease than any other factor. Smokers also experience increased risk for other respiratory problems, have more protracted respiratory symptoms following mild viral illness, and are at greater risk for postoperative respiratory complications (HEW 1979b:6–7).

In addition to heart and lung diseases and cancer, the habit of smoking has been shown to have other severe deleterious effects on health. As noted in chapter 2, babies carried by women who smoke are at greater risk for fetal growth retardation resulting in low birth weight. They also are more prone to fetal death due to maternal complications during delivery and to sudden infant death syndrome. Finally, cigarette smokers appear to be at increased risk of developing peptic ulcers, hazardous drug interactions, and allergic reactions.

The Policy Issues. Cigarette smoking, like alcohol abuse, is a potentially deadly habit. Unlike alcohol consumption, however, the deleterious effects of smoking probably are not limited to the individual who smokes. Considerable research attention and public consternation is currently being directed toward the health effects of involuntary or passive smoking, i.e., the inhalation of smoke contaminants by persons in close proximity to smokers. Efforts to prohibit smoking on airlines and in public places reflect this concern. Although research findings to date are neither uniform nor conclusive, there is growing evidence of potential harm to nonsmokers from exposure to sidestream cigarette smoke (Lenfant and Liu 1980). If, indeed, secondary smoke is hazardous to the health of nonsmokers, then this personal habit takes on another policy dimension. Not only are smokers responsible for increasing health care costs to society because of injury they do to themselves, but they may also be contributing directly to the health problems of those persons around them who are forced to breath the air they have polluted. Under these circumstances, developing preventive measures requires a multifaceted approach designed to discourage individuals from smoking for the sake of their own health as well as for the health of the public around them.

In part because of the conclusive evidence of the hazards of smoking and the potential harm to involuntary participants, but also because cigarettes offer an easy target for excise taxes, no other lifestyle practice has been attacked more vocally. Public policy toward smoking, however, is ambivalent because governments depend heavily on continued smoking for the revenue produced by tobacco excise taxes. Also, tobacco is a major crop in the southern United States. Federal subsidies of the tobacco industry are significant, and the industry itself has a powerful lobby in Washington. The result has been to establish policies that support the product but stigmatize those who use it. In addition to paying heavy taxes on cigarettes, most of which are funnelled into unrelated programs, smokers are the target of ordinances designed to reproach their habit and of increased insurance premiums to help pay for their heightened health risk.

Interwoven with these conflicting threads of policy are paternalistic efforts to encourage people to quit smoking for their own health. The mass media antismoking campaign has been, by far, the most consistent and ambitious attempt to influence a lifestyle choice in the United States. For the last two decades, cigarette smokers have been the target of the efforts of public and private agencies to discourage smoking by pointing out the health dangers and, more subtly, by altering public perceptions of the smoking habit and counteracting tobacco industry advertising. Current attempts to stigmatize smokers and prohibit their smoking in public places demonstrate that pressures on smokers to quit are becoming more coercive. One extension of this antismoking atmosphere could be the creation of policies designed to specifically ration medicine away from those persons who continue to smoke. Although these efforts to alter personal behavior obviously conflict with the freedom of individuals to choose their own lifestyles, a value so central to our prevailing belief system, cigarette smoking appears to be in the first wave of personal behaviors to be seriously challenged through public policy.

Diet and Health

The scientific evidence on the association between diet and health is impressive and expanding. Cardiovascular disease, cancer, prenatal injury, and other risk factors are tied to lifestyle patterns and, of these, diet is emerging as more critical than previously assumed. Although it is comforting to know that cancer and cardiovascular disease are largely preventable, from a public health standpoint it is frustrating because of the difficulty of translating scientific evidence into the behavioral change necessary to reduce or avoid the risk. However, along with cigarette smoking, alcohol abuse, and an array of other lifestyle factors, diet represents a controllable element in the etiology of many diseases.

Comparative risk incidence data across countries consistently demonstrate wide variation in cancer rates. Age-adjusted rates of breast cancer and colon cancer in the United States are over five times as high as in many other countries. Moreover, genetic factors do not appear to explain these differences. When people move from one country to another, they tend to acquire the pattern of cancer that is characteristic of their new location (Adelstein, Staszewski, and Muir 1979). Through comparisons between the highest and lowest national cancer incidence rates for specific types of cancer, researchers estimate that approximately 90 percent of cancers in the United States are caused by environmental, largely lifestyle, factors.

Although manufactured chemicals are clearly responsible for numerous cancer deaths among workers in the high-risk occupations (Oppenheimer 1984), overall, individual behaviors and habits are more important determinants of cancer. Doll and Peto (1981) estimate that at most only 4 percent of cancers are directly related to occupational exposure. They contend that environmental pollution, the most touted villain of the 1970s, is a relatively minor cause of cancer. According to a recent National Research Council committee (1982), the observation that the incidence of many types of cancer is high in nonindustrialized countries indicates that the most common cancers are primarily related, not to industrial pollution, but to various persistent features of lifestyle, particularly diet.

While stressing that any estimates remain tentative within the context of current epidemiological data, Doll and Peto (1981) calculate that 35 percent of cancers in the United States may be caused by components of the diet. In addition to diet, other causes are smoking (30 percent), alcohol (4 percent), sexual practices, probably through viral transmissions (7 percent), and other viruses and infections (10 percent). Heredity is estimated to be the primary cause in 2 percent of cases, although it also might be indirectly linked to other causes by heightening susceptibility or lowering tolerance levels to chemicals or other substances. Food additives are estimated to account for 1 percent, nonoccupational environmental and medical exposure to radiation for 1 percent, and unknown etiology approximately 5 percent.

Even if these estimates are exaggerated, it is becoming obvious that some lifestyle choices are strongly associated with heightened incidence rates of many cancers. Among all of these factors, the contribution of diet is most surprising, mainly because most attention to date has focused on the link between cigarette smoking and lung cancer. Upon examination of hard data indicating that certain substances in foods are carcinogenic in animals, and soft data that statistically link people who eat certain foods with the incidence of cancer, two findings emerge. On the one hand, some foods—i.e., those with high fat content, or foods which have been salt-cured or smoked—should be avoided because they contain known carcinogens or are linked to heightened rates of cancer among people who consume them. On the other hand, other foods should become a regular part of the diet because they appear to inhibit carcinogenesis. The National Research Council (NRC), for example, recommends that the daily diet include whole grain cereals and fruits and vegetables, especially those high in vitamin C and B-carotene, which have been found to inhibit the formation of cancer-causing chemicals or reduce cancer incidence in other ways (NRC 1982:11). Contrarily, the NRC suggests that the proportion of calories in the diet provided by fats should be reduced from 40 percent to 30 percent, because fats, although they do not in themselves cause cancer, seem to act as promoters that enhance the activity of carcinogens.

In a recent article on dietary carcinogens and anticarcinogens, Bruce Ames (1983) illustrates correlations between high fat intake and increased rates of colon, breast, and prostate cancers. Conversely, colon cancer risk appears related to low fiber consumption, while very low levels of vitamin A are associated with a heightened risk of lung and bladder cancers (Willett and MacMahan 1984). Because these cancers account for a large number of cancer deaths per year in the United States (i.e., colon-rectum, 50,000; breast, 40,000; prostate, 24,000) the importance of the diet-cancer linkage currently is being stressed by the National Cancer Institute and the American Cancer Society as well as the cancer research community. Although the level of knowledge on the specific mechanisms of diet and cancer remains primitive, according to the NRC, "the weight of evidence suggests that what we eat during our lifetimes strongly influences the probability of developing certain kinds of cancer" (NRC 1982:16). It might never be possible to specify a diet that protects all people against all forms of cancer, but we now know enough to demonstrate that major alterations in the American diet are warranted as a preventive approach.

Despite the mounting evidence of the importance of diet in averting many cancers, the data are unlikely to effect major changes in the diet of most Americans, because the linkage is ambiguous. Considerably more impressive evidence is available to show that a diet low in fat and high in fiber reduces substantially the risk of cardiovascular disease. At present, deaths from cardiovascular diseases account for half of the mortality in the United States (HHS 1981). A significant proportion of the risk of dying of cardiovascular disease can be accounted for by three major and controllable risk factors: cigarette smoking, hypertension, and elevated serum cholesterol level. The two latter factors are associated with diet.

Studies of groups with extremely low cardiovascular risk such as Seventh-Day Adventists indicate reduced rates of coronary heart disease (Cooper et al. 1984). Initially, all of the observed health advantages were attributed to the absence of cigarette smoking among Seventh-Day Adventists. Subsequent studies, however, have demonstrated that while not smoking contributes to lowered cardiovascular risk, other differences in lifestyle, specifically dietary ones, also contribute (Phillips et al. 1980). The group's extremely low-cholesterol vegetarian diet and their high intake of polyunsaturated fat apparently explain at least in part the reduced mortality rates of this population as opposed to the general population. According to Cooper and associates (1984), the lifestyle adopted by this population has much to offer as a general public health model.

As noted in chapter 2, there is no doubt that nutrition is a critical factor during pregnancy. The diet of the mother is directly linked to the health of the fetus; the fetus is completely dependent upon the mother for nutritional sustenance. Adequate caloric intake, good overall nutrition, and minimal levels of specific vitamins and minerals are essential to proper fetal development. Unlike much of the research on diet and disease in adults which focuses on the deleterious effects of what we ingest, most attention regarding maternal diet centers on the effects of malnutrition or of a deficiency of specific nutrients that are crucial for adequate development of the fetus.

The Policy Issues. Although few observers dismiss diet as a concern or argue that it is not linked to health, there is considerable controversy over what, if any, public action ought to be initiated. In 1985, the NIH Consensus Development Conference on Lowering Blood Cholesterol to Prevent Heart Disease recommended that all individuals beyond the age of two should follow fat-modified diets in the interest of preventing coronary disease, regardless of their sex, age, or the presence of other risk factors. In agreement with the Consensus Panel, Harlan and Stross (1985) propose that a massive education program should be launched for professionals and the public concerning the benefits of a dietary intervention program. In a JAMA editorial on the subject, Rahimtoola (1985) also recommends diet modification in addition to advice on weight control, smoking, and exercise.

In contrast, Olson (1986) argues against mass programs. The data, he feels, are far too equivocal to make recommendations to the general public along the lines presented by the consensus panel: "With these data at hand, what are we promising the American people by recommending a fat-modified diet? A possible fall in cardiac events with a probable increase in noncardiac mortality? These statistics offer no proof of life extension" (1986:2205). Similarly, Ahrens concludes that the diet-heart question has not been settled. He raises several subordinate questions which are similar to Olson's:

1) Can the public be promised a reduced incidence of coronary heart disease if a prudent diet is widely adopted?
2) Is the prudent diet safe and effective for everyone over the age of 2 years?
3) Is the diet recommended the best of several recommended to reduce plasma cholesterol levels?
(Ahrens 1985)

Ahrens contends that the answers to these questions are not resolvable with current data. Because only 50 percent of the risk of heart disease at present can be accounted for by known risk factors, Olson (1986) rejects the mass dietary intervention program proposed by the Consensus Panel and favors instead screening for high-risk persons only, with very selective intervention.

Thus, even now the medical establishment continues its heated debate over the appropriateness of intervention in the dietary practices of the public, even through the relatively unobtrusive method of an educational program. Taking a more cautious approach than the Consensus Conference, the Food and Nutrition Board (1980) cautions that before recommending adoption of any new public health program for disease prevention, public officials must evaluate the potential effectiveness of the effort. Particularly in the case of diseases with multiple causes and poorly understood etiology, such as cancer and heart disease, the Board considers the assumption that dietary change will be effective as a preventive measure to be debatable. Despite the impressive statistical linkages between diet and health, then, the controversy over what public policy approach ought to be pursued is bound to continue.

Infertility and Rationing

As discussed in chapter 2, infertility is increasing as a perceived health problem in the United States and leading to heightened demands for an array of reproductive technologies. The rapid transition of techniques such as in vitro fertilization and embryo flushing from the status of experiments to routine procedures in a matter of several years has been spurred by the demands for a cure for infertility, or at least for a temporary circumvention of it. As these procedures have become routine, pressures have mounted for third-party coverage, resulting in the establishment in Massachusetts and other states of medical insurance policies that include coverage for these expensive interventions. More states and third-party payers will soon acquiesce to these pressures, thus encouraging expanded access to these techniques and further raising public expectations.

The demand for access to fertility-aiding technologies emerges from the heavy emphasis in American society on the right to reproduce. If all persons have the right to reproduce, then those individuals who are unable to do so without intervention have a claim to those techniques and procedures which are capable of overcoming the problem. If reproduction is a fundamental right, as the Supreme Court has declared (*Skinner* v. *Oklahoma*, 1942; *Roe* v. *Wade*, 1973), then ability to pay should not be the determining factor. Infertile persons without the requisite resources to pay for procedures which would enable them to have children seem to have a legitimate claim on society to provide access to them. As in all areas of health care, however, society must establish reasonable limits to such claims. As asked earlier, does a woman who is physically or emotionally unable to carry a fetus herself have a right to a state-funded surrogate mother? If not, can we justify a $20,000 series of in vitro fertilization attempts on a woman who has blocked fallopian tubes, but the capacity to bear a child? Or what about state funding of AID for a couple in which the husband is infertile? Does the fact that the cost here is minimal compared to in vitro fertilization and surrogate motherhood make this claim on societal resources more legitimate? Also, if reproduction is a basic human right, does a lesbian woman have the right to expect development and availability of egg fusion techniques, or the transsexual male a right to expect research leading to male pregnancy?

These claims have already been expressed and it is expected that they will become more intense in the near future. Increasingly, decision makers will be forced to make allocation and rationing decisions concerning this vast and rapidly expanding array of reproductive technologies. These decisions will be made within the cultural context of the individuals right to reproduce and the social context of heightened public expectations. As a result, any decisions to limit the availability of these techniques or establish constraints on their use will be highly controversial.

Allocation and rationing of reproductive technologies becomes more problematic because an increasing proportion of human infertility is caused by personal behavior. The fallopian tubes, especially, are extremely sensitive to infection and easily blocked by the resulting inflammation and scarring. One cause of increased infertility in adult women is acute salpingitis which, in turn, is linked to greater frequency of sexual intercourse among adolescents and to the increasing prevalence of several sexually transmitted diseases, particularly that caused by Chlamydia trachomatis. The epidemic spread of Chlamydia during the recent decade is reflected in estimates of 3 million infections per year in the United States (Holmes 1981). Most critical is its concentration in adolescents, who are more vulnerable to developing salpingitis. According to Westrom (1980), sexually active 15-year-old girls are ten times more likely to develop salpingitis than their 25-year-old counterparts (1:8 versus 1:80). Assuming that the infertility rate following a single bout of salpingitis is 10 percent, then almost 1 percent of sexually active teenage girls will become infertile as a result of salpingitis each year. This data leads Schachter and Shafer (1985) to question whether today's adolescents infected with Chlamydia are not tomorrow's candidates for in vitro fertilization.

Acute salpingitis is a major public health problem with direct medical costs well in excess of $1 billion. More importantly, the future problems of dealing with the results of this disease are potentially staggering both in monetary and policy terms. Its direct contribution to tubal factor infertility, and the resultant need to either reverse the damage through reconstructive surgery or bypass the damage through techniques such as in vitro fertilization, will produce difficult allocation decisions. Should society continue to place high priority on curative medicine that treats largely preventable conditions? It seems more logical to put considerably greater effort into developing workable policies to control the epidemic of sexually transmitted diseases that are contributing to the increase in infertility. Stone, Grimes, and Magder (1986), for instance, contend that persons at high risk for sexually transmitted diseases should be encouraged to modify their sexual behavior as a preventive measure.

A debate that has received considerable attention within the medical community as well as in the popular press concerns the extent to which the fertility of women declines with age. Although data have consistently corroborated the assumption that fertility does indeed decrease with age both in men and women, a heated controversy was sparked by a French study of 2,193 women who were undergoing artificial insemination because of sterile husbands (Schwartz and Mayaux 1982). This study reported that while 26 percent of the women under 30 were infertile, 39 percent of those 31 to 35 were unable to bear children within prescribed time limits. In an editorial response to this article, DeCherney and Berkowitz boldly declared: "If the decline of fecundity after 30 is as great as the French investigation indicates, new guidelines for counseling on reproduction may have to be formulated" (1982). In a statement designed to be highly controversial, they suggested that "the third decade should be devoted to childbearing and the fourth to career development."

Reaction against this editorial as well as to other interpretations of the French data was immediate and often hostile. Attacks were directed against both the statistical inferences drawn from the French data and the basic premises concerning parenthood (Bongaarts 1982). The unique sample in the French study and its operationalization of infertility based on the mean proportion of women conceiving per cycle, it was argued, led to highly inflated infertility estimates. Although it is universally accepted that fertility declines with age, critics contend that the level of decline is nowhere near that of the French sample. Generally accepted U.S. data show approximately 5.5 percent infertility among women 25 to 29, 9.4 percent among those aged 30 to 34, and 19.7 among those 35 to 39. Ironically, even though these overall percentages are substantially lower than the French figures and imply that women over 30 are considerably less prone to be infertile than that study suggests, the rate of increase between the last two groups in the U.S. data is actually greater, representing about a 70 percent increase. Certainly, the scope of the infertility problem for women over 30 seems exaggerated by the French data. It seems clear, however, that women do bear a greater risk of having fertility problems with increasing age; only the extent of the decline in fertility is open to question.

This debate is most meaningful because of current trends in the United States toward women postponing parenting until their mid- to late thirties, after establishing their careers. On the one hand, some clinicians argue that women must make a choice: to delay childbirth with an increased risk of becoming infertile, or to have children during their peak reproductive years, the mid-twenties, and then begin a career. However, many women work to supplement or provide family income and the career-or-children choice is not always a viable one. In contrast, other clinicians contend that the increased risk of infertility is negligible and that other personal, economic, and emotional factors are essential in producing a favorable environment for parenthood. They argue that parenthood is more than simply producing children at the most optimal biological age, and that the biologically optimal period of procreation is not a realistic time for parenthood for many women in our highly complex society.

Despite the disagreement about the interpretation of available data and the necessity of looking at the personal/social context of childbearing, it appears that the risk of infertility does increase with age and that women who postpone childbearing until their mid-thirties should be aware of this. This consideration raises a wide range of questions concerning the role of women in the family and, to some extent, counteracts significant efforts by feminists to minimize the biological parameters of parenthood. It also demonstrates why the demand for reproductive technologies is bound to intensify as many women who were unaware of these patterns in fertility attempt to bear children later in life.

Will women of the future who delay childbearing, only to find themselves infertile, face the possibility of being denied expensive reproductive technologies should they be unable to pay for them? Here again the question of rationing resources on the grounds of lifestyle choice is raised. Although this problem might be resolved by the development of affordable alternatives to in vitro fertilization and embryo flushing, the possibility of rationing such treatments is more threatening than other forms of lifestyle rationing because it is primarily applicable to women, it deals with the fundamental right of reproduction, and more is involved than discrete behavior or personal habits. Rationing reproductive health care on the basis of the age at which a woman is trying to bear children would require intrusion into choices that allow women to organize and plan their entire lives. As such, it would be more insidious than rationing medicine on the grounds of personal habits deemed unhealthy.

A problem for the formulation of policy is that to be effective, any preventive effort must include measures that clash with the cultural values of individual autonomy and free choice of lifestyle, and that clash is particularly acute when adolescents' sexual habits are at issue. For instance, prominent among the measures endorsed by Schachter and Shafer (1985:100) for halting the spread of Chlamydia infection are the screening of high-risk populations, the routine identification and treatment of sexual contacts, and increased education concerning the risks and symptoms of such infection. Additionally, they suggest that presumptive therapy is appropriate for populations in which Chlamydia is known to occur at relatively high rates. All but the last of these measures includes what might be interpreted to be intrusions into the privacy of individuals. Although it is likely that such intervention would withstand constitutional scrutiny, it demonstrates once more that prevention necessitates changing lifestyles, most likely through some combination of education and more coercive measures.

As with smoking, alcohol abuse, and inadequate diet, the question eventually comes down to the extent to which policymakers are willing to ration medicine on the basis of lifestyle choice. Although it now seems inconceivable that treatment preference could be given to those persons who have not contributed directly to their disease, as medical resources become more scarce, such rationing is not beyond imagination. This policy could be effected either by making a macro-allocation decision not to devote any resources to programs designed to overcome infertility, or by allocating limited funds for that purpose such that rationing becomes essential. Whereas the former policy would deny treatment to all infertile persons, including those whose behavior has not led to their condition, the latter rationing policy could be designed to take into account individual responsibility. Similarly, third-party payers could refuse to reimburse for any treatments that were necessitated a patient's habits or behavior. For instance, if the examining physician could demonstrate that scarred fallopian tubes were the result of personal behavior, treatment could be denied, or at least not covered by a third party. Given the possibility of sophisticated and inclusive medical data banks in the future, it is not implausible that personal history data could be specific enough to trace the cause to individual behavior. Although rationing on this basis would not resolve the problem for those persons now affected, it might have a long-term influence on behavior and thus serve a preventive function. Conversely, such a policy would be contrary to conventional medical ethics and most difficult to administer equitably. Physicians would understandably be most reluctant to make such judgments and would most likely view the intrusion of such a public policy into the physician-patient relationship as unacceptable.

The Dilemma of the Wood Stove

One paradox in environmental health centers on the cumulative impact of the actions of many individuals who believe, in large part, that they are contributing to a healthier environment. In recent years a considerable amount of the air pollution in western cities has been traced to the widespread use of wood-burning stoves. Up to 95 percent of the pollution during air inversions in mountain and northwestern states has been attributed to wood burning by individuals (*Lewiston Morning Tribune*, December 23, 1985). In the winter of 1985, this led to numerous air quality advisories and warnings to persons at high risk for respiratory illness. This is ironic, because wood-burning stoves have been highly touted in recent decades as a safe and effective alternative source of heat. To date, the efforts of the environmental health movement have been directed at power companies and industrial pollution, even though in some parts of the country, at least, residential sources, cumulatively, are the primary cause of the problem.

Genuine preventive efforts to eliminate this health problem require constraints on individual practices. Although some combination of education, incentives, and regulation is probably necessary, the immensity of the task makes aggressive government action improbable. Also, because the government actively encouraged wood-burning stoves and other alternative energy sources during the 1970s, any efforts now to discourage use would appear ridiculous. This example does illustrate, however, the difficulty both of identifying practices that affect health and of taking effective and feasible action to ameliorate the situation. Finally, it demonstrates how a relatively innocuous practice by a few people can become a meaningful health threat when practiced by many individuals simultaneously.

Free Will and Individual Responsibility

Critics who charge that any effort to assign individual responsibility for behaviors that result in ill health amounts to "blaming the victim" appear all too willing to dismiss individual accountability for action. The assumption that persons are victims implies a lack of free will on their part. Individuals, in this approach, are viewed as incapable of making rational decisions when it comes to selecting healthy as opposed to unhealthy practices. Such critics may argue, for instance, that cigarette smokers smoke because of peer pressure as shaped and reinforced by media advertising, and are therefore simply reflecting societal influences. Recent suits against tobacco companies by cigarette smokers whose habit has led to disease exemplify this reasoning, in which the person who made the choice to smoke would be absolved of responsibility.

According to this viewpoint, individuals are dupes, the products of societal forces that mold their personal behavior. This argument can be heard from both ends of the ideological spectrum. Although the most vocal proponents of this view come from the left, fundamental religions contend that society perpetuates promiscuity, pornography, and so forth through the mass media and assume that individuals have little capacity to act in ways counter to what the media tells them. This environmental determinist view concedes to individuals little free will to choose a healthy lifestyle.

Ironically, this argument against the free will and accountability of individuals for their actions is manifested as well in genetic arguments which would appear to be the antithesis of the environmentalist approach. Increasingly, evidence is offered to support the contention that unhealthy personal habits might be genetically preconditioned. Recently, the heightened genetic susceptibility of persons to alcoholism (Schuckit 1985) and obesity (Price 1987) has been suggested as a cause of these problems. The search for genetic markers that determine susceptibility is ongoing and undoubtedly will result in the identification of some genes that are found in higher proportions among persons with specific behavioral patterns (Lewin 1987). As with strict social environmental determinism, if the genetic argument is stated in the extreme, it will suggest that individuals lack the free will to make certain choices concerning their personal behavior because they are, in effect, the product of their genes.

Both of these theoretical perspectives are important contributors to our understanding of personal behavior. Certainly, as humans we are products of both the social environment and our genetic heritage. Many personal practices are shaped by the value system and institutional structure of a particular culture—there is no disputing this. Furthermore, current scientific evidence suggests that a genetic base to behavior is often present, particularly in creating susceptibility to a behavior. Although it is unlikely that alcoholism, for instance, is genetically determined, human twin studies as well as experimental animal research demonstrate a genetic predisposition. Some people, then, might have less resistance than others to alcohol addiction or might have a genetic predisposition toward obesity. In neither case does this negate the dimension of free will or individual responsibility for behavior.

Any policies that ration medicine on the basis of lifestyle choices or that otherwise discriminate against those persons who engage in self-destructive or unhealthy habits must take into account the social and genetic contributions to that behavior. If it is found that people are unable to exercise free choice within the context of the mass media or other societal incentives toward the unhealthy practice, then that incentive structure should be modified. Conversely, until society actually does use lifestyle choices to ration scarce resources, there is little disincentive for such behavior. Within our technological fix mentality, it is not uncommon for those persons engaging in unhealthy behaviors to rationalize their actions by assuming that science will provide a cure for problems that might accrue in the long run. Would persons change this behavior if they knew that medical resources would be unavailable to them because of a rigid social policy against the deployment of scarce resources to individuals who knowingly contribute to their own ill health? If one assumes that social environment is critical to individual choice, then a responsible public policy to alter the current incentive/disincentive structure is necessary.

Unfortunately, many of those observers with a social-environmental determinist leaning reject strong action by the state to discourage deleterious personal behavior. Such efforts, they argue, represent illegitimate state interference in individual choice. Rationing of medicine on lifestyle grounds is bound to be attacked by these individuals as a further attempt to blame the victim. The circularity of their argument is obvious. Unless society takes steps to strongly discourage harmful behaviors, it in effect encourages such behaviors. Particularly if individuals lack the free will to make and thus be responsible for their own decisions, it is up to society to shape their practices in a positive manner. By denying free will and also rejecting societal intervention, the proponents of this approach offer no logical means out of this dilemma. Although the provision of education programs and adequate social support systems to ensure that a free, informed choice is possible should be a first priority, it is unlikely that the problems of alcohol abuse, smoking, poor diet, and so forth will be overcome by these means alone. More ambitious and intrusive steps by society, however, are destined to be fought by critics who appear to want it both ways.

Similarly, it is difficult to apply the genetic model without severe implications for individual choice. If we accept the assumption that behavior has a significant genetic component, we have several options. We can choose to ignore evidence of genetic propensities, but in the process forfeit any advantages that would accrue from designing social policy that would target these individuals for special education, counseling, or treatment programs. Alternately, we could utilize this information to categorize children on the basis of the genetic markers they carry and establish preventive programs to avert behavioral patterns that, combined with their genetic susceptibility, would put these persons at risk.

The second option can be perceived as either expanding the person's free choice by fully setting forth the risks, or constraining it by defining what is socially responsible action in light of the information. In other words, although such information may or may not be valuable for a particular individual, designing social policy around it might be seen as constrictive of free choice. Furthermore, the social stigma of simply being identified as having heightened genetic susceptibility might be critical enough to impugn the fairness of any such policy, not to mention its questionable effectiveness as a preventive strategy. Once this type of information is available, however, it may be difficult for a society concerned with the health of its citizens not to utilize it. It is feasible that genetic information of this type might be included among the criteria for rationing medicine in the foreseeable future and be an integral part of a preventive program. Both the environmental and genetic models, then, could be used to justify intrusive governmental policies designed to alter individual behavior that is deemed to be unhealthy. By assuming that individual free will and responsibility for behavior are limited by either the societal or genetic factors, these approaches could conceivably lead to severe constraints being imposed upon individual lifestyle choices if used as rationales for public policy.

Prevention and Lifestyle Choice

In a recent article, Lenn and Madeleine Goodman (1986) argue that "prevention" is a badly misused term which has been subject to an overselling of its benefits, an underestimation of its secondary effects,

and overextension, through which moral, social, and political problems are treated as though they were health problems. Although the
Goodmans acknowledge that the idea of prevention rests on real,
though limited, achievement, they maintain that the fashionable tendency to rely too heavily on prevention has troubling implications. In
addition to creating a blame-the-victim atmosphere, there is a danger
of imparting a false sense of security. This is especially important when
prevention centers on statistical inference of reduced health risks. By
placing heavy emphasis on prevention as a cure-all for potential health
problems we practice deception and place blame on individuals when
they are struck by disease (Goodman and Goodman 1986).

The Goodmans present a variety of examples of extreme proposals
and arguments for prevention, including prophylactic hysterectomies
and mastectomies. Misuse of prevention is not limited to faddists or
propagandists, however, as is illustrated by the misguided swine flu
vaccination campaign which they characterize as follows:

The decision-making process throughout was characterized by concern
about blame, eagerness to showcase preventive medicine, and a crisis mentality, all of which tended to eclipse clinical and epidemiological evidence.
The rhetoric deployed at each level effectively forced the hand of those who
would carry the decision to the next. Earnestness and vigor proved insufficient
guides to policy. Assigning greater weight to reified notions of prevention than
to hard information about disease, vaccine modalities, and risks had seriously
discredited the hitherto conservative and respected image of preventive medicine. (1986:29–30)

In addition to problems that center on exploitation of the concept
of prevention, a heavy emphasis on prevention aimed at changing
individual behavior does have the effect of shifting responsibility from
the health sector to the individual. Although I contend that the individual must bear considerably more responsibility for his or her health
status, the abrogation of society's responsibility for the health of its
members does not follow. If anything, the social responsibility to
educate and counsel individuals is heavier, and it is in this area of
responsibility for encouraging healthful behavior where our institutions have failed. I also contend that medicine in general has always
been used as a surrogate for deeper social reforms. That is why we
have used the medical model to frame the issues of abortion, child
abuse, drug abuse, and so forth. Prevention is not the only area of

health care in which we have evaded making major social reforms. Although I agree with Neubauer and Pratt (1981) that assigning to the individual the major responsibility for preventive health shifts the onus away from social agencies, I argue that it does so justifiably only after society has made considerable effort to inform and educate individuals. This societal commitment must also include making research into lifestyle choice and health a major priority, so that the individual has the best information possible upon which to base his or her choices. Instead of abrogating social responsibility, prevention, even when targeted at individual lifestyle, primarily redirects responsibility away from the provision of curative technologies toward the provision of information and education.

Prevention in the United States has always been less popular than in other western democracies. Fein (1981:52) sees this as a result of our tendency to value private decision making over public choice. Because we prize the freedom of the individual to choose his or her own lifestyle even if it is self-destructive, we hesitate to compel prevention. One logical assumption that follows from this attitude is that if prevention is possible and yet illness or injury is present, then people have voluntarily chosen to take the risk and they have lost. This assumption is based however on the premise that the individual has the information on risks needed to make an informed choice, and that it is a free choice.

In a society predisposed against public prevention programs on the basis that they interfere with individual choice, it is easy to slip into a blame-the-victim mentality and argue that prevention should be a private, as opposed to a public, matter. The idea of shifting the costs of unhealthy behavior to those individuals who engage in it, making them pay for the results of their voluntary choices, engenders sympathy among rugged individualists. Prevention, from this perspective, becomes a means not to reduce human misery, but rather to shift costs to those persons who create the need for medical services. The primary goal of this type of preventive approach is not to raise the general level of health for its own sake, but rather to shift responsibility and the cost burden to individuals and thereby encourage them to alter their lifestyles.

It may well be that corporations, not the government, will take the lead in initiating this shift toward prevention as an individual responsibility. As noted by Thurow (1985:611), whereas government measures to contain costs focus attention on the poor and elderly and are most likely to directly affect those groups, corporate measures focus on the middle class, and thus might become more widely accepted. Thurow (1985:612) contends that once the idea of prevention becomes legitimate for middle class workers, the government will then extend it to the poor and elderly.

Joseph Califano's (1986) description of Chrysler Corporation's initiatives in mounting a major health promotion and disease prevention effort illustrates the array of positive and negative incentives available to effect these goals. "We tell them about the benefits of a healthy life-style and warn them about alcohol and drug abuse. We inform them about the dangers of smoking and urge them to quit. We are beginning to provide financial incentives as well: life insurance rates are 75 percent higher for smokers" (Califano 1986:84). According to Califano, business has a duty to "market healthy life-styles" to its employees. In addition to encouraging exercise, providing information about proper diet, and upgrading assistance for alcohol and drug abusers, business must make "health and life insurance more expensive for smokers, heavy drinkers, and overweight employees" in order to cut health care costs, reduce absenteeism, and raise productivity (Califano 1986:89).

Although reasonable efforts by business to instill healthy lifestyles in their employees are laudable, overly ambitious attempts by corporate America to intervene in lifestyle choice could lead to severe inconsistencies in the allocation of resources. Also, as noted in chapter 3, health benefits managers already have considerable influence in determining the scope and type of health coverage of employees, and are involved in a kind of rationing. I argue that, in the name of fairness, health promotion efforts must ultimately be part of a national health policy. In the words of Balfe and associates (1985), in their article describing the AMA-initiated Health Policy Agenda for the American People: "Piecemeal decision making in both the public and private sectors has been counterproductive and has resulted in a hodgepodge of inconsistent laws and policies that are ineffective as a guide for the future direction of health care in the United States."

Rationing Preventive Medicine

The emphasis of this book has been directed thus far toward the rationing of high-cost curative or rescue technologies. To this point, preventive medicine has been spared similar scrutiny. A substantial proportion of preventive efforts, however, concentrate on the use of increasingly sophisticated diagnostic procedures which allow for the identification of rare conditions. Serious outcomes that require major medical intervention can often be avoided by early diagnosis and treatment, but only if large numbers of persons at risk are screened. Examples of this type of preventive effort include cervical cancer screening, blood pressure screening, preoperative chest x-rays, whole body scans, and alpha-fetoprotein tests for spina bifida, to name a few. The problem with these efforts, however, is that because the risk of such problems is so low, extensive screening will avert only a small number of cases at substantial expense.

Within the context of scarce medical resources, diagnostic services might be too expensive under some circumstances even though effective techniques are available to avoid severe disability or even death. In a study for the British National Health Service, Roberts, Farrow, and Charny (1985) contend that here too as well as in curative medicine, difficult choices must be made that may preclude use of certain preventive or early diagnostic services, thereby denying benefits which are technically feasible. They explain that the clinical effectiveness of a service is no longer the only dimension which has to be considered before allocating resources for that purpose. Also considered are the prevalence of the outcome to be avoided in the population at large and the cost of the procedure itself. As noted above, even though the cost of a single procedure might be reasonable, if the condition is rare, a large number of such procedures might be necessary to identify and prevent one case.

The sad truth for some conditions might be that it is more cost-effective to forgo the screening program and bear the full costs of the outcome in those few instances where it occurs. Gerald Leach (1970:292), for instance, argues that "mass prevention campaigns against disease" are generally not efficient investments. In her seminal work on prevention, Russell (1986) argues that while the appeal of prevention is straightforward—it is better to avoid a disease than to try to repair damage later—in reality preventing disease involves risks and, in some instances, large financial costs. Although prevention can be a worthwhile investment in better health, and should be evaluated on those grounds, not cost alone, it is not the complete solution to the problem of rising medical expenditures. According to Russell (1986:110), even after allowing for savings in treatment, prevention usually adds to the costs of health care, contrary to the popular view that it reduces them. Proposals that would make important changes in individual lives therefore deserve careful evaluation, she believes, before action is taken. In contrast, a recent editorial in the *Journal of Public Health Policy* argues for a comprehensive prevention program for noninfectious and infectious diseases, maternal and child care, and protection from environmental hazards: "A substantial investment in these programs will achieve extraordinarily high dividends in terms of reduction in illness, disability and death, as well as in the need for costly treatment services" (*Journal of Public Health Policy* 1984:12). The assumption that preventive programs are always preferable to curative medicine continues to elicit controversy, at least over allocating scarce resources such that benefits are maximized across society.

Roberts, Farrow, and Charny (1985) argue that under these circumstances, acceptable limits on what the British National Health Service (NHS) can afford to spend on achieving different levels of benefit from preventive procedures must be defined. They base their criteria on a measure termed the "benefit:premium ratio." Although the specific figures they use and assumptions they make are open to question, the result is to rank a variety of preventive programs as to cost acceptability. Given the amount of money available for programs directed toward the avoidance of death and the prevention of long-term disability, they arrive at a cut-off point above which the NHS cannot afford to provide the service (Roberts, Farrow, and Charny 1985:90). The "outcome" cost is defined as the cost of intervention for each individual in the screened group divided by the effectiveness of intervention in avoiding one death or long-term disability.

Table 5.2 lists the estimated costs in pounds to the NHS for various procedures. The broken line represents the cut-off between services with acceptable and unacceptable costs. The authors conclude that the great majority of services which save a life or prevent severe disability withstand this analytical scrutiny. Problems arise when diagnostic pro-

Table 5.2
Costs of Averting One Death or Permanent Disability

Procedure	Cost in Pounds
Preoperative chest x-ray	900,000
Cervical cancer screening	300,000
Breast cancer screening	80,000
Prenatal test for open spina bifida	19,000
Sudden death syndrome surveillance	14,000
Whole body scan	10,000
Routine hemoglobin test	200
Blood pressure screening	100

Source: Robert, Farrow, and Charny 1985.

cedures are used on the population at large to identify those at risk from a condition which is not widespread (i.e., Pap smears to detect cervical cancer, or breast cancer screening), or when procedures whose per unit cost is high are used on those in the hospital (i.e., preoperative skull or chest x-rays). The low per unit cost of some population screening procedures may obscure their true cost, which is the cost of achieving the desired outcome for the few who will benefit. Although technologically Britain could reduce the frequency of death from breast cancer by screening, of the birth of surviving bifida babies by prenatal screening, and of brain damage by means of skull radiology, the total costs of each procedure exceed what Roberts and associates estimate the NHS can afford.

This concern over the cost effectiveness of preventive measures obviously follows from the emphasis on cost containment. Less obviously, however, it reflects an alteration in the nature of preventive medicine itself. Most of the benefits expected to accrue from traditional public health measures have already been achieved, thus subjecting present and future efforts to the law of diminishing returns. As a result, prevention now must focus on changing lifestyles and identifying the early signs of serious disease through screening and education. Under these conditions, any preventive measure must be evaluated in terms of how successful it is in actually changing behavior.

Furthermore, as discussed earlier, many of the ties between lifestyle and health remain speculative and are based on statistical data, not on rigorous clinical trials. Even where evidence of danger is strong, there is considerable debate over how effective any preventive measures might be. Jennett (1985:169) argues that even where clear causative relationships have been established, as with smoking, the effectiveness of preventive measures that limit the hazard has been slight. He contends that to discover the dangers of smoking without discovering how to make smokers stop is, in fact, a half-way prevention, just as many curative applications have been denigrated as half-way medicine.

According to the National Center for Health Services Research (1984:3), one of the reasons health counseling is not more commonly practiced by primary care providers may be the belief that patients will not follow the advice. The results of lifestyle changes can be only stated to the individual patient in terms of probability. Moreover, any illness resulting from potentially harmful behavior is likely to appear in the distant future. For this reason, considerable research is needed to test the effectiveness of more immediate rewards or tangible incentives for motivating patients to modify unhealthy behavior or lifestyle. Until we are capable of devising acceptable and effective methods of altering lifestyle choices, monies spent to that end will be largely wasted.

As noted above, preventive services are as vulnerable to rationing as curative procedures. Recent arguments to the effect that attempts at mass screening for coronary risk factors are unproductive, and that to be effective, attention must be targeted to persons identified as being at high risk, are arguments for a form of rationing, because at least some persons at low risk will develop the disease if they are not screened. Jennett (1985:169) also contends that potential deleterious effects of preventive measures on the quality of life are frequently understated. For the people affected, prevention might be worse than the risk of developing the disease. Efforts to change behavior will fail unless they are directed toward those individuals who are willing to alter their behavior.

The Courts and Rationing

In regard to rationing medicine, the United States is in a more awkward situation than other western nations. With our emphasis on the individual's legal right to health care, once a procedure is available there is a tendency to use the courts to obtain the treatment, even if at great expense with little or no benefit. The legal system, moreover, is not designed to deny such appeals on grounds of economics alone. Instead, it is intended to serve as a protector of the rights of individual citizens vis-à-vis the government and others in society. Furthermore, the tort system encourages lawsuits that challenge specific instances of treatment or nontreatment. In this process, the courts legitimize and mandate certain standards of care. It is unlikely that within this legal context, the courts will become rationers of medical care. Instead, they will serve as a difficult hurdle in the way of any attempts to ration treatment. Asks Stone, "How will a jury respond when economic rather than medical considerations are offered as the reason for a diagnostic or treatment decision that has led to a malpractice claim?" (1985:310). Whether or not the courts would be willing to take lifestyle considerations into account, or factor in responsibility for the results of a person's own habits, is yet to be seen.

One area of recent court activity that might presage judicial reaction to lifestyle choices in general centers on the rash of suits in the late 1960s challenging the constitutionality of the mandatory motorcycle helmet laws of the states. In all but several instances, the courts overwhelmingly rejected the suits, largely on the grounds of the social impact of individual behavior. In a 1972 case, upheld by the Supreme Co..rt (*Simon* v. *Sargent*), the court stressed the economic costs that would be borne by society if individuals were free to choose whether or not to wear a safety helmet:

From the moment of injury [society] picks up the person off the highway; delivers him to a municipal hospital and municipal doctors; provides him with unemployment compensation if, after recovery, he cannot replace his lost job, and if the injury causes permanent disability, may assume the responsibility for his and his family's continued subsistence. We do not understand the state of mind that permits plaintiff to think that only he himself is concerned.

On the basis of this ruling it might be posited that the courts will not reject out of hand policies that intervene in individual choices which could be proven to place an unavoidable economic burden upon society.

At present, the courts can parcel out blame in tort claims, but in the end those who have the resources often pay the full amount of the damages, no matter what level of responsibility the court determined they bore. This approach is illustrated in a California case in which a drunken driver with no insurance killed a person in a head-on collision. Although the court determined that the city was 1 percent responsible for the accident because of the design of the highway which had been in existence 100 years, the city ended up paying 100 percent of the settlement of well over $1 million (Gettinger 1986:153). In contrast, in several cases the courts have rejected claims against tobacco companies for health damages suffered when the plaintiffs used their product. The courts agreed that the smokers bore responsibility for their actions because they knew the risks and continued to smoke in spite of this knowledge.

The problem with depending on the courts to provide meaningful policies on rationing and on the question of lifestyle choice is twofold. First, the courts argue that they do not make policy, but instead judge each case on its own merits. Despite this hesitancy to make public policy, the courts do have strong influence on it through the precedents they set. Although the debate over the policymaking role of the courts will not end, the argument seems largely to be a semantic one at present. Unless one defines policymaking very narrowly, the courts always have and will continue to make policy through their decisions. Second, and more important, because the courts' first responsibility is to resolve the specific case at hand and render justice on the merits of that case, virtually any decision is possible in a specific court, at a specific time, under specific circumstances. This piecemeal, case-by-case approach only establishes confusing and, many times, contradictory policy guidelines. Stone (1985:310) sees a clash between standards of practice that might result from the response of physicians to legally imposed economic constraints such as DRGs and other incentives intended to lower the aggregate cost of health care, and the body of law that pushes physicians to ignore costs. In a highly specialized and frequently speculative field such as medicine, it is dangerous to make public policy on the grounds of specific court cases or even on the basis of the general pattern of the decisions of many courts over time.

Despite these caveats, the courts are critical in setting guidelines for rationing medicine. Through their handling of the tort cases in which plaintiffs contend they have been denied access to lifesaving technologies, and through the standards of care the courts accept as adequate, they will have substantial influence. Even prior to this, anticipation of expected court reaction to statutory legislation and administrative regulations will, to some extent, shape those more recognized policymaking mechanisms.

Public Expectations and the Media

The mass media are predisposed toward focusing on the more spectacular achievements of medicine and, in the process, have a tendency to simplify and sensationalize technological breakthroughs. Seldom is there the time or inclination to temper optimism with realism, or to qualify claims for these medical breakthroughs with caveats about their limitations, complexity, and social implications. As a consequence, expectations frequently are falsely raised. By dwelling on technologies, procedures, and health programs that promise the quick fix, the press and particularly the electronic media promote a "disease of the week" mentality. This tendency is aggravated by the public's apparently short attention span for news. As a result, the search goes on for newsworthy events to give the public a continual flow of dramatic yet superficial stories about medical developments.

A substantial proportion of the content of the mass media news stories that reaches the public is in the form of summaries of studies from medical journals, particularly the *New England Journal of Medicine* or *JAMA*. Again, however, these extracts tend to emphasize the news aspects, thus failing to analyze the "breakthrough" objectively. The discovery of the AIDS antibodies becomes a potential cure to that disease; artificial heart transplants become a promise of a mechanical fountain of youth; and the war on cancer portends a cure. What is not stressed are the facts that identifying antibodies to the HTLV-III virus, although significant, does not represent a cure for AIDS; artificial heart transplants raise severe questions concerning the quality of life and the use of scarce resources; and no all-encompassing cure for cancer exists. Without exposure to the negative aspects and the uncertainty of medical science, the public is given a narrow vision of medical technology.

Despite these limitations, the mass media, particularly television, are for most of the public the most constant and powerful sources of information. Because of the directed coverage of medicine by the media, with few exceptions the public is not exposed to comprehensive, systematic, and critical analysis of medical developments. The media coverage heightens the public's already strong trust in the technological fix. It reinforces the assumption that if we as a society only put our collective mind and resources to a task, we will achieve it. Often cited as support for this assumption are the elimination of small pox, polio, and other communicable diseases. The assumptions that diagnosis of a disease will lead to treatment and treatment to a cure are also central to news coverage of medicine. One danger in this overoptimism is that the public comes to expect near-miracles that medicine cannot deliver. Eventually, this must lead to a reaction against a medical community that delivers much less than it supposedly promised. Public resentment against the amount of resources put into the cancer program reflects in part the perceived lack of progress in what the media portrayed as the effort to eradicate cancer. By reporting only the positive and sensational aspects of medical research and development, the media is in effect creating unrealistic expectations about the power of medicine. In the end, this pattern of coverage is counterproductive and obscures the difficult real decisions that must eventually be made.

When a crisis occurs, the media also has a tendency to exaggerate the consequences for the public. The media handling of the AIDS "epidemic" created unsubstantiated fears in the public by dramatizing and thus overestimating the danger of its spread across the heterosexual population. Again, because the media was the only source of information for many persons, the myths soon became fact for the public. Fear of transmittal of AIDS by casual contact resulted in children with HTLV-III antibodies being barred from attending school in some localities and triggered action on a variety of state legislative efforts to reduce the spread of this virus to the general public. Given the media coverage, it is no surprise that public support for a variety of public health measures, including the quarantine of AIDS carriers, is high. Public expectations, then, are heavily dependent on the content and tone of media coverage. It is critical that the mass media exercise this powerful influence responsibly and with caution. Unfortunately, competition between the news services and pressures to sell their products leads them to produce potentially misleading coverage of health care allocation and rationing issues.

Conclusions: Rationing Medicine in the United States

This book has described many approaches to rationing health care resources. Some approaches, such as rationing by physicians, which appeared to work reasonably well in the past when medical intervention was more limited, are no longer adequate or acceptable. Other approaches now operative, such as rationing by litigation, public relations, or ability to pay or obtain third-party coverage, are patently unfair and lead to incongruous medical decision making. Still others, such as computerized rationing, or explicit rationing by a central authority on the basis of rigid criteria, would be anathema to prevailing social values in the United States.

In spite of problems inherent in each approach to rationing, I maintain, along with the many scholars cited throughout this book, that the rationing of medical technologies will become more prevalent and overt. George Annas (1985:188) is correct in suggesting that the customary approach to rationing medicine, in which it is practiced by health care providers but not explicitly acknowledged, gives us the illusion that we do not have to make these choices—but only at the cost of mass deception. Moreover, this deception has contributed to the misconception that as a society we can avoid making explicit rationing decisions because we have managed to do so thus far. It is natural, when faced with painful choices, to take solace in approaches that appear to free us from the necessity of making those decisions. It is becoming increasingly clear, however, that American society can no longer escape facing the problems of rationing head-on. Although some persons remain content in the illusions and evasions of our present approach, high-technology medicine, accompanied by the array of demographic and social trends discussed here, makes it impossible for this to continue. Abram and Wolf arrive at the same conclusion: "As we are forced to place limits on health care for financial reasons and reconcile competing claims to increasingly capable medical technology, we will face agonizing dilemmas with extraordinary political implications" (1984:631).

Although explicit rationing of medical resources is alien to our rights-oriented value system, there is no escape from making such decisions. In the absence of coordinated, consistent national criteria, rationing decisions will continue to be made on an ad hoc, reactive basis by a combination of public and private mechanisms including legislatures, courts, corporations, insurance companies, public relations firms, ethics committees, and physicians. The most appropriate question is not whether rationing ought to be done but rather, who should establish procedures that are fair and reasonable. To this end, a first order of business is to initiate a public dialogue over societal goals and priorities that includes determining the preferred agents for rationing medical resources. This initial enterprise could take the form of Milbrath's (1986) Council for Long-Range Societal Guidance, Abram and Wolf's (1984) temporary government committee, or other proposed mechanisms discussed in chapter 4. Although direct government involvement in the deliberations of such a group would have to be limited, I argue that the effort has to be initiated by the national government and must be viewed as legitimate and critical by public officials.

I agree with Engelhardt and Rie (1986:1159) that society must determine at what point undesirable standards of health care are simply "unfortunate," but not "unfair," in the sense of constituting a claim on further resources. The fundamental question here, however, is what constitutes "society." Even among those observers who agree that limits on the use of medical resources must be established, there is disagreement as to how and by whom the decisions ought to be made. Certainly the most acceptable means of allocating and rationing health care resources would be through some consensus or at least reasonably common agreement as to the most just distribution. As emphasized throughout this book, however, the diversity of interests in our society and the respective demands they place on the health care system make such agreement impossible.

Although a consensus on how medical resources should be distributed is unlikely, agreement is more possible on the procedures through which society will approach these problems. If we can agree that the procedures are fair, and understand that we are bound by them, specific applications, though difficult, might be perceived as unfortunate but not unfair. As noted earlier, one of the reasons we as individuals and health providers tend to reject the notion of rationing or any attempt to withhold treatment is that there is no guarantee that the resources thus saved will be used fairly or even more efficiently. If I as an individual forgo a liver transplant, most likely its cost will not be spent on prenatal care, but rather on a transplant for someone else—someone who is perhaps less "deserving." The problem then is partly a lack of confidence in the fairness of present procedures for allocating treatment in the United States.

As discussed in detail in chapters 3 and 4, there is considerable concern that macro-allocation decisions are being made, not through open, democratic procedures, but by corporations, courts, public relations firms, and special interest groups. Engelhardt and Rie (1986:1160) contend that outcomes can be unfair due to the absence of "free and open participation" in fashioning allocation policy. Their discussion of the need to establish criteria for admission of individuals to intensive care units can easily be generalized to allocation and rationing decisions at all three levels. The lack of explicit and clear priorities and goals for health care does nothing to inspire confidence in the current process. Engelhardt and Rie (19786:1164) are correct in their conclusion that both the government and third-party payers should explicitly state that funds will not be available under specified circumstances. Policies must be announced in advance, particularly if resources become rationed.

Any attempts to ration medicine by edict, particularly if they are based on lifestyle choices, will fail in a society such as ours which stresses individual rights over other societal priorities. Furthermore, it would be foolish to presume that it will be easy to moderate the expectations, demands, and behavior of a public that has come to expect unlimited access to technological progress in medicine. Mechanic notes that, even though public expectations may be unrealistic, it is "unlikely that the American population would support the rationing of expensive high technology in the fashion characterizing England's National Health Service" (1986:215). Moreover, because officeholders gain so little political credit for trying to convince people that they are largely responsible for their own health problems, one can hardly expect many elected officials to publicly advocate an explicit rationing policy that incorporates lifestyle considerations. Elections and political careers are lost, not won, on such issues. The difficulty of the issue, however, does not reduce the need and urgency of facing it.

A central element in any effort to ration medical resources in such a way as to be fair yet efficient is education designed to counter the technological imperative. If candidates for organ transplants and other surgical interventions were fully apprised of the risks and side effects of the proposed treatment and counseled as to the quality of life they could expect after the surgery, some individuals would most likely remove themselves from the pool of candidates. The danger in this approach is the possible use of this education effort by some persons to discourage use of a procedure by exaggerating its negative aspects. The possibility of bias on the part of the providers could also be manifested through charging various groups in society differential rates for the same procedure.

Despite these potential pitfalls, some means must be established to counter the prevailing tendency of Americans to view medical technologies as able to conquer all disease. Without a countervailing emphasis on the risks and dangers inherent in each proposed medical intervention, it is not surprising that we as a society are conditioned to embrace the technologies. As a result, there are many patients who expect and demand treatment only to regret their decision after the resources have been used. Our failure to assess realistically the limits of medicine and the long-term consequences of high-technology interventions and to communicate this knowledge to the public produces a situation in which we ask for the intervention first and give it serious thought only after the fact. Public expectations must be revised to take into account the limits on what medical science can accomplish both for society and for the individual.

As discussed earlier, I believe the government has a responsibility to educate the public both as to the links between lifestyle choices and health and the need to moderate its expectations. This educative approach must be accompanied by a significant shift at the allocation level toward preventive and primary health care programs, which recently have received shrinking shares of our health care dollar. This shift will be difficult, in part because of the momentum toward more profitable curative/restorative medicine, and in part because of the strength of prevailing perceptions of health care. Unfortunately, the trend continues toward more emphasis on high-technology interventions at the exclusion of preventive measures and education. Ongoing decisions by third-party payers, including the states and Medicare, to fund heart and liver transplants imply that such a transformation is not imminent.

The most controversial aspect of rationing medicine discussed here is the advocacy of a shift toward individual responsibility for health. Given the large proportion of health care resources expended on illnesses that are linked to individual behaviors, however, any rationing policy, if it is to be effective, must place considerable emphasis on the ultimate responsibility of the individual not only for his or her own health, but also for reducing the overall costs of health care to society both present and future.

It is unfortunate that the health benefits of changes in behavior tend to come late in life, while the personal sacrifices come substantially earlier. Given the present-oriented, live-for-today mentality of American society, it is not surprising that many persons are unwilling to forgo the pleasures and conveniences of less healthy lifestyles, especially if their choice merely puts them at heightened risk of ill health in some distant future. This individualistic worldview, combined with our presumption that health care resources will be available to us when required and our faith that technology will solve the health problems we help create, leads to a complacency unmatched in western democracies about personal contributions to health.

We urgently need a more future-oriented perspective both for individual health and societal survival. "There will be little meaning to political freedom, or freedom of choice, if our society fails to prepare for predictable crises," according to Milbrath (1986:33). Although the emphasis on lifestyle and individual responsibility for health does conflict with strongly held notions of free choice in a liberal society, failing to recognize the crisis and take action now, even at the expense of some freedom of choice, risks the loss of considerably more freedoms in the future. The assumption that each individual has rights to unlimited medical resources is collectively disastrous when resources are finite.

Increasingly, constraints on the use of medical resources will result in situations where the decision is made not to initiate lifesaving treatment. Although such decisions have always been made, they were not perceived as the product of an explicit rationing policy. Often the dispute over whether or not to initiate aggressive treatment to save a particular person's life revolves around the question of how much the life of a disabled infant, for instance, or of a potential organ transplant patient is worth. Quality-of-life distinctions always have and will continue to be made in this allocation process. The broader question of how much a human life ought to be worth also depends on the value assigned life or a particular life by society. Our willingness to expend hundreds of thousands of dollars to save one life, while largely ignoring the worldwide deaths of millions of children each year from diarrhea and other readily avertable causes, demonstrates our selectivity in assigning values to human life.

A crisis over the allocation of large sums of money for the treatment of severely ill persons is inevitable, because such treatment is in direct competition with other health priorities. Thus, the question becomes not how much a particular human life is worth but what priority we put on that life versus another life or lives. Every decision we make to allocate extensive resources (money, equipment, blood, trained personnel) to save one life diverts those resources from other potentially lifesaving treatments, albeit less dramatic ones. The decision to save the life of a disabled infant through aggressive medical intervention also raises critical questions concerning the long-term commitment of society to providing the substantial downstream resources needed to maximize the potential of that infant. Until now, we have shown more interest in technologically saving the life than in the less dramatic but more difficult task of caring for those persons we have rescued. As discussed in chapter 2, before we rush into aggressive treatment of newborns, including those with multiple serious malformations and severe prematurity, we must ask whether we are willing to expend the essential long-term resources to care for those saved. Similarly, before we establish a program to fund heart or liver transplants, we must test our long-term commitment to the counseling and emotional aid that transplant patients require. We must ask the difficult questions, not only about who should make the decision to rescue and on the basis of what criteria, but also about who should pay the enormous costs, both tangible and intangible.

Each of the four areas of medical treatment discussed in this book exemplifies the current dilemmas facing society regarding the allocation and rationing of scarce medical resources. Together, they dramatize the need for all concerned persons to participate in a dialogue over what the goals and priorities of society ought to be. The trade-offs inherent in any decision must be clarified if we are to appraise realistically the options available to us. Unfortunately, our choices are being increasingly constrained by the lack of adequate resources through which to utilize all the technologies needed to save the lives of all persons. Rationing these technologies, although not a popular option, is becoming a necessary one. As a society, we must ensure that rationing is carried out in as rational and fair a manner as possible.

References

Aaron, Henry J. and William B. Schwartz. 1984. *The Painful Prescription: Rationing Hospital Care.* Washington, D.C.: Brookings Institution.

Abram, Morris B. and Susan M. Wolf. 1984. "Public Involvement in Medical Ethics: A Model for Government Action." *New England Journal of Medicine* 310(10):627–632.

Abrams, N. E. and J. R. Primack. 1980. "The Case of Radioactive Waste Management." *Environment* 22:14–20.

Adelstein, A. M., J. Staszewski, and C. S. Muir. 1979. "Cancer Mortality in 1970–1972 Among Polish-Born Migrants to England and Wales." *British Journal of Cancer* 40:464–475.

Ahrens, E. H. 1985. "The Diet-Heart Question in 1985: Has it Really Been Settled?" *The Lancet,* May 4, pp. 1085–1087.

Allegrante, John P. and Lawrence W. Green. 1981. "When Health Policy Becomes Victim Blaming." *New England Journal of Medicine* 305 (25): 1528–1529.

Altman, Drew E. and Robert J. Blendon, eds. 1979. *Medical Technology: The Culprit Behind Health Care Costs?* Washington, D.C.: GPO.

American Academy of Pediatrics. 1984. "Guidelines Announced for Infant Bioethics Committees." *News and Comment* (June), 35(6):1.

American Cancer Society. 1982. *Cancer Facts and Figures.* New York: American Cancer Society.

American Medical Association, Judicial Council. 1982. *Current Opinions.* Chicago: AMA.

Ames, Bruce N. 1983. "Dietary Carcinogens and Anticarcinogens." *Science* 221:1256.

Anderson, Gerald F. and Earl P. Steinberg. 1984. "Hospital Readmissions in the Medicare Population." *New England Journal of Medicine* 311(21):1349–1353.

Annas, George J. 1984. "Ethics Committees in Neonatal Care: Substantive Protection or Procedural Diversion?" *American Journal of Public Health* 74(8):843–845.

—— 1985. "The Prostitute, the Playboy, and the Poet: Rationing Schemes for Organ Transplantation." *American Journal of Public Health* 75(2):187–189.

Annis, Linda F. 1978. *The Child Before Birth*. Ithaca: Cornell University Press.

Antonov, A. N. 1947. "Children Born During the Seige of Leningrad in 1942." *Journal of Pediatrics* 30:250–259.

Arehart-Treichel, J. 1980. "Questioning the New Genetics." *Science News* 116:155–156.

Ashley, John T. 1986. Letter to the Editor. *JAMA* 256(3):350.

Austen, W. Gerald and A. Benedict Cosimi. 1984. "Editorial Retrospective: Heart Transplantation After 16 Years." *New England Journal of Medicine* 311(22):1436–1438.

Avery, Gordon B., ed. 1981. *Neonatology*. 2d ed. Philadelphia: Lippincott.

Avorn, Jerry. 1984. "Benefit and Cost Analysis in Geriatric Care: Turning Age Discrimination into Health Policy." *New England Journal of Medicine* 310(20):1294–1301.

Balfe, Bruce E., Joseph F. Boyle, Severine J. Brocki, and Kathleen R. Lane. 1985. "A Health Policy Agenda for the American People: Phase I: The Principles." *JAMA* 254(17):2440–2448.

Baltimore, David. 1983. "Can Genetic Science Backfire? 'That's the Chance We Take.' " *U.S. News and World Report*, March 28, pp. 52–53.

Bayer, Ronald. 1982. "Women, Work, and Reproductive Hazards." *Hastings Center Report* 2(5):14–19.

Bazelon, David L. 1983. "Governing Technology: Values, Choices, and Scientific Progress." *Technology in Society* 5:19.

Beauchamp, Tom L. and James F. Childress. 1979. *Principles of Biomedical Ethics*. New York: Oxford University Press.

Belloc, Nedra B. and Lester Breslow. 1972. "Relationship of Physical Health Status and Health Practices." *Preventive Medicine* 1:419.

Berkman, Lisa F. and Lester Breslow. 1983. *Health and Ways of Living: The Alameda County Study*. New York: Oxford University Press.

Bernbaum, Judy and Marsha Hoffman-Williamson. 1986. "Following the NICU Graduate." *Contemporary Pediatrics* 3:22–37.

Bingham, Eula. 1980. "Some Scientific and Social Hazards of Identifying Reproductive Hazards in the Workplace." In Peter F. Infante and Marvin S. Legator, eds., *Proceedings of a Workshop on Methodology for Assessing Reproductive Hazards in the Workplace*. Washington, D.C.: National Institute for Occupational Safety and Health.

Blank, Robert H. 1984. "Judicial Decision Making and Biological Fact: Roe v. Wade and the Unresolved Question of Fetal Viability." *Western Political Quarterly* (December), 37:584–602.

—— 1986. "Emerging Notions of Women's Rights and Responsibilities During Gestation." *The Journal of Legal Medicine* 7(4):441–469.

Blendon, Robert J. 1986. "Health Policy Choices for the 1990s." *Issues in Science and Technology* 2(4):65–73.

Blendon, Robert J. and Drew E. Altman. 1984. "Public Attitudes About Health-Care Costs: A Lesson in National Schizophrenia." *New England Journal of Medicine* 311(9):613–616.

Boffey, Philip M. 1976. "NSF: New Program Criticized as 'Appalling' Subsidy to Activists." *Science* 194:306, 347–349.

—— 1976a. "Office of Technology Assessment: Bad Marks on Its First Report Card." *Science* 193:213–215.

Bongaarts, J. 1982. "Infertility After Age 30: A False Alarm." *Family Planning Perspectives* 14(2):75–78.

Bosy, Linda. 1987. "A Cold 'Nuclear Winter': Blood Bankers Collect Fewer Units as Tests, Lack of Donors Threaten Volunteer System." *American Medical News*, February 20, pp. 2, 17.

Boulding, Kenneth E. 1982. "Science and National Defense: A Speculative Essay and Discussion." In Albert H. Teich and Richard Thornton, eds., *Science, Technology, and the Issues of the Eighties: Policy Outlook*. Boulder: Westview Press.

Bowes, Watson A. and Brad Selgestad. 1981. "Fetal Versus Maternal Rights: Medical and Legal Perspectives." *Obstetrics and Gynecology* 58 (2):209–214.

Bowes, Watson A. and Michael Simmons. 1980. "Improved Outcome in Very Low-Birth Weight Infants." *American Journal of Obstetrics and Gynecology* 136(8):1080.

Bowie, Norman E. and Robert L. Simon. 1977. *The Individual and the Political Order: An Introduction to Social and Political Philosophy*. Englewood Cliffs, N.J.: Prentice-Hall.

Boyle, Joseph F. 1984. "The Health Policy Agenda for the American People." *JAMA* 249(15):2073.

Brandon, William P. 1982. "Health-Related Tax Subsidies: Government Handouts for the Affluent." *New England Journal of Medicine* 307(15): 947–950.

Brazil, Percy. 1986. "Cost Effective Care is Better Care." *Hastings Center Report* 16(1):7–8.

Brent, R. L. 1980. "Radiation-Induced Embryonic and Fetal Loss from Conception to Birth." In I. H. Porter and Ernest B. Hook, eds., *Human Embryonic and Fetal Death*. New York: Academic Press.

Breslow, Lester and James E. Enstrom. 1980. "Persistence of Health Habits and Their Relationship to Mortality." *Preventive Medicine* 9:478–479.

Brewer, Gary D. and Peter de Leon. 1983. *The Foundations of Policy Analysis*. Homewood, Ill.: Dorsey.

Brooks, Harvey. 1976. "Technology Assessment as a Process." *International Social Science Journal* 25(3):247–256.

Brown, E. Richard. 1983. "The Rationing of Hospital Care." In President's Commission for the Study of Ethical Problems in Medicine and Biomedical and Behavioral Research, *Securing Access to Health Care*, vol. 3. Washington, D.C.: GPO.

Brown, J. H. U. 1978. *The Health Care Dilemma: Problems of Technology in Health Care Delivery*. New York: Human Sciences Press.

Brunswick, Ann F. and Peter Messeri. 1986. "Drugs, Lifestyle, and Health:

A Longitudinal Study of Urban Black Youth." *American Journal of Public Health* 76(1):52–57.

Butler, N. R., H. Goldstein, and E. M. Ross. 1972. "Cigarette Smoking in Pregnancy: Its Influence on Birth Weight and Perinatal Mortality." *British Medical Journal* 2:127–130.

Cady, Blake. 1982. "Cost of Smoking." *New England Journal of Medicine* 308(18):1105.

Caldwell, Lynton K. 1983. "Biotechnology Versus the Life Sciences? The Politics of Biocracy." Paper presented at the annual meeting of the Western Political Science Association, March 25, Seattle.

Califano, Joseph A., Jr. 1986. "A Corporate Rx for America: Managing Runaway Health Costs." *Issues in Science and Technology* 2(3):81–90.

Caplan, Arthur L. 1983. "How Should Values Count in the Allocation of New Technologies in Health Care?" In Ronald Bayer, Arthur L. Caplan, and Norman Daniels, eds., *In Search of Equity: Health Needs and the Health Care System*. New York: Plenum Press.

Capron, Alexander M. 1975. "Legal Issues in Fetal Diagnosis and Abortion." In Charles Birch and Paul Abrecht, eds., *Genetics and the Quality of Life*. Sydney: Pergamon Press.

Carey, William D. 1982. "Observations: Racing the Time Constraints." In Albert H. Teich and Richard Thornton, eds., *Science, Technology, and the Issues of the Eighties: Policy Outlook*. Boulder: Westview Press.

Casper, B. 1976. "Technology Policy and Democracy: Is the Proposed Science Court What We Need?" *Science* 194:29–35.

Centers for Disease Control. 1986. "Alcohol-Related Traffic Fatalities." *JAMA* 255(4):450.

Chapman, Fern Schumer. 1985. "Deciding Who Pays to Save Lives." *Fortune*, May 25, pp. 39–43.

Chernoff, G. 1977. "The Fetal Alcohol Syndrome in Mice: An Animal Model." *Teratology* 15:223–230.

—— 1980. "The Fetal Alcohol Syndrome: Clinical Studies and Strategies of Prevention." In M. K. McCormack, ed., *Prevention of Mental Retardation and Other Developmental Disabilities*. New York: Marcel Dekker.

Christoffel, Tom. 1982. *Health and the Law: A Handbook for Health Professionals*. New York: Free Press.

Coates, Joseph F. 1971. "Technology Assessment: The Benefits . . . The Costs . . . The Consequences." *Futurist* no. 5: pp. 225–231.

—— 1978. "What is a Public Policy Issue?" In K. R. Hammond, ed., *Judgment and Decision in Public Policy Formation*. Boulder: Westview.

Cobb, R. W. and C. D. Elder. 1972. *Participation in American Politics: The Dynamics of Agenda-Building*. Boston: Allyn and Bacon.

Coleman, Samuel, Phyllis T. Piotrow, and Ward Rinehart. 1979. "Tobacco—Hazards to Health and Human Reproduction." *Population Reports* L-1:L1–L37.

Collingridge, David. 1980. *The Social Control of Technology*. New York: St. Martin's Press.

Comroe, J. H. 1978. "The Road from Research to New Diagnosis and Therapy." *Science* 200:931–937.

Conley, R. W. 1973. *The Economics of Mental Retardation*. Baltimore: Johns Hopkins University Press.

Consensus Conference. 1985. "Lowering Blood Cholesterol to Prevent Heart Disease." *JAMA* 253(14):2080–2086.

Cook, Philip J. 1984. "The Economics of Alcohol Consumption and Abuse." In L. J. West, ed., *Alcoholism and Related Problems: Issues for the American Public*. Englewood Cliffs, N.J.: Prentice-Hall.

Cooper, Richard, Arline Allen, Ronald Goldberg, Maurizio Trevisan, and Linda Van Horn. "Seventh-Day Adventist Adolescents—Life-Style Patterns and Cardiovascular Risk Factors." *The Western Journal of Medicine* (March), 140(3):411–477.

Corey, Lawrence. 1982. "Dx and Rx Changes in Primary Care for Genital Herpes." *Illustrated Medicine* 1(2):1–8.

Council on Scientific Affairs. 1983. "Fetal Effects of Maternal Alcohol Use." *JAMA* 249(18):2517–2521.

Crane, Diana. 1975. *The Sanctity of Social Life: Physician's Treatment of Critically Ill Patients*. New York: Russell Sage Foundation.

Cullen, D. J. 1981. "Surgical Intensive Care: Current Perceptions and Problems." *Critical Care Medicine* 9:263.

Cwiek, Mark A. 1984. "Presumed Consent as a Solution to the Organ Shortfall Problem." *Public Law Forum* 4(8):81–99.

Daniels, Norman. 1986. "Why Saying No to Patients in the United States is So Hard: Cost Containment, Justice, and Provider Autonomy." *New England Journal of Medicine* 314(21):1380–1383.

Danzon, Patricia M. 1985. "Testimony Before the Committee on Labor and Human Resources, U.S. Senate, July 10, 1984." *Duke Law Magazine* (Winter), 3(1):11–15.

DeCherney, Alan H. and Getrud S. Berkowitz. 1982. "Female Fecundity and Age." *New England Journal of Medicine* 306(7):424–426.

Demkovich, Linda E. 1984a. "Administration Boosts Medicare Rates to Keep Peace with Hospital Industry." *National Journal*, September 15, pp. 1721–1722.

—— 1984b. "Mimicking Medicare." *National Journal*, September 8, p. 1678.

—— 1984c. "Mondale Moves on Medicare Issue by Hitting Reagan's 'Secret Plan.' " *National Journal*, October 20, pp. 1984–1985.

Detsky, A. S., S. C. Stricker, A. G. Mulley, and G. E. Thibault. 1981. "Prognosis, Survival, and the Expenditure of Hospital Resources for Patients in an Intensive Care Unit." *New England Journal of Medicine* 305(12):667–672.

Devine, Donald J. 1982. *The Political Culture of the United States*. Boston: Little, Brown.

DeVito, Anthony J. 1984. "Abuse of Litigation: Plague of the Medical Profession." *New York State Bar Journal*, (July), pp. 23–25.

Devore, Nancy E., Virginia M. Jackson, and Susan L. Piening. 1983. "TORCH

Infections." *American Journal of Nursing* (December), pp. 1660–1665.

Diamond, E. F. 1977. "The Deformed Child's Right to Life." In D. J. Horan and D. Mall, eds., *Death, Dying, and Euthanasia.* Washington, D.C.: University Publishers of America.

Doll, Richard and Richard Peto. 1976. "Mortality in Relation to Smoking." *British Medical Journal* (December), 2:1525–1536.

—— 1981. *The Causes of Cancer.* New York: Oxford University Press.

Doubilet, Peter, Milton C. Weinstein, and Barbara J. McNeil. 1986. "Use and Misuse of the Term 'Cost Effective' Medicine." *New England Journal of Medicine* 314(4):253–255.

Drucker, Peter F. 1981. "New Technology: Predicting Its Impact." In Albert H. Teich, ed., *Technology and Man's Future.* 3d ed. New York: St. Martin's Press.

Duff, R. S. and A. G. M. Campbell. 1973. "Moral and Ethical Dilemmas in the Special-Care Nursery." *New England Journal of Medicine* 289(17):890–894.

Dyer, Allen R. 1986. "Patients, Not Costs, Come First." *Hastings Center Report* 16(1):5–7.

Eckhardt, Michael J., T. C. Harford, C. T. Kaelber, E. S. Parker, and L. S. Rosenthal. 1981. "Health Hazards Associated with Alcohol Consumption." *JAMA* 246(6):648–666.

Eisner, Victor, Joseph V. Brazie, Margaret W. Pratt, and Alfred C. Hexter. 1979. "The Risk of Low Birthweight." *American Journal of Public Health* 69(9):887–893.

Engelhardt, H. Tristram, Jr. 1984. "Shattuck Lecture—Allocating Scarce Medical Resources and the Viability of Organ Transplantation." *New England Journal of Medicine* 311(1):66–71.

Engelhardt, H. Tristram, Jr. and Michael A. Rie. 1986. "Intensive Care Units, Scarce Resources, and Conflicting Principles of Justice." *JAMA* 255(9):1159–1164.

Etzioni, Amitai. 1973. *Genetic Fix: The Next Technological Revolution.* New York: Harper and Row.

—— 1978. "Individual Will and Social Conditions: Toward an Effective Health Maintenance Policy." *Annals of the Association for the Advancement of Political and Social Sciences* 437:62–73.

Evans, Roger W. 1983. "Health Care Technology and the Inevitability of Resource Allocation and Rationing Decisions: Part II." *JAMA* 249(6):2208–2219.

—— 1986. "The Heart Transplant Dilemma." *Issues in Science and Technology* 2(3):91–101.

Fein, Rashi. 1981. "Social and Economic Attitudes Shaping American Health Policy." In John B. McKinlay, ed., *Issues in Health Care Policy.* Cambridge: MIT Press.

Feinberg, Joel. 1973. *Social Philosophy.* Englewood Cliffs, N.J.: Prentice-Hall.

Feinstein, Alvan R., Daniel M. Sosin, and Carolyn K. Wells. 1985. "Stage Migration and New Diagnostic Techniques as a Source of Misleading Statistics for Survival on Cancer." *New England Journal of Medicine* 213 (25):1604–1608.

Ferkiss, Victor. 1978. "Technology Assessment and Appropriate Technology: The Political and Moral Dimensions." *National Forum* (Fall), pp. 3–7.

Fielding, Jonathan E. 1982. "Appraising the Health of Health Risk Appraisal." *American Journal of Public Health* 72(4):337–339.

Fleischman, Alan R. (1986). "An Infant Bioethical Review Committee in an Urban Medical Center." *Hastings Center Report* 16(3): 16–18.

Fletcher, John C. 1983. "Emerging Ethical Issues in Fetal Therapy." In Kare Berg and Knut E. Tranoy, eds., *Research Ethics*. New York: Alan R. Liss.

Florio, James J. 1985. "Regulation in Biotechnology." In Sandra Panem, ed., *Biotechnology: Implications for Public Policy*. Washington, D.C.: Brookings Institution.

Food and Nutrition Board. 1980. *Toward Healthful Diets*. Washington, D.C.: National Academy of Sciences.

Forsythe, Alan B., Barbara Griffiths, and Sidney Reiff. 1982. "Comparison of Utilization of Medical Services by Alcoholics and Non-Alcoholics." *American Journal of Public Health.* 72(6):600–602.

Fredrickson, Donald S. 1978. "The Public Governance of Science." *Man and Medicine* 3(2):77–88.

Freedman, Steve A. 1985. "Megacorporate Health Care: A Choice for the Future." *New England Journal of Medicine* 312(9):579–582.

Freeman, David M. 1974. *Technology and Society: Issues in Assessment, Conflict and Choice*. Chicago: Rand McNally.

Freiherr, Greg. 1985. "Applying Personal Computers to Patient Care." *Research Resources Reporter* (November), 9(11):1–6.

Friedrich, Otto. 1984. "One Miracle, Many Doubts." *Time*, December 10, pp. 70–77.

Fuerst, Mark L. 1985. "Shopping Center Medicine: The New Conception." *Generics* (January), pp. 50–55.

Gallup Report. 1983. (June), 213:11–12.

—— 1984a. (January/February), 220/221:26.

—— 1984b. (July), 226:17.

—— 1986. (September), 252:28–29.

Gambitta, Richard A.L., Marlynn L. May, and James C. Foster. 1981. "Introduction." In A.L. Gambitta, M.L. May, and J.C. Foster, eds., *Governing Through Courts*. Beverly Hills: Sage.

Gapen, Phyllis. 1984. "New Program Aids Physicians in Making Diagnosis." *American Medical News*, October 26, pp. 18–19.

Gettinger, Stephen. 1986. "Liability Insurance Squeeze Spurs Pleas to Hill for Relief." *Congressional Quarterly Weekly Report*, January 25, pp. 148–153.

Goggin, Malcolm L. 1984. "Reagan's Revival: Turning Back the Clock on the Health Care Debate." In Anthony Champagne and Edward J. Harpham, eds., *The Attack on the Welfare State.* Prospect Heights, Ill.: Waveland Press.

Goodman, Lenn E. and Madeleine J. Goodman. 1986. "Prevention—How Misuse of a Concept Undercuts Its Worth." *Hastings Center Report* 16(2):26–37.

Green, H. P. 1973. "Mechanisms for Public Policy Decision-Making." In Bruce Hilton, ed., *Ethical Issues in Human Genetics.* New York: Plenum Press.

—— 1976. "Law and Genetic Control: Public Policy Questions." *Annals of the New York Academy of Sciences* (January), 265:170–177.

Hale, Ellen. 1984. "Is There Life After Transplant?" *American Health* (January/February), pp. 58–62.

Hallstrom, Alfred P., Leonard A. Cobb, and Roberta Ray. 1986. "Smoking as a Risk Factor for Recurrence of Sudden Cardiac Arrest." *New England Journal of Medicine* 314(5):271–275.

Halpern, Stephen C. and Charles M. Lamb, eds. 1982. *Supreme Court Activism and Restraint.* Lexington, Mass.: Lexington Books.

Hamburg, David A. 1982. "Health and Behaviors." *Science* 217:4558.

Hanson, J. W. 1980. "Reproductive Wastage and Prenatal Ethanol Exposure: Human and Animal Studies." In I. H. Porter and Ernest B. Hook, eds., *Human Embryonic and Fetal Death.* New York: Academic Press.

—— 1981. "Counseling and Fetal Alcohol Syndrome." In S. R. Applewhite et al., eds., *Genetic Screening and Counseling: A Multidisciplinary Perspective.* Springfield, Ill.: Charles C. Thomas.

Hanson, J. W., K. L. Jones, and D. W. Smith. 1976. "Fetal Alcohol Syndrome: Experience With 41 Patients." *JAMA* 235(14):1458–1460.

Hanson, J. W., A. P. Streissguth, and D. W. Smith. 1978. "The Effects of Moderate Alcohol Consumption During Pregnancy on Fetal Growth and Morphogenesis." *Journal of Pediatrics* 93(3):457–460.

Hardin, Garrett. 1974. "The Moral Threat of Personal Medicine." In M. Lipkin and P. Rowley, eds., *Genetic Responsibility: On Choosing Our Children's Genes.* New York: Plenum Press.

Harlan, William R. and Jeoffrey K. Stross. 1985. "An Educational View of a National Initiative to Lower Plasma Lipid Levels." *JAMA* 253(14):2087–2090.

Harrigan, J. 1980. "Prenatal and Obstetrical Factors in Mental Retardation." In M. K. McCormack, ed., *Prevention of Mental Retardation and Other Developmental Disabilities.* New York: Marcel Dekker.

Harris, Louis and Associates. 1983. *The Equitable Health Care Survey: Options for Controlling Costs.* New York: Equitable Life Assurance Society.

Harron, Frank, John Burnside, and Tom Beauchamp. 1983. *Health and Human Values.* New Haven: Yale University Press.

Harsanyi, Zolt and R. Hutton. 1981. *Genetic Prophecy: Beyond the Double Helix.* New York: Rawson, Wade.

Hartz, Louis. 1955. *The Liberal Tradition in America*. New York: Harcourt, Brace and World.

Hastings Center Report. 1983. "Case: AID and the Single Welfare Mother." *Hastings Center Report* 13(1):22–23.

Havighurst, Clark C. 1983. "Decentralized Decision Making: Private Contract Versus Professional Norms." In J. Meyer, ed., *Market Reforms in Health Care*. Washington, D.C.: American Enterprise Institute.

—— 1985. "Testimony Before the Committee on Labor and Human Resources, U.S. Senate, July 10, 1984." *Duke Law Magazine* (Winter), 3(1):16–20.

HCFA (Health Care Financing Administration). 1986. "Projections in Health Care Spending to 1990." *Health Care Financing Review* 7(3):1–36.

HEW (Department of Health, Education, and Welfare). 1964. *Smoking and Health: Report of the Advisory Committee to the Surgeon General*. Washington, D.C.: GPO.

—— 1979a. *Healthy People: The Surgeon General's Report on Promotion and Disease Prevention*. Washington, D.C.: GPO.

—— 1979b. *Smoking and Health: A Report of the Surgeon General*. Washington, D.C.: GPO.

HHS (Department of Health and Human Services). 1981. *Arteriosclerosis*. Bethesda, Md.: National Institutes of Health.

—— 1983. *Alcohol and Health*. Washington, D.C.: GPO.

Hiatt, Howard H. 1975. "Protecting the Medical Commons: Who Is Responsible? *New England Journal of Medicine* 293(5):235–240.

Hill, J. D., J. R. Hampton, and J. R. A. Mitchell. 1978. "A Randomized Trial of Home Versus Hospital Management of Patients with Suspected Myocardial Infarction." *The Lancet*, April 22, pp. 837–841.

Holmes, K. King. 1981. "The Chlamydia Epidemic." *JAMA* 245(17):1718–1723.

Hook, Janet. 1984a. "Compromise Set on Aiding Child Protection Programs." *Congressional Quarterly Weekly Report*, September 22, p. 2305.

—— 1984b. "Senate 'Baby Doe' Floor Compromise Readied." *Congressional Quarterly Weekly Report*, July 21, p. 1796.

Horowitz, D. I. 1977. *The Courts and Social Policy*. Washington, D.C.: Brookings Institution.

Howard, Linda G. 1981. "Hazardous Substances in the Workplace: Rights of Women." *University of Pennsylvania Law Review* 129:798–845.

Idaho Health Systems Agency. 1986. "Rationing By Default." *IHSA News* 9(1):6.

Infante, Peter F., Joseph K. Wagoner, Anthony J. McMichael, Richard J. Waxweiler, and Henry Falk. 1976. "Genetic Risks of Vinyl Chloride." *The Lancet*, April 3, pp. 734–735.

Ingelfinger, Franz J. 1980. "Medicine: Meritorious or Meretricious." In Philip H. Abelson, ed., *Health Care: Regulation, Economics, Ethics,*

Practice. Washington, D.C.: American Association for the Advancement of Science.

IOM (Institute of Medicine). 1979. *Medical Technology and the Health Care System: A Study of Equipment Embodied Technology.* Washington, D.C.: National Academy of Sciences.

—— 1980. *Alcoholism, Alcohol Abuse, and Related Problems: Opportunities for Research.* Washington, D.C.: National Academy Press.

—— 1982. *Health and Behavior: Frontiers of Research in the Biobehavioral Sciences.* Washington, D.C.: National Academy Press.

—— 1983. *A Consortium for Assessing Medical Technology.* Washington, D.C.: National Academy of Sciences.

—— 1985a. *Preventing Low Birthweight.* Washington, D.C.: National Academy Press.

—— 1985b. *Report of Committee for Evaluating Medical Technologies in Clinical Use: Assessing Medical Technologies.* Washington, D.C.: National Academy Press.

Jasper, H. N. 1974. "Congressional Interests in the Ethical Problems of Biomedical Technology." In M. Lipkin and P. Rowley, eds., *Genetic Responsibility: On Choosing Our Children's Genes.* New York: Plenum Press.

Jeffe, Douglas and Sherry Bebitch Jeffe. 1984. "Losing Patience with Doctors: Physicians vs. the Public on Health Care Costs." *Public Opinion* (February/March), pp. 45–47, 55.

Jelliffe, Roger W. 1985. Interview in "Managing Patients by Computer." *Research Resources Report* (December), 9(12):8–12.

Jennett, Bryan. 1985. "High Technology Medicine: How Defined and How Regarded." *Milbank Memorial Fund Quarterly* 63(1):141–173.

Johnson, Dana E. 1984. "Life, Death, and the Dollar Sign: Medical Ethics and Cost Containment." *JAMA* 252(2):223–224.

Jones, K. L., David W. Smith, D. N. Ulleland, and A. P. Streissguth. 1973. "Pattern of Malformation in Offspring of Chronic Alcoholic Women." *The Lancet,* June 9, pp. 1267–1271.

Jonsen, Albert R. 1986. "The Artificial Heart's Threat to Others." *Hastings Center Report* 16(1):9–11.

Journal of Public Health Policy. 1984. "A National Health Program for the United States." Editorial. *Journal of Public Health Policy* 5:10–17.

Kaplan, M. B. 1975. "The Case of the Artificial Heart Panel." *Hastings Center Report* 5(5):41–48.

Kass, Leon R. 1981. "Making Babies Revisited." In Thomas A. Shannon, ed., *Bioethics* 2d ed. Ramsey, N.J.: Paulist Press.

Kirkley, William H. 1980. "Fetal Survival—What Price." *American Journal of Obstetrics and Gynecology* (August), 137:873.

Klein, Rudolf. 1981. "Economic Versus Political Models in Health Care Policy." In John B. McKinlay, ed., *Issues in Health Care Policy.* Cambridge: MIT Press.

Knaus, William A. 1986. "Rationing, Justice and the American Physician." *JAMA* 255(9):1176–1177.

Knowles, John D. 1977. "The Responsibility of the Individual." *Daedalus* 106(1):57–80.

Kressley, Konrad M. 1981. "Diffusion of High Technology Medical Care and Cost Control—A Public Policy Dilemma." *Technology in Society* 3:304–322.

Krimsky, Sheldon. 1978. "A Citizen Court in the Recombinant DNA Debate." *Bulletin of the Atomic Scientists* 8:37–43.

—— 1982. *Genetic Alchemy: The Social History of the Recombinant DNA Controversy.* Cambridge: MIT Press.

Kristein, Marvin M., Charles B. Arnold, and Ernst L. Wynder. 1980. "Health Economics and Preventive Care." In Philip H. Abelson, ed., *Health Care: Regulation, Economics, Ethics, Practice.* Washington, D.C.: American Association for the Advancement of Science.

Lappe, Marc. 1972. "Moral Obligations and the Fallacies of 'Genetic Control.' " *Theological Studies* (September), 33:411–427.

Lappe, Marc and P. A. Martin. 1978. "The Place of the Public in the Conduct of Science." *Southern California Law Review* 52:1535–1539.

Lawrence, Diane B. and Clifton R. Gaus. 1983. "Long-Term Care: Financing and Policy Issues." In David Mechanic, ed., *Handbook of Health, Health Care, and the Health Professions.* New York: Free Press.

Leach, Gerald. 1970. *The Biocrats.* New York: McGraw Hill.

Lenfant, C. and B. M. Liu. 1980. "(Passive) Smokers versus (Voluntary) Smokers." *New England Journal of Medicine* 302(13):742–743.

Lewin, Roger. 1987. "National Academy Looks at Human Genome Project, Sees Progress." *Science* 235:747–748.

Lieber, Charles S. 1978. "Pathogenesis and Early Diagnosis of Alcoholic Liver Injury." *New England Journal of Medicine* 298(16):888–893.

—— 1982. *Advances in Alcohol and Substance Abuse.* New York: Haworth Press.

Light, Paul. 1985. *The Politics of Social Security Reform.* New York: Random House.

Loewy, Erich H. 1980. "Cost Should Not Be a Factor in Medical Care." *New England Journal of Medicine* 302(12):697.

Longo, Lawrence M. 1982. "Health Consequences of Maternal Smoking." In National Research Council, *Alternative Dietary Practices and Nutritional Abuses in Pregnancy.* Washington, D.C.: National Academy Press.

Lowrance, William W. 1982. "Choosing Our Pleasures and Our Poisons: Risk Assessment for the 1980s." In A. H. Teich and R. Thornton, eds., *Science, Technology, and Issues of the Eighties: Policy Outlook.* Boulder: Westview Press.

Luce, Bryan R. and Stuart O. Schweitzer. 1978. "Smoking and Alcohol Abuse: A Comparison of Their Economic Consequences." *New England Journal of Medicine* 298(10):569–571.

Luft, Harold S. 1983. "Health Maintenance Organizations and Rationing of Medical Care." In *Report of the President's Commission on Securing Access to Health Care.* Washington, D.C.: GPO.

Lundberg, George D. 1983. "Rationing Human Life." *JAMA* 249(16):2223–2224.

Lyon, Jeff. 1985. *Playing God in the Nursery.* New York: Norton.

Marmor, Theodore R. and Jon B. Christianson. 1982. *Health Care Policy: A Political Economy Approach.* Beverly Hills: Sage.

Marston, R. Q. 1978. "Influence of NIH Policy Past and Present on the University Health Education Complex." In H. H. Fudenberg and V. L. Melnik, eds., *Biomedical Scientists and Public Policy.* New York: Plenum Press.

Matheny, Albert R. and Bruce A. Williams. 1981. "Scientific Disputes and Adversary Procedures in Policy Making." *Law and Policy Quarterly* (July), 3(3):341–364.

Mathieu, Deborah. 1984. "The Baby Doe Controversy." *Arizona State Law Journal* 1984(4):602–626.

Matthews, Donald R. and James A. Stimson. 1975. *Yeas and Nays: Normal Decision Making in the U.S. House of Representatives.* New York: Wiley.

Maugh, Thomas H. 1982. "Cancer is Not Inevitable: National Research Council Panel Recommends Change in Diet to Reduce the Risk of Cancer." *Science* 217(2):36–37.

May, Marlynn L. 1981. "Governing Standards of Medical Care." In R. A. L. Gambitta, M. L. May, and J. C. Foster, eds., *Governing Through Courts.* Beverly Hills: Sage.

McCall, N. and H. S. Wai. 1981. *An Analysis of the Use of Medicare Services on the Continuously Enrolled Aged.* Menlo Park, Calif.: Sorin Research Institute.

McCormick, Marie C. 1985. "The Contribution of Low Birth Weight to Infant Mortality and Childhood Morbidity." *New England Journal of Medicine* 312(2):82–89.

McDowell, G. L. 1982. *Equity and the Constitution: The Supreme Court, Equitable Relief, and Public Policy.* Chicago: University of Chicago Press.

Mechanic, David. 1977. "The Growth of Medical Technology and Bureaucracy: Implications for Medical Care." *Milbank Memorial Fund Quarterly* 55(1):61–78.

—— 1981. "Some Dilemmas in Health Care Policy." *Milbank Memorial Fund Quarterly* 59(1):1–15.

—— 1986. *From Advocacy to Allocation: The Evolving American Health Care System.* New York: Free Press.

Mendeloff, John. 1985. "Politics and Bioethical Commissions: 'Muddling Through' and the 'Slippery Slope.' " *Journal of Health Politics, Policy, and Law* 10(1):81–92.

Meyer, Mary B. 1982. "Smoking and Pregnancy." In Jennifer R. Niebyl, ed., *Drug Use in Pregnancy.* Philadelphia: Lea and Febiger.

Milbrath, Lester W. 1986. "A Governance Structure Designed to Help a Society Learn How to Become Sustainable." Paper presented at the annual meeting of the American Political Science Association Meeting, August 30, Washington, D.C.

Miller, Arthur S. 1982. "In Defense of Judicial Activism." In S. C. Halpern and C. M. Lamb, eds., *Supreme Court Activism and Restraint*. Lexington, Mass.: Lexington Books.

Miller, C. Arden. 1984. "The Health of Children, A Crisis in Ethics." *Pediatrics* 73(4):550–558.

Miller, Francis H. and Graham A. H. Miller. 1986. "The Painful Prescription: A Procrustean Perspective." *New England Journal of Medicine* 314(21):1383–1385.

Miller, H. C., K. Hassanein, and P. A. Hemsleigh. 1976. "Fetal Growth Retardation in Relation to Maternal Smoking and Weight Gain in Pregnancy." *American Journal of Obstetrics and Gynecology* 125(1):55–60.

Miller, Jon D., Robert W. Suchner, and Alan M. Voelker. *Citizenship in an Age of Science: Changing Attitudes Among Young Adults*. New York: Pergamon Press.

Moreno, Jonathan D. and Ronald Bayer. 1985. "The Limits of the Ledger in Public Health Promotion." *Hastings Center Report* 15(16):37–41.

Mulley, Albert G. 1983. "The Allocation of Resources for Medical Intensive Care." In *Report of the President's Commission on Securing Access to Health Care*. Washington, D.C.: GPO.

Murray, Thomas H. 1984. "Ethics and Health Care Allocation." *Public Law Forum* 4:41–50.

Naeye, R. L. 1980. "Effects of Maternal Nutrition on the Outcome of Pregnancy." In I. H. Porter and Ernest B. Hook, eds., *Human Embryonic and Fetal Death*. New York: Academic Press.

Nakamura, Robert T. and Frank Smallwood. 1980. *The Politics of Policy Implementation*. New York: St. Martin's Press.

National Academy of Sciences. 1975. *Assessing Biomedical Technologies: An Inquiry into the Nature of the Process*. Washington, D.C.: National Science Foundation.

National Center for Health Services Research. 1984. "The Role of Market Forces in the Delivery of Health Care: Issues for Research." In *Program Notes* (October). Washington, D.C.: Public Health Service.

National Governors' Association. 1983. *Governors' Priorities: 1983*. Washington, D.C.: National Governors' Association.

Nelkin, Dorothy. 1977. "Technology and Public Policy." In I. Spiegal-Rosing and Derek deSolla Price, eds., *Science, Technology, and Society*. Beverly Hills: Sage.

—— 1980. "Science and Technology Policy and the Democratic Process." In vol. 12 of *Five Year Outlook*. Washington, D.C.: National Science Foundation.

Nelson, W. B., J. M. Swint, and C. T. Caskey. 1978. "An Economic Evaluation of a Genetic Screening Program for Tay-Sachs Disease." *American Journal of Human Genetics* 30:160–166.

Neubauer, Deane and Richard Pratt. 1981. "The Second Public Health Revolution: A Critical Appraisal." *Journal of Health Politics, Policy, and Law* 6:205–228.

Newhouse, J. P., W. G. Manning, C. N. Morris, L. L. Orr, and N. Dean. 1981. "Some Interim Results from a Controlled Trial of Cost Sharing in Health Insurance." *New England Journal of Medicine* 305(25)1501–1507.

NIAAA (National Institute on Alcohol Abuse and Alcoholism). 1978. *Alcohol and Health.* No. 3. Washington, D.C.: GPO.

Noble, Ernest P., ed. 1978. *Third Special Report to the U.S. Congress on Alcohol and Health.* U.S. Department of Health, Education, and Welfare. Washington, D.C.: GPO.

NRC (National Research Council). Committee on Diet, Nutrition, and Cancer. 1982. *Diet, Nutrition, and Cancer.* Washington, D.C.: National Academy Press.

Office of Health Economics. 1979. "Scarce Resources in Health Care." *Milbank Memorial Fund Quarterly* 57(2):265–287.

Olson, Robert E. 1986. "Mass Intervention vs. Screening and Selective Intervention for the Prevention of Coronary Heart Disease." *JAMA* 255(16):2204–2207.

Oppenheimer, Steven B. 1984. *Cancer Prevention Guidebook.* Minneapolis: Burgess.

Organization for Economic Cooperation and Development. 1981. *Science and Technology Policy for the 1980s.* Paris: Organization for Economic Cooperation and Development.

OTA (Office of Technology Assessment). U.S. Congress. 1976. *Development of Medical Technology: Opportunities for Assessment.* Washington, D.C.: GPO.

—— 1981. *The Costs and Effectiveness of Neonatal Intensive Care.* Case Study no. 10. Washington, D.C.: GPO.

—— 1982. *Strategies for Medical Technology Assessment.* Washington, D.C.: GPO.

—— 1987. *OTA Proposal: Infertility Prevention and Treatment.* Washington, D.C.: OTA.

Overcast, Thomas D., Karen J. Merrikin, and Roger W. Evans. 1985. "Malpractice Issues in Heart Transplantation." *American Journal of Law and Medicine* 10:363–396.

Peacock, James E. and Felix A. Sarubbi. 1983. "Disseminated Herpes Simplex Virus Infection During Pregnancy." *Obstetrics and Gynecology* 61(3):13S–18S.

Pellegrino, Edmund D. 1986. "Rationing Health Care: The Ethics of Medical Gatekeeping." *Journal of Contemporary Health Law and Policy* 2:23–46.

Perry, Seymour. 1986. "Technology Assessment: Continuing Uncertainty." *New England Journal of Medicine* 314(4):240–243.

Phillips, R. L., J. W. Kuzman, and W. L. Beeson. 1980. "Influence of Selection Versus Life-Style on Risk of Fatal Cancer and Cardio-vascular Disease Among Seventh-Day Adventists." *American Journal of Epidemiology* 112:296–314.

Pitner, S. E. and C. J. Mance. 1973. "An Evaluation of Stroke Intensive Care Results in a Municipal Hospital." *Stroke* 4:737–741.

Pollak, Victor E. 1985. "The Computer in Medicine: Its Application to Medical Practice, Quality Control, and Cost Containment." *JAMA* 253(1):62–68.

Powledge, T. M. and L. Dach, eds. 1977. *Biomedical Research and the Public.* Report prepared for the Senate Subcommittee on Health and Scientific Research. 95th Congress, 1st sess. Washington, D.C.: GPO.

Pozgar, George D. 1983. *Legal Aspects of Health Care Administration.* 2d ed. Rockville, Md.: Aspen Systems.

President's Commission for the Study of Ethical Problems in Medicine and Biomedical and Behavioral Research. 1982. *Splicing Life.* Washington, D.C.: GPO.

—— 1983. *Deciding to Forego Life-Sustaining Treatment.* Washington, D.C.: GPO.

—— 1983a. *Securing Access to Health Care.* Washington, D.C.: GPO.

Price, David K. 1978. "Endless Frontier or Bureaucratic Morass?" *Daedalus* 107(2):75–92.

Price, R. Arlen. 1987. "Genetics of Human Obesity." *Annals of Behavioral Medicine* 9(1):9–14.

Prinz, Patricia N., T. A. Roehrs, P. P. Vitaliano, M. Linnoila, and E. D. Weitzman. 1980. "Effect of Alcohol on Sleep and Nightime Plasma Growth Hormone and Cortisol Concentrations." *Journal of Clinical Endocrinology and Metabolism* 51(4):759–764.

Prospective Payment Assessment Commission. Department of Health and Human Services. 1985. *Report and Recommendations to the Secretary of the Department of Health and Human Services.* Washington, D.C.: GPO.

Rahimtoola, S. H. 1985. "Cholesterol and Coronary Heart Disease: A Perspective." *JAMA* 253(14):2094–2095.

Ramsey, Paul. 1970. *Fabricated Man: The Ethics of Genetic Control.* New Haven: Yale University Press.

Raup, Mitchell D. 1985. "Medicaid Boycotts by Health Care Providers: The Noerr-Pennington Defense." *Duke Law Magazine* (Winter), 3(1):27–36.

Rawls, R. L. 1980. "Reproductive Hazards in the Workplace." *Chemical and Engineering News* (February), pp. 28–30.

Redisch, M. A. 1978. "Physician Involvement in Hospital Decision Making." In Mark Zubkoff, L. A. Raskin, and Ruth S. Hanft, eds., *Hospital Cost Containment.* New York: Prodist.

Reiser, Stanley J. 1984. "The Machine as Means and End: The Clinical Introduction of the Artifical Heart." In Margery W. Shaw, ed., *After Barney Clark: Reflections on the Utah Artifical Heart Program.* Austin: University of Texas Press.

—— 1985. "Responsibility for Personal Health: A Historical Perspective." *The Journal of Medicine and Philosophy* 10:7–17.

Relman, Arnold S. 1984. "Are Teaching Hospitals Worth the Extra Cost?" *New England Journal of Medicine* 310(19):1256–1257.

Rettig, R. A. 1982. "Applying Science and Technology to Public Purposes: A Synthesis." In A. H. Teich and R. Thornton, eds., *Science, Technology, and the Issues of the Eighties: Policy Outlook.* Boulder: Westview Press.

Rhoden, Nancy K. and John D. Arras. 1985. "Withholding Treatment from Baby Doe: From Discrimination to Child Abuse." *Milbank Memorial Fund Quarterly* 63(1):18–51.

Ricardo-Campbell, Rita. 1982. *The Economics and Politics of Health Care.* Chapel Hill: University of North Carolina Press.

Rist, Ray C. and Ronald J. Anson, eds. 1977. *Education, Social Science, and the Judicial Process.* New York: Teachers College Press.

Roberts, D. J., S. C. Farrow, and M. C. Charny. 1985. "How Much Can the NHS Afford to Spend to Save a Life or Avoid a Severe Disability?" *The Lancet*, January 12, pp. 89–91.

Robertson, John A. 1975. "Involuntary Euthanasia of Defective Newborns: A Legal Analysis." *Stanford Law Review* (January), 27:213–267.

—— 1982. "The Right to Procreate and In Utero Therapy." *The Journal of Legal Medicine* 3(3):333–366.

—— 1983. "Procreative Liberty and the Control of Conception, Pregnancy, and Childbirth." *Virginia Law Review* 69(3):405–464.

Rodgers, Joann Ellison. 1984. "Liver Politics: Cruel Decisions." *American Health* (January/February), pp. 62–63.

Rogers, Harrison L., Jr. 1986. "Resisting Pressure." *American Medical News* (June 27/July 4), p. 4.

Rom, William N. 1980. "Effects of Lead on Reproduction." In Peter F. Infante and Marvin S. Legator, eds., *Proceedings of a Workshop on Methodology for Assessing Reproductive Hazards in the Workplace.* Washington, D.C.: National Institute for Occupational Safety and Health.

Rosen, Paul L. 1972. *The Supreme Court and Social Science.* Urbana: University of Illinois Press.

Rosenblatt, Rand E. 1981. "Rationing 'Normal' Health Care: The Hidden Legal Issues." *Texas Law Review* 59:1401–1420.

Rothman, Kenneth J. 1986. "Tobacco Habits." *American Journal of Public Health* 76(2):133.

Rush, D., and E. H. Kass. 1972. "Maternal Smoking: A Reassessment of the Association with Perinatal Mortality." *American Journal of Epidemiology* 93(3):183–196.

Russell, Louise B. 1986. *Is Prevention Better Than Cure?* Washington, D.C.: Brookings Institution.

Saward, Ernest and Andrew Sorensen. 1980. "The Current Emphasis on Preventive Medicine." In Philip H. Abelson, ed., *Health Care, Regulation,*

Economics, Ethics, Practice. Washington, D.C.: American Association for the Advancement of Science.

Schachter, Julius and Mary-Ann Shafer. 1985. "Female Adolescents with Chlamydia: Tomorrow's Candidates for In Vitro Fertilization?" *Western Journal of Medicine* (July), 143(1):100.

Schechner, Sylvia. 1980. "For the 1980s: How Small is Too Small?" *Clinics in Perinatology* (March), 7:142.

Schoenberg, Bernard. 1979. "Science and Anti-Science in Confrontation." *Man and Medicine* 4(2):79–102.

Schramm, Carl J. 1984. "Can We Solve the Hospital-Cost Problem in Our Democracy?" *New England Journal of Medicine* 311(11):729–732.

Schuck, Peter H. 1981. "Malpractice Liability and the Rationing of Care." *Texas Law Review* 59:1421–1425.

Schuckit, Marc A. 1985. "Genetics and the Risk for Alcoholism." *JAMA* 254(18):2614–2617.

Schwartz, William B. 1984. "The Most Painful Prescription." *Newsweek,* November 12, p. 24.

Schwartz, D. and M. J. Mayaux. 1982. "Female Fecundity as a Function of Age." *New England Journal of Medicine* 306(7):404–406.

Senior, John R. 1983. "Digestive Diseases Information Center Fact Sheet." *Alcoholic Liver Disease* 2:16–20.

Sever, J. L. 1980. "Infectious Causes of Human Reproductive Loss." In I. H. Porter and Ernest B. Hook, eds., *Human Embryonic and Fetal Death.* New York: Academic Press.

Sexton, Mary and J. Richard Hebel. 1984. "A Clinical Trial of Change in Maternal Smoking and Its Effect on Birth Weight." *JAMA* 251(7):911–915.

Shapiro, Donald L. and Paul Rosenberg. 1984. "The Effect of Federal Regulations Regarding Handicapped Newborns." *JAMA* 252 (15):2031–2033.

Shapiro, Sam, M. C. McCormick. B. H. Starfield, J. P. Krisher, and D. Boss. 1980. "Relevance of Correlates of Infant Deaths for Significant Morbidity at One Year of Age." *American Journal of Obstetrics and Gynecology* 136(3):363–366.

Shepard, D. S. and A. J. Ghanotakis. 1979. *Hospital Costs in Massachusetts: A Report on the Massachusetts Funds Flow Project.* HRP-0029335. Springfield, Va.: National Technical Information Service.

Sher, George. 1983. "Health Care and the 'Deserving Poor.' " *Hastings Center Report* 13(2):9–12.

Shick, Alan. 1977. "Complex Policy Making in the United States Senate." In *Policy Analyses on Major Issues Prepared for the Commission on the Operation of the Senate.* U.S. Senate. Washington, D.C.: GPO.

Siegler, Mark. 1986. "Ethics Committees; Decisions by Bureaucracy." *Hastings Center Report* 16(3):22–24.

Singer, Daniel E., P. L. Carr, A. G. Mulley, and G. E. Thibault. 1983. "Rationing Intensive Care: Physician Responses to a Resource Shortage." *New England Journal of Medicine* 309(19):1155–1160.

Sirageldin, Ismail, David Salkever, and Richard W. Osborn, eds. 1983. *Evaluating Population Programs: International Experience with Cost-Effectiveness Analysis and Cost-Benefit Analysis*. New York: St. Martin's Press.

Slavin, Gerard, F. Martin, P. Ward, J. Levi, and T. Peters. 1983. "Chronic Alcohol Excess is Associated with Selective but Reversible Injury to Type 2B Muscle Fibers." *Journal of Clinical Pathology* 36(7):772–777.

Smith, C. A. 1947. "Effects of Maternal Under-Nutrition Upon the Newborn Infant in Holland, 1944–1945." *Journal of Pediatrics* 30:229–241.

Smith, J. M. 1977. "Congenital Minimata Disease: Methyl Mercury Poisoning and Birth Defects in Japan." In E. Bingham, ed., *Proceedings: Conference on Women and the Workplace*. Washington, D.C.: Society for Occupational and Environmental Health.

Smithells, R. W., M. J. Seller, R. Harris, D. W. Fielding, and C. J. Schorah. 1983. "Further Experience of Vitamin Supplementation on Prevention of Neural Tube Defects." *The Lancet* May 7, pp. 1027–1031.

Somers, Anne R. 1982. "Moderating the Rise in Health-Care Costs." *New England Journal of Medicine* 307(15):944–947.

Spilhaus, A. 1972. "Ecolibrium." *Science* 175:711–715.

Starr, Paul. 1982. *The Social Transformation of American Medicine*. New York: Basic Books.

Stone, Alan A. 1985. "Law's Influence on Medicine and Medical Ethics." *New England Journal of Medicine* 312(5):309–312.

Stone, Katherine M., David A. Grimes, and Laurence S. Magder. 1986. "Primary Prevention of Sexually Transmitted Diseases." *JAMA* 255(13):1763–1766.

Strauss, Michael J., J. P. LoGerfo, J. A. Yeltatzie, N. Temkin, and L. D. Hudson. 1986. "Rationing of Intensive Care Unit Services: An Everyday Occurrence." *JAMA* 255(9):1143–1146.

Strom, Terry B. and Rolf Loertscher. 1984. "Cyclosporine-Induced Nephrotoxicity: Inevitable and Intractable." *New England Journal of Medicine* 311(11):728–729.

Strong, Carson. 1983. "The Tiniest Newborns." *Hastings Center Report* 13(5):14–19.

Stuart, Bruce A. and Lee Bair. 1971. *Health Care and Income: The Distributional Impacts of Medicaid and Medicare Nationally and in the State of Michigan*. 2d ed. Lansing: Michigan Department of Social Services.

Susser, M. and Z. Stein. 1980. "Prenatal Diet and Reproductive Loss." In I. H. Porter and Ernest B. Hook, eds., *Human Embryonic and Fetal Death*. New York: Academic Press.

Swint, J. M., J. M. Shapiro, V. L. Corson, L. W. Reynolds, and G. H. Thomas.

1979. "The Economic Returns to Community and Hospital Screening Programs for a Genetic Disease." *Preventive Medicine* 8(4):463–470.

Tancredi, Lawrence R. and Jeremiah A. Barondess. 1980. "The Problem of Defensive Medicine." In Philip H. Abelson, ed., *Health Care: Regulating Economics, Ethics, Practice.* Washington, D.C.: American Association for the Advancement of Science.

Tarrance, Lance and Associates. 1983. *Public Opinion on Health Care Issues: 1983.* Chicago: American Medical Association.

Task Force of the Presidential Advisory Group on Anticipated Advances in Science and Technology. 1976. "The Science Court Experiment: An Interim Report." *Science* 193:653–656.

Taylor, A. K. and W. R. Lawson, Jr. 1981. "Employer and Employee Expenditures for Private Health Insurance." *NCHSR National Health Care Expenditures Study Data Preview* 7. Department of Health and Human Services Publication no. PHS 81-3297. Washington, D.C.: GPO.

Thibault, G. E., Albert G. Mulley, and G. O. Barnett. 1980. "Medical Intensive Care: Indications, Interventions, and Outcomes." *New England Journal of Medicine* 302(17):938–942.

Thurow, Lester C. 1985. "Medicine Versus Economics." *New England Journal of Medicine* 313(10):611–614.

Tribe, Lawrence H. 1973. *Channeling Technology Through Law.* Chicago: Bracton Press.

—— 1973a. "Technology Assessment and the Fourth Discontinuity: The Limits of Instrumental Rationality." *Southern California Law Review* (June), 46:617–660.

Turnbull, A. D., G. Carlon, R. Baron, W. Sichel, and C. Young. 1979. "The Inverse Relationship Between Cost and Survival in the Critically Ill Cancer Patient." *Critical Care Medicine* 7:(1)20–23.

Valentine, Jeannette M. and Alonzo L. Plough. 1983. "Protecting the Reproductive Health of Workers: Problems in Science and Public Policy." *Journal of Health Politics, Policy, and Law* 8(1):144–163.

Vaupel, James W. 1980. "Prospects for Saving Lives: A Policy Analysis." In *Hearings on Comparative Risk Assessment.* House Subcommittee on Science, Research, and Technology of the Committee on Science and Technology. 96th Congress, 2d. sess. Washington, D.C.: GPO.

Van Den Berg, B. J. 1977. "Epidemiological Observations of Prematurity: Effects of Tobacco, Coffee, and Alcohol." In D. M. Reed and F. J. Stanley, eds., *The Epidemiology of Prematurity.* Baltimore: Urban and Schwarzenberg.

Veatch, Robert M. 1980. "Voluntary Risks to Health: The Ethical Issues." *JAMA* 243(1):50–55.

—— 1986. "DRGs and the Ethical Reallocation of Resources." *Hastings Center Report* 16(3):32–40.

Verni, Thomas and John Kelly. 1981. *The Secret Life of the Unborn Child.* New York: Summit Books.

Warner, Kenneth. 1983. "The Benefits and Costs of Antismoking Policies." Report prepared for the National Center for Health Services Research (June), ch. 9, p. 16.

—— 1986. "Smoking and Health Implications of a Change in the Federal Excise Tax." *JAMA* 255(8):1028–1032.

Warner, Kenneth E. and Hillary A. Murt. 1983. "Premature Deaths Avoided by the Antismoking Campaign." *American Journal of Public Health* 73(6):672–677.

Warner, R. H. and H. L. Rosett. 1975. "The Effects of Drinking on Offspring: An Historical Survey of the American and British Literature." *Journal of Studies on Alcohol* 36:1395–1420.

Wehr, Elizabeth. 1984a. "Congress Passes Compromise Organ Transplant Legislation." *Congressional Quarterly Weekly Report*, October 6, p. 2479.

—— 1984b. "National Health Policy Sought for Organ Transplant Surgery." *Congressional Quarterly Weekly Report*, February 25, pp. 453–458.

Weiner, Charles. 1982. "Relations of Science, Government, and Industry: The Case of Recombinant DNA." In A. H. Teich and R. Thornton, eds., *Science, Technology, and the Issues of the Eighties: Policy Outlook.* Boulder: Westview Press.

Wenk, Edward. 1981. "Political Limits in Steering Technology." In Albert H. Teich, ed., *Technology and Man's Future.* New York: St. Martin's Press.

West, Louis J. 1984. "Alcoholism and Related Problems: An Overview." In L. J. West, ed., *Alcoholism and Related Problems: Issues for the American Public.* Englewood Cliffs, N.J.: Prentice-Hall.

Westrom, L. 1980. "Incidence, Prevalence, and Trends of Acute Pelvic Inflammatory Disease and Its Consequences in Industrialized Countries." *American Journal of Obstetrics and Gynecology.* 138:880–892.

Wikler, Daniel I. 1978. "Persuasion and Coercion for Health: Ethical Issues in Government Efforts to Change Life-Styles." *Milbank Memorial Fund Quarterly* 56(3):303–338.

Wildavsky, Aaron. 1977. "Doing Better and Feeling Worse: The Political Pathology of Health Policy." *Daedalus* 106(1):105–123.

Willett, Walter C. and Brian MacMahon. 1984. "Diet and Cancer—An Overview." *New England Journal of Medicine* 310(10):633–638.

Williams, S. V. 1980. "The Consequences of Premature Discharge from the Medical Intensive Care Unit." Paper presented at the symposium, Critical Issues in Medical Technology, April, Boston.

Williams, Wendy W. 1981. "Firing the Woman to Protect the Fetus: The Reconciliation of Fetal Protection with Employment Opportunity Goals Under Title VII." *Georgetown Law Journal* 69:641–704.

Winick, Myron. 1976. *Malnutrition and Brain Development.* New York: Oxford University Press.

Wolf, Stewart. 1984. "Alcohol and Health: The Wages of Excessive Drinking." In L. J. West, ed., *Alcoholism and Related Problems: Issues for the American Public.* Englewood Cliffs, N.J.: Prentice-Hall.

Wolf, Susan M. 1986. "Ethics Committees in the Courts." *Hastings Center Report* 16(3):12–15.

Wooddell, W. Jeff. 1980. "Liver Disease in Alcohol-Addicted Patients." In Sharon V. Davidson, ed., *Alcoholism and Health.* Germantown, Md.: Aspen.

Yankelovich and White, Inc. 1982. *Health and Health Insurance: The Public's View.* Washington, D.C.: Health Insurance Association of America.

Yellin, Joel. 1981. "High Technology and the Courts: Nuclear Power and the Need for Institutional Reform." *Harvard Law Review* 94(3):489–560.

Young, Ernle W. D. 1983. "Caring for Disabled Infants." *Hastings Center Report* 13(4):15–18.

Youngblood, J. Craig and Parker C. Folse III. 1981. "Can Courts Govern? An Inquiry into Capacity and Purpose." In R. A. L. Gambitta, M. L. May, and J. C. Foster, eds., *Governing Through Courts.* Beverly Hills: Sage.

Zook, Christopher J. and Francis D. Moore. 1980. "High-Cost Users of Medical Care." *New England Journal of Medicine* 302(18):996–1002.

Index